Dear Reader:

The book you are about to read is the latest bestseller from the St. Martin's True Crime Library, the imprint *The New York Times* calls "the leader in true crime!" Each month, we offer you a fascinating account of the latest, most sensational crime that has captured the national attention. St. Martin's is the publisher of Tina Dirmann's VANISHED AT SEA, the story of a former child actor who posed as a yacht buyer in order to lure an older couple out to sea, then robbed them and threw them overboard to their deaths. John Glatt's riveting and horrifying SECRETS IN THE CELLAR shines a light on the man who shocked the world when it was revealed that he had kept his daughter locked in his hidden basement for 24 years. In the Edgar-nominated WRITTEN IN BLOOD, Diane Fanning looks at Michael Petersen, a Marine-turned-novelist found guilty of beating his wife to death and pushing her down the stairs of their home—only to reveal another similar death from his past. In the book you now hold, A TWISTED FAITH, *New York Times* bestselling true crime author Gregg Olsen presents a story of betrayal and religious zeal, in which a minister used his faith as a tool of seduction.

St. Martin's True Crime Library gives you the stories behind the headlines. Our authors take you right to the scene of the crime and into the minds of the most notorious murderers to show you what really makes them tick. St. Martin's True Crime Library paperbacks are better than the most terrifying thriller, because it's all true! The next time you want a crackling good read, make sure it's got the St. Martin's True Crime Library logo on the spine—you'll be up all night!

Charles E. Spicer, Jr.
Executive Editor, St. Martin's True Crime Library

"Olsen writes the way a surgeon cuts—precisely exposing the personality riddles that lie concealed within each of the players."
                                    —Anthony Flacco, author of
                                         The Road Out of Hell

"A horrifying tale of spiritual and physical seduction, and murder . . . [*A Twisted Faith*] draws its power from the strong and subtle hand of a master storyteller."
                              —Kate Flora, Edgar-nominated author of
                       Finding Amy: A True Story of Murder in Maine

"A very strange but fascinating journey into the heart of a religious community torn asunder by sex and murder."
                                    —Harry MacLean, author of
                                         The Past is Never Dead

"Everybody should read Gregg Olsen's book . . . What an eye-opener!"
                                                  —*Book Reporter*

"I was hooked on page one . . . An extremely difficult book to put down."
                                    —*True Crime Book Reviews*

BITTER ALMONDS

"A real page-turner."
                                    —Jonathan Kellerman

"Absolutely fascinating . . . one of the most devious female minds in crime history."
                                    —Ann Rule

"A truly remarkable book. The trailer-park babes of *Bitter Almonds* leap off the page, fingernails sharpened and aimed for your eyes."

                                    —Jack Olsen, author of
                       Son: A Psychopath and His Victims
                    and *"I": The Creation of a Serial Killer*

ABANDONED PRAYERS

"A searingly tragic look behind the headlines that broke America's heart. Brilliantly researched, wonderfully written."
—Ann Rule

"A riveting and deeply disturbing chronicle of true crime. Olsen has done a superior job." —*Cleveland Plain Dealer*

"Among the top true crime books published. Once picked up, it's hard to put down." —*New Philadelphia Times Reporter*

"A superior true crime account that should not be missed."
—Jack Olsen

CRUEL DECEPTION

"A tough new voice rises in the ranks of true-crime writers."
—*Seattle Post-Intelligencer*

"Gregg Olsen's work is absolutely top notch, masterful. With [*Cruel Deception*], Gregg takes his rightful place among crime masters." —Dennis McDougal, author of *In the Best of Families* and *Whatever Mother Says*

"Compelling . . . suspenseful . . . Gregg Olsen is masterful in creating this incredible story. As he brings his characters to life, he evokes emotions in us, as we hope against hope that the inevitable crime will not happen."
—Rod Clovin, author of *Evil Harvest*

"A must read for all true-crime junkies . . . It picks up speed with each page and rapidly moves from absorbing to riveting, sweeping the reader along . . . Combines diligent, exhaustive research with a crisp, captivating style."
—Steven Nickel, author of *Torso*

Also by Gregg Olsen

A
Twisted
Faith

**A MINISTER'S
OBSESSION AND
THE MURDER
THAT DESTROYED
A CHURCH**

Gregg Olsen

St. Martin's Paperbacks

A TWISTED FAITH

Copyright © 2010 by Gregg Olsen.

For information address St. Martin's Press, 175 Fifth Avenue, New York, NY 10010.

ISBN:978-1-250-12449-4

Printed in the United States of America

St. Martin's Press hardcover edition published 2010
St. Martin's Paperbacks edition / April 2011

St. Martin's Paperbacks are published by St. Martin's Press, 175 Fifth Avenue, New York, NY 10010.

P1

For Dawn

DRAMATIS PERSONAE

Annette Anderson　Christ Community Church member; married to Craig; mother of four and confidante of Sandy Glass

Craig Anderson　Salesman; married to Annette

Yvonne Basso　An Oregon pastor's wife; friend of Annette Anderson

Robert Bily　Apostle; married to Pamela; father of three, including son Adam

Julie Conner　Married to Christ Community Church board member Gary; mother of seven

Julia DeLashmutt　Christ Community Church secretary

Michael DeLashmutt　Student

Jimmy Glass　Carpenter; married to Sandy Glass; son of church members James and Mary Glass

Sandy Glass　Prophetess of Christ Community Church; married to Jimmy; mother of four boys

Dan Hacheney　Auto mechanic; Nick's father; married to Sandra Hacheney

Dawn Hacheney   Credit union employee; married to Nick; daughter of Don and Diana Tienhaara

Nick Hacheney   Youth pastor, Christ Community Church; married to Dawn Hacheney

Holly Kloven   Married to contractor Einar; mother of three; close friend of Sandy Glass

Sally LaGrandeur   Married to Rich; mother of Sara and Ed Matheson

Nicole Matheson   Housecleaner; estranged from husband, Ed; mother of two

Richard Maxwell   Christian counselor with Alpha Counseling in Poulsbo, Washington

Ron McClung   Christ Community Church pastor; married to Carol; father of Jon

Scott Nickell   Navy officer; confidante of Sandy Glass

Bob "PB" Smith   Longtime pastor of Christ Community Church; married to Adele; father of Lindsey and Kim

Lindsey Smith   Daughter of PB and Adele Smith; sister to Kim Smith Selembo; along with Sara LaGrandeur, one of Nick's "little disciples"

Diana Tienhaara   Dawn Hacheney's mother; married to naval shipyard worker Donald

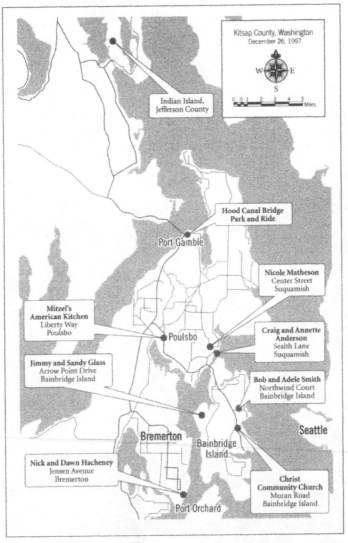

Map by Bill Webb

PROLOGUE

December 26, 1997
Bremerton, Washington

I T WAS THE DAY AFTER CHRISTMAS 1997 IN BREMERTON, a navy town across Puget Sound from Seattle, Washington. Contractor Jeff Richardson, age thirty-four, pulled into an East Bremerton neighborhood to pick up his employee Tim Pitts, thirty-three, for work. The split second Jeff planted his foot on Jensen Avenue, he turned with a start toward the sound of a jagged crackle and the whooshing of air. It was coming from a small brown vertical-sided house across the street. A fire had sucked in a window, and black smoke poured from the splintered gash.

A neighbor's house was on fire.

Jeff hurried to the Pitts' door, where he machine-gun knocked and called out about the emergency. It was 7:13 A.M., and Amy Pitts, startled from bleary-eyed to wide awake, went straight for the telephone. Her call to 911 was one of several that came in around the same time.

The burning 1942-built rambler belonged to Nick and Dawn Hacheney. The Pitts knew the Hacheneys only in passing, based on occasional conversations on the street. Nick was a youth pastor for a church on nearby Bainbridge Island, and Dawn a loan officer at the Kitsap Federal Credit Union in Silverdale. He seemed outgoing, the kind of fellow with a quick word and a smile; she was nice but a bit more reserved—not cool, just the type of person who waited for others to approach her, not the other way around. Nick liked to hunt and had set up a tented structure in the backyard that some assumed he was testing as a prototype for a hunting shelter he'd erect elsewhere. The Hacheneys had a couple of Labs, yellow and chocolate, named Hope and Faith. None of the neighbors had been inside the house, but there was evidence—sounds of hammering and construction supplies being brought in—that the place was in the midst of a much-needed remodeling. That was about the sum of what they knew.

Having roused the Pitts, Jeff Richardson immediately sprinted up the steep concrete steps to the Hacheneys' door and pounded it until his fist stung. Tim Pitts, who had joined his boss, called out to see if anyone was inside.

"Hey! You're on fire!"

A voice came from the other side of a shaggy hedge. "They're not home!"

This report from the unseen neighbor gave Tim and Jeff a momentary flash of relief, but in the chaotic first moments of emergencies, relief is almost always short-lived. Tim had noticed Dawn's blue Dodge Neon parked in front. It appeared someone *could* be home.

Jeff kicked the door; the frame splintered and the door swung open. Tim was right behind him, coughing from the smoke yet feeling the rush that propels a man toward danger. Crouching, Jeff tried to make his way deeper inside the house, but the force of the smoke and heat that blasted his face made him wince. He retreated, then tried again. Amy, now at the Hacheneys' door, proffered a pair of water-soaked bath towels, and Jeff held one to his face as he started to crawl farther into the burning house. He could barely see through the heavy, dark smoke. He bumped into furniture, pushing chairs aside, forcing his way down the hallway toward the master bedroom.

On his next attempt, the would-be rescuer saw the red blush of burning embers and the yellow buzz saw of flames lapping at the woodwork around the doorway. *It's too hot. Too dangerous.* Although he'd done what lesser men might not have, given the perilous conditions, the young contractor knew that he could not save anyone trapped inside. He backed out. As swiftly as he could, Tim retrieved a garden hose, thinking that he could slow the blaze somewhat until the fire department arrived. But no water came through the hose. Another window burst.

Although less than ten minutes had elapsed between the time Amy dialed 911 and the moment when sirens could finally be heard, it seemed a good deal longer. A fire truck and an aid car parked nearby and a squad of firefighters unfurled hoses, grabbed axes, ran up the steps. Hoses unleashed jets of water, and steam shot out of the bedroom, the only room burned by the inferno.

Outside in the street, some neighbors were worried about the Hacheneys' dogs; they speculated that the animals might have run off during the commotion. No one was thinking the worst. The house was small, and the occupants were young and able-bodied. Surely they'd made it out safely, as the fire seemed to have affected only the master bedroom. It was the holidays; they probably weren't even home.

The clock spun to the next hour, and as the smoke began to clear, everyone held their breath.

When it became safe enough to do so, a team of geared-up firefighters trudged down the hallway, their boots leaving tracks in the sodden carpet and debris scattered in the fire's blowback. Their flashlights pierced the darkened space, cutting through the heavy air and the acrid odor firefighters know at first whiff.

The smell of flesh consumed by a blaze.

The dogs?

When they entered the bedroom, the crew was unsure exactly what they were seeing. Water spray had knocked the room's contents into a maelstrom of disarray. Fragments of clothing collected in the corners. A melted plastic alarm clock slumped. Bits of charred paper stuck everywhere. The conflagration had generated a tornado of heat, smoke, and circulating rubble.

The Hacheneys' bed had nearly been sucked into the floor.

A fireman found the source of the odor. It was not a missing dog, but the barely distinguishable form of a human being.

"There," he said, pointing a gloved finger. It was small, limbless, a child or a woman. Although the remains were so badly burned that dental records or DNA analysis would be necessary to confirm just who it was, those on the scene at the Jensen Avenue fire made an assumption right away. The small body folded into the oozing rubble was Dawn Hacheney, twenty-eight, and not her husband, Nick.

As tight-lipped as fire department and police personnel can be, it was apparent to the bystanders witnessing to the emergency that something extremely grave had occurred in the house.

There was nothing to do—just wait and watch.

Around 10 A.M., Nick Hacheney, twenty-seven, emerged from his grimy late-model Jeep parked on the other side of the police and fire department barricade. He wore hunting gear and had one of the missing dogs by his side. He was a chubby figure, with a pleasant round face and receding hairline. His brown eyes were awash with worry as he looked past the red truck, the gawkers, the police cars with blue lights still strobing the alert. With each step, Nick quickened his gait.

Someone identified him as the missing husband, and the chief deputy coroner from the Kitsap County Coroner's Office in Port Orchard moved in his direction. Slow, fast, faster yet. She scarcely needed words to convey what had happened.

Nick began to cry as he confirmed that only he and his wife lived there. No roommates. No children.

The body that the firefighters had found could only be Dawn.

The assistant coroner led Nick to the back of a truck, where he sat, his face in his hands. His body shuddered in inconsolable grief.

Everyone watching felt the deep emotion that accompanies such scenes, when the unthinkable can no longer be denied by hope. It reminded the cadre of onlookers how in an instant everything can change. A young woman on their street had lost her life. She'd been so vital the last time they'd seen her.

A life had been inexplicably eclipsed by a tragedy.

The fire department left and the police secured the scene. There was nothing more to see, so the neighbors returned to their houses, their Christmas leftovers, the gifts that they would choose to keep or return. Some cried. Some just shrugged it off. Others pondered how it was that Dawn Hacheney hadn't made it out alive.

What happened on that smoky Bremerton morning more than a decade ago seemed so final, so devastating in its outcome, that none involved could know that they were in the middle of a story. Not the beginning.

And far, far from the end.

BOOK
ONE

Prophecy of Murder

God told me Dawn is going to die on December 18. He showed me that Nick and I will be together.

—Sandy Glass

BY THE MID-1990S, BERRY PATCHES AND CREOSOTE-cured pilings protruding from the waters of Puget Sound were no longer the prevailing features of Bainbridge Island, Washington. Faux châteaus and gargantuan Craftsman-style homes had arisen, as ubiquitous as strawberry farms and shorefront sawmills had once been. For the old-timers, it was a time of boom and bust. Property values had made rich people out of mobile-home dwellers on forested acreage. Weekend beach cottages had long since been razed by Seattle yuppies with lots of money and a scant sense of proportion. Those who grew up on the island lamented that though their property values had skyrocketed, the friendly rural character of their community was fading. Long gone were the days when everyone knew everyone and chatted while they waited for the ferry to Seattle, just across Puget Sound.

Connected by Agate Pass Bridge to the Kitsap Peninsula to the north and by the state ferry system to Seattle to the east, Bainbridge was isolated and insular—which was a blessing, as far as newcomers were concerned. Islanders hated being part of Kitsap County, the poorest of the major counties around Puget Sound. To resist the influence of a county that allowed chain stores like Wal-Mart to take root like so many scattered weeds, the entire island incorporated as a city in 1991.

It was that kind of insularity and attitude that brought

members of Christ Community Church close together and, ultimately, set tragedy in motion.

Many of the Christ Community Church faithful were part of the island's old guard. Families like the Glasses, Klovens, LaGrandeurs, and Smiths were of somewhat-modest means. While some were ferry ticket-takers, checkers, housecleaners, or baristas, several, like building contractor Einar Kloven, had their own businesses. Dan Hacheney ran an auto repair shop a few doors down from the ferry landing with service to Seattle. Dan and Suzy Claflin owned a restaurant. James Glass and his son Jimmy were skilled carpenters.

Some congregants, like the Andersons and the Mathesons, lived off the island on tribal land in Suquamish, the birthplace and final resting place of Chief Sealth, for whom the city of Seattle was named. Suquamish was a quick drive over the Agate Pass Bridge. A few miles down the road was Poulsbo, an orderly enclave best known for its Norwegian bakeries and a marina that on a summer's day boasted a rainbow of spinnakers from one side of Liberty Bay to the other.

RAISED MOSTLY ON THE OUTSKIRTS OF POULSBO, NICK Hacheney came from a troubled family. Observers would later suggest that Nick had been somewhat neglected as a child in a chaotic household, and that it was that lack of attention that had shaped him more than anything else. He was the fat kid without many friends. He was the one who always tried to be outgoing but still managed to be a loner. It wasn't until he picked up a Bible and dug deep into the meaning of God's Word that he seemed to find his place. It was God's calling, he insisted, that gave him strength and shaped every bit of his character. In his family, he became the rock, the point person for every family calamity. When his brother Todd, a drug addict, was rendered brain-dead after being hit by a car on Bainbridge Island, it was Nick who instructed his parents to remove Todd from life support.

"My parents didn't have the stomach for it," he told a friend much later. "But I knew what God wanted."

Nick was seen as the strongest and most responsible

member of his family. Nick's mother, Sandra Hacheney, was a fiercely independent woman who ran a home day care and took in foster children whenever the spirit moved her, which was quite frequently. Nick would later gripe that his mother favored his brothers, his sister, and even the foster kids over him.

"I don't think she ever loved me," he told a friend. "Actually, I think she hated me."

For her part, Sandra Hacheney seldom said a cross word about her youngest.

Dan Hacheney always knew his greatest legacy would be his children, especially Nick. Even when he was a little boy, there was no doubt among the Hacheneys that Nick was the golden child. He had a backstory that confirmed it. Dan and Sandra Hacheney told the story often. Nick recited it too, albeit with a sheepish sense of burden.

"You have no idea," he told a friend, "what it is like to be handed over to God."

IT WAS 1970 AND DAN AND SANDRA HACHENEY WERE IN A state of terror. Nicholas Daniel was turning a deep shade of blue. As the auto mechanic and his wife jumped into the car and drove to a Bremerton hospital, they were sure the youngest of their four children was going to die.

At twenty-eight, Dan was a rare combination of toughness and gentleness. His hands were never clean, always stained with motor oil from a job that kept food on the table and Sandra washing coveralls. A year younger than her husband, Sandra could be a somewhat sullen figure, given to what some believed were long bouts of depression. She had dark eyes and hair, like Dan and their baby.

Nick gasped for air in his mother's arms and Dan knew only one thing to do. So convinced was he that he couldn't get to the hospital in time, he parked the car on the edge of the roadway.

He began to pray.

"Dear God, don't let him die. If you let him live, I'll give him over to you right now, forever. Please, God, you raise my son! You be his father! Please, God, don't let this boy die."

A moment later, the blue cast on his son's face was transformed to the rosy flush of a healthy baby.

"Thank you, Jesus," Dan said.

BREMERTON, THE BLUE-COLLAR HEART OF KITSAP COUNTY, had its positive attributes: decent-paying jobs, cheap housing, mountain and water views at every turn. Kitsap County's largest city was home to a U.S. Navy shipyard, submarine base, and port for aircraft carriers, and for many years that meant nothing more than topless bars, tattoo parlors, sailors on leave, and the women they left behind on the prowl when ships and subs departed for tours of the Pacific. Things had improved somewhat in Bremerton, though it was still "Bummertown" to many, the butt of Seattle jokes. But in 1990 a great irony came to pass when *Money* magazine named Bremerton "America's Most Livable City." Even locals, proud as they were of the completely unexpected designation by a well-known publication, wondered out loud if *Money*'s editors had bothered to visit the town in person.

Dawn Tienhaara had been raised in Bremerton. Her father, Donald, was a shipyard worker; her mother, Diana, a homemaker. Dawn was the oldest and the only girl in a brood that included three brothers—all named with the initial *D*. She was a honey blonde with pretty green eyes, a tiny birthmark above her upper lip, and a knack for memorization that, when she was a schoolgirl, took her all the way to the Rose Garden of the White House and a meeting with President Ronald Reagan when she competed in the Scripps National Spelling Bee.

Diana Tienhaara was an anxious woman who by her own admission required more love than she could get from her husband, Donald. Diana wanted a happy marriage, but she didn't quite know how to achieve it. Her search for affection and acceptance sometimes brought turmoil. In February 1980, Diana left her husband, daughter, and son, Dennis, to live with the father of a baby she named Daron, whom she con-

ceived during an extramarital affair. After some soul searching and a flood of tears, she returned to the family home on
Rimrock Avenue in East Bremerton. She didn't tell her youngest son about his true parentage until he was a young adult.
During the difficult times, Dawn lent her mother as much
support as a child could. Sometimes Diana would find small
notes from her daughter under her pillow. *You are great,
Mom! I love you.*

THAT NICK AND DAWN WOULD FALL IN LOVE AT NORTH-
west College of the Assemblies of God—known informally
as Northwest Bible College but celebrated and mocked by
some as "Northwest *Bridal* College"—in Kirkland, Washington, was hardly a foregone conclusion. Those who attended
the east-of-Seattle college with the young couple were surprised by the relationship. Dawn was an achiever, after all.
She wasn't gorgeous, but she was pretty in a girl-next-door
way. Her roommates at the time saw Nick, on the other hand,
as a loser—a guy "who tried too hard" and was clueless about
it. He was brash and pushy, but Dawn was no match for his
everlasting persuasion. Always a little overweight and with
his hairline starting to recede while he was still in his teens,
Nick was more concerned about the spiritual than the physical. No one would have said he was handsome. And yet, he
had a kind of magnetism that some couldn't resist.

Nick proposed marriage to Dawn over Oreo cookies and
milk on Alki Beach, not far from her grandparents' home in
West Seattle, and the two married soon after, on April 20,
1991. They moved into a place in Bremerton; Dawn found
work at the credit union and Nick set his sights on his long-
held dream: to be a youth pastor under the tutelage of his
beloved pastor, Bob Smith, at Christ Community Church on
Bainbridge Island.

Despite being so capable—she was, after all, her high
school valedictorian—Dawn surprised many with how
quickly she abdicated all decision making to Nick. She appeared to go along with the fundamentalist edict that submitting to her husband's authority was God's plan and the greatest

gift a woman could give him. When Nick's decisions seemed foolish, Dawn backed him all the way. If he wanted to take in a troubled congregant, she agreed, although she longed for privacy. When he charged hundreds of dollars in music CDs for church friends on his credit card, Dawn shrugged it off, even though she'd had her eye on a new Jaclyn Smith outfit for work.

YEARS LATER, A WOMAN WHO LIVED WITH NICK AND DAWN in the early days of their marriage stumbled onto a cache of dildos and other sex toys in the master bathroom of a house they were remodeling on Nipsic Avenue in East Bremerton. Crystal Gurney, a twenty-year-old church member going through a bad patch with a new marriage at the time, wasn't horrified by what she'd discovered. She'd lived a tough life of her own and had seen plenty. Long after her friend's death, though, Crystal grappled with her observation. "It just didn't seem like Dawn at all. Not the girl I knew. I wondered how it was that Nick got her into that."

ALL GREAT THINGS START WITH A DREAM. SOMETIMES two. Pastor Bob Smith; his wife, Adele; and their little girls, Kim and Lindsey, joined hands with other members of Bainbridge Christian Assembly to pray and rejoice. A new church was coming. *Their church.* Tall bigleaf maples and cedars were spared as the ground was sliced with the blade of a backhoe in the construction zone for a church on Moran Road. It was to be a twelve-thousand-square-foot structure that looked Northwest contemporary in its architecture, more like a large new home or even professional offices than a house of worship.

On this day in the mid-1980s, drivers whizzing by on Highway 305, which bisects the island from Agate Passage to the ferry landing, scratched their heads, wondering just what was being built where the ground was broken. A bank? New restaurant?

There was no marker to proclaim what it would be.

Finally, in what would one day prove to be a twist of irony, Einar Kloven, who had volunteered countless hours of labor, made a sign and hung it up facing the highway: NEW PRISON.

No one laughed with more gusto than Pastor Bob, or "PB," as congregants called him. He could take a joke. He was the kind of pastor who'd cry with the hurting, feed the hungry from his own plate, and shoulder the burdens of those who could no longer carry them alone. Growing up in a rural Northwest community had taught him not only to love God but to cherish the relationships that united the disparate. PB and Adele were married after he graduated from Northwest College in 1972. After he'd served as a pastor on the Yakama Indian Reservation in south-central Washington, the young family moved to Kitsap County, first leading a church in Bremerton and then, in 1982, moving to Bainbridge Island to oversee an Assemblies of God congregation.

The new Pentecostal church on Moran Road was the culmination of a dream. Everything was coming together as it had been mapped out, every nail lovingly hammered into place. One hundred Bainbridge area families had joined forces to build a house of God.

YET PB SMITH AND HIS CONGREGANTS WEREN'T THE ONLY ones with a dream that involved the church on Moran Road. Far away, in California, a woman named Pamela Bily had a vision—a gift God had given her on many occasions—that her pastor husband, Robert, and their children would live on the northeast side of an island near Seattle. It was a remarkable and vivid dream. Like putting a pin in a wall map, God had shown her just where it was.

It was Bainbridge Island, Washington.

When Pamela told her husband, Robert, about it, there was only one thing to do.

IN HIS FORTIES, ROBERT BILY, AN EXCEEDINGLY FIT 173-pound six-footer, was a Stanford University graduate who had been a senior manager in his father's cheese-processing and distribution business, a leader in a financially troubled church in San Jose, and an investor and board member of a computer company that went kaput. Each endeavor brought new burdens, mostly financial. He came to the Seattle area in the early 1990s to work with TV cook Graham Kerr, a devout Christian who had achieved worldwide fame as the flamboyant host of TV's *The Galloping Gourmet*. The two had conversations about marketing a soy-based foodstuff that Robert had developed to feed the Christian masses. There was also talk of books, a new television program, and a worldwide network. But egos clashed and the project dragged on until, like other good-intentioned endeavors that Robert dove into headfirst, it failed.

Along with Pamela and their children, Robert arrived on Bainbridge Island with the remnants of a once-luxurious California life: Persian rugs, a Mercedes-Benz, and stylish wardrobes. Robert was undeterred by any setback. Pamela's dream had brought them there. God had a plan.

He told Robert to work for Him at the church led by Bob Smith.

ROBERT BILY WAS AN UNFALTERING PROPONENT OF THE apostolic approach to Christianity, which sought the creation of new churches made of nondenominational congregants. Robert brought strengths: management skills, a deep understanding of the Bible and how it should be used as a blueprint for modern lives, and the ambition to make the church into something greater than it had been. Robert saw Bob Smith's church as the launching pad for a profound and ultimately world-changing movement. The way to get there was to listen very carefully to God, act upon His wishes, follow His direction, and, above all, understand that being a Christian was more than just believing in the Word of God; it was living it. All day. Every day.

At first Robert taught Sunday-school classes in which he recast some of the themes to better reflect his beliefs that church denominations were divisive and against God's message of Christian unity.

He convincingly pointed to passages in the Bible that illustrated what it was that God had truly sought, and that man—through *church denominations*—had corrupted the message of God. He pointed to the etymology of specific words, pulling out scriptural passages and historical references. He had a lawyer's mind for presenting his point of view in a conclusive and logical manner.

Over time, Robert went from teaching children to offering sermons. He was powerful and persuasive. When he preached from the pulpit that one of the accepted tenets of

the Assemblies of God church—that every Spirit-filled believer would speak in tongues—was in error, he had biblical
backup at his fingertips.

"Robert knows better than I do," PB said to a church
member who wondered aloud if they were on the right track.

Some members of the congregation were uncomfortable
with the transfer of power. Although by this point Robert had
been a part of Christ Community for years, it was still seen as
PB's church. PB was a gentle and caring man. Robert seemed
to try his best, but neither sympathy nor empathy appeared to
be in his repertoire. Nevertheless, PB and the church board
promoted him to pastor.

Not long after Robert managed a toehold in the church
leadership, Nick Hacheney, then in his early twenties, arrived
to serve as a youth pastor. It was a surprise appointment,
made by PB. Nick and PB had known each other since Nick
was a kid. Both men, with almost a father-son bond between
them, saw as essential the nurturing of youth in their understanding of the love and power of the Lord.

A FORM OF DELIVERANCE COUNSELING HAD BECOME THE
primary method of helping church members forge stronger
relationships with God. The sessions were intense, dramatic,
and steeped in fear and shame, with Robert and PB praying
and screaming at demons to exit the afflicted church members.

Have you ever had an abortion?
Had sex with more than one person at a time?
With an animal?
With a person of the same sex?

As church members understood it, the casting out of demons was genuine proof of God's anointing of Robert, a true
gift of miracles that validated his apostleship.

Another aspect of church doctrine guided its course even
more than the gut-wrenching deliverance sessions: the view
that God talked directly to select members of the congregation. Sometimes God spoke of small things, like that a person's illness would wane or that a baby would be born on a

certain day. Whatever the message, it was heeded as if the Almighty had sent a telegram.

Others were bigger. The greatest was the one that stirred most church members into action. God told Pamela Bily about an immense earthquake coming to wreak havoc on the Pacific Northwest.

The earthquake prediction—be it from Pamela, the Bilys' son Adam, or a congregant named Sandy Glass, who also reported prophetic communication from God—altered the lives of those attending their church. So confident were some in the prophecies that they refused to go to work on the specific days named. They didn't take their children to horseback-riding lessons across the Agate Pass Bridge for fear of its collapse. They stockpiled foodstuffs.

Each prophecy pointed a sure finger at the tiny island congregation. God, its members believed, had chosen them to heal and feed the injured and raise the dead of the Seattle area.

That the killer earthquake never jostled the region didn't stop the pronouncement of additional prophetic dreams. At nearly every service, someone would come forward with a Word from God. Some were shared from the pulpit by PB, Robert, or Nick. Sometimes they were typed up and distributed as little slips of paper to be tucked into Bibles or hymnals. Surprisingly, the vaguest messages from God were given the most credence. A congregant could see what he or she wanted to see, like a reader sizing up a horoscope in the daily paper.

And despite the innumerable prophecies, the congregation failed to stop the greatest impending tragedy: a devoted follower dying in a fire.

In the spring of 1996, some incidents involving discipline reflected an underlying and growing fear among the membership. The first occurred when a longtime congregant pointedly refused to accept Robert as an apostle—and could no longer hold his tongue about it. The subject of the service that day was yet another prophecy Pamela Bily brought forth about an imminent earthquake.

As Robert reiterated the prophecy that day in May, the disgruntled churchgoer spoke up.

"This is wrong," he said. "Robert is a false apostle."

All mouths were agape as the man and his wife left the sanctuary.

Two days later, PB delivered a ten-page single-spaced letter of excommunication to the couple's island home. It was a scathing missive in every way, questioning the man's love of Christ, his ability to serve the Lord, and his denial of the need to repent for his sins. Even the fellow's love of baseball was chastised as "idolatry."

Mostly, however, it was a relentless defense of Robert. In fact, Robert Bily's name appeared in the document an astounding seventy times.

> Robert has never arrogantly proclaimed his apostolic position or used it as a means to exercise authority over people. That's a despicable lie that attacks God's leadership. . . .

PB made it very obvious that the man being booted from the congregation had made Robert the scapegoat for his own shortcomings.

> He makes a good target for you to lie about in an effort to cover up your serious sins and your need to repent. Despite your lies and hypocrisy, you are unable to show us or anyone legitimate historical record of Robert's sins in the same way that we have given you a legitimate historical record of your sins.

THE WORDS KEPT COMING TO ANOTHER CHURCH MEMBER, Lavern Melson, as she sat in the comfortable living room of her house hugged by firs in the woods of Poulsbo. The messages were coming louder and louder. *Save PB. Save his wife, Adele. Save them from the doom of Robert's false teachings.* She continued to pray on it. Over the course of a three-day period, ending on May 11, 1996, she wrote a letter to PB indicating that she felt Robert's apostolic teachings were false, that he was more concerned with his own pride and ego than the building of a free and loving ministry.

> I know that you will immediately go to Robert with this letter. . . . Robert will then critique it, dissect it, and cut and dice it, then pronounce it worthless and send you on your way.

It was more than a month before PB answered Lavern. On a crisp white sheet of Christ Community Church letterhead, he wrote how he hadn't given the letter to Robert out of fear that it would "wound" him. He also let her know that her comments were destructive and misguided.

> Over the past few weeks we have had total strangers (to me) approach members of this church and state that they have heard we are now a cult and that Pastor Robert Bily writes my sermons.

PB told her that whatever discipline the church applied was in line with the gospel. The hope for any church-sanctioned discipline, he said, was always to restore the fallen member to the body of Christ. But no matter what resolve PB demonstrated in his letter to Lavern, deep down, he felt a flush of worry.

MANY YEARS LATER, OVER COFFEE IN A BREMERTON RES-taurant, one former congregant was circumspect about the church senior leadership and who was responsible for what transpired on December 26, 1997.

"Look, Bob [PB] can say whatever he wants after the fact, but he bought in to Robert's apostleship. Really, there's no oversight for any apostle. Just show up somewhere and say you are one and—boom, that's what you are. I don't doubt that Robert believed he was an apostle, but Bob didn't question it. I think he thought Robert was smarter and closer to God than he was."

3

THE RIFT BETWEEN BOB SMITH AND ROBERT BILY was, at first, nearly imperceptible to those outside the inner circle. After all, from the outset, PB seemed to be Robert's chief supporter. Robert had been pressing for his apostolic church model for years, which would mean the creation of a nondenominational network of home-based worship groups. And while PB also wanted to serve God in a bigger, better way, he had misgivings about severing his long-standing ties with the Assemblies of God.

Robert felt that he'd proven his concepts, his teachings, and himself to the congregants and the members of the board. To his way of thinking, the sole stumbling block was PB. Robert's patience was ebbing. So was Pamela's. Sweet as she was, she had desires and needs. She had come from a family of means and had grown weary of living hand to mouth, as so many ministers' wives do. She'd waited all those years for the soy-food concept to take off or the money for a lawsuit against the failed computer company to pay off. A stylish blonde with an almost ethereal beauty, Pamela wasn't a greedy woman; she was just tired of never-ending delay.

Robert decided to push PB and the others harder. He used his formidable personality—direct, cool, and unbreakable—to let congregants know that the time to do something was now, not later. He felt his role was to remind people what they needed to *do* to be better Christians. Words were never enough.

"I'm just trying to do what's scriptural," he said.

In the pages of the Bible, Robert found scriptural edicts that suggested what people should eat (high-protein foods, whole grains, no sugar), how they should dress (modestly), how they should teach their children (homeschooling), and how Christ would help them get to where they needed to go (He wants you to have whatever you dream).

For a few worshippers, that was too much. Some felt the dietary requirements mandating whole and natural foods, in particular, were too strict. PB Smith, with his thickset frame, was hardly the best example of success in the diet department. He liked a big slice of pizza now and then. The idea that God would urge his believers to fulfill all their personal desires also provided further contention and conflict. Some were ringing up skyrocketing credit card balances just to keep up with their wants and desires as God had promised them.

The mantra coming out of the church sanctuary could not have been clearer: "You name it, claim it. God wants you to be happy! Take the land. Take what's yours!"

In sermons, writings, or counseling sessions, Robert freely conceded that people would stumble. Being a Christian wasn't supposed to be easy. It was about creating faith by making sacrifices. Rewards would come from those sacrifices. When people griped, Robert, Bible in hand, gave them intense one-on-one counseling that left no doubt: He was right; they were weak.

Sometimes those who'd been challenged by Robert would circumvent his authority by going to see Pastor Bob. PB, always the peacemaker, tried to smooth things over.

"Robert, you've got a blind spot," PB said on more than one occasion. "You get too aggressive."

LIKE OTHERS NOT QUITE IN THE INNER CIRCLE, ED MATHE-son's mother, Sally LaGrandeur, had been feeling things were on a desperate course since Robert Bily came onto the scene. Nearly a decade later, sitting in her cozy cluttered home on Bainbridge Island with her husband, Rich, her sister Suzy, and Suzy's husband, Danny Claflin, she spoke for all of them. She recalled an encounter she had had with the pastors.

"I always felt like PB was the pastor and suddenly he was giving everything over to Bily and, I thought, *That's really weird. That's not right.* I met with PB and Bily in the office, them and me. I was really nervous, and I said, 'This isn't right that one person has all the control. What if you decide to take over the church or something?' I said it like a joke!"

Robert, to whom the question was addressed, answered that it could *never* happen. "If I did something like that, then no one would follow me, so why would I do that? You could all just leave."

Sally glanced at her husband, who nodded knowingly all those years later. "Pastor Bob was sitting there, saying, 'Yeah, that's not going to happen, so don't worry about it.'"

CERTAINLY IN THE BEGINNING ROBERT BILY HAD LITTLE use for Nick Hacheney. He considered Nick PB's surrogate son, and whatever differences he had with his rival were readily transferred to Nick. But in Nick, Robert began to see something that he hadn't allowed himself to accept at first: Nick desired to grow in his understanding of God.

"Robert," Nick said one time, "I really want you to take greater interest and involvement in my development. I'm here at the office. I'm working with PB, and we never do anything. I don't want his culture to affect me and to cause me to become like him."

The words surprised Robert, and he was unsure how to respond. PB, after all, was Nick's father figure. They hunted together, went on trips, and went to Sawatdy's for Thai. Robert and Nick, meanwhile, shared no such camaraderie.

"Nick, I'm a pastor here, but I'm not yet *senior* pastor."

Nick persisted and Robert eventually gave in.

Nick's energy was undeniable, and his compassion for others seemed to run deep. Despite being in his twenties, Nick appeared adept at counseling church members. Robert saw all of it as supernatural proof that true grace can come when least expected. Nick, young as he was, was the right man at the right time. He could, with the right guidance, be a key player in the apostolic church Robert had envisioned.

Only one thing seemed amiss. A couple of the people Nick was counseling complained that his focus was on private, sexual matters. One woman even broke up with her betrothed because of Nick's insistence that they discuss things she considered too personal.

"All he wants to do is talk about sex," she told Robert.

4

T HE FIRST MONTHS OF 1997 WERE COLD, GRAY, AND wet, typical for the Pacific Northwest. Kids prayed for snow. Adults, of course, hoped for rain instead, which would ensure children would be in the classroom and not underfoot. The higher elevations got a decent dusting of snow that January, but the streets around Bremerton stayed shiny and damp: too close to the water to allow for snow to last and, at sea level, never quite high enough to catch the coldest puff of a winter day.

Nick Hacheney found an East Bremerton fixer-upper on Jensen Avenue and immediately pronounced it perfect for a trip up the property ladder. Dawn, working as a loan officer at Kitsap Federal Credit Union, where she earned eighteen thousand dollars a year, reluctantly agreed. It wasn't that she wasn't interested in a new house; she simply had grown weary of moving, as this was their third address in as many years. She told friends that she hated living out of boxes or cooking in kitchens coated with drywall dust. Dawn loathed the feeling of the chalkiness of the boards and the putty; she double-pumped vanilla hand lotion whenever she could.

Dawn's father, Donald Tienhaara, didn't think much of the couple's latest real estate investment and told Nick so. He pointed at the cement stairs that climbed from street level to the walkway to the front door. The nine-hundred-square-foot house was perched on a sliver of solid ground.

"Not a good place to raise kids," he said.

When Nick didn't answer, Donald took his son-in-law's

uncharacteristic silence to mean that children weren't in the offing.

"I know she wanted to be a mother," Donald said many years later, "but I guess Nick had other ideas."

HEAVY WINDS ARE NOTORIOUS FOR KNOCKING OUT POWER in Kitsap County, sometimes for days at a time. The winds bully the shoreline and batter the power lines with a force that occasionally seems otherworldly. Kitsap County is often one of the last areas of the Puget Sound to get back on the grid after a storm.

During such outages, couples spend their time either in bed or at each other's throats. Violence spikes; tempers flare. In their home in the Suquamish Shores neighborhood, Craig and Annette Anderson, two of the church's faithful, found themselves stuck in the dark with three children under five. Things quickly went ugly. Annette was frustrated with Craig. He was frustrated with *her*. It didn't get violent, but it did get vocal.

Annette, age twenty-nine, knew that any argument with Craig, nine years older, was a no-win stalemate. In such cases, one of them would retreat before reaching any real resolution.

"Let's go to the church," she said. "At least they'll have heat."

Barely speaking to each other, they packed up their brood and headed across the bridge. It was late in the afternoon when they went inside, past the pastors' offices—PB's, Robert's, and Nick's—to the nursery, where they sat down to glare at each other. They were at another impasse, a divide fueled by the power outage and the forced interaction that came with it.

An advertising sales representative, Craig was a handsome man with black hair and olive skin who had chased demons of his own for most of his life. He'd had substance-abuse problems since he was seventeen, a disastrous first marriage, and an employment history that included the sort of jobs he wanted to leave off his résumé. Christ Community Church was the key to his personal salvation and he knew it.

Annette and Craig had met in Portland, Oregon. She'd been through some hard knocks, having come from a devout religious family that sometimes missed the big problems brewing at home. She'd fallen victim to predatory men. Some of the things that happened to her as a young woman were so dark that she could scarcely talk to anyone about them. She camouflaged her beauty with ill-fitting attire, clunky shoes, and long hair more suited to a 1960s hippie than a young wife and mother in the 1990s. She cleaned houses for extra income.

"On Bainbridge there was the working class and the wealthy," Annette said many years later, "and not really much in between. Craig and I were on the working-class end of things, for sure. I cleaned houses for those on the upper end of the spectrum, including Robert and Pamela Bily. There were financial pressures there, I'm sure. I remember how they were selling off furniture, Persian rugs, and Lalique crystal as they kept waiting for money to come in. That was before Robert set his eyes on taking over the church, though."

"YOU GUYS OKAY?"

Annette and Craig looked up. It was Nick Hacheney. The twenty-seven-year-old pastor always had a knack for reading people, although the rift between Craig and Annette was palpable enough that anyone would have sensed it.

Nick took a seat in a beat-up donated rocker, facing the Andersons in the nursery. The children were preoccupied with a shopping cart and other toys scattered across the carpeted floor. Nick's tone was serious and buoyant at the same time; it was as if he'd been sent to the room to make peace.

"Maybe I can help you work through some things," he said.

Neither said it, but they had a very real sense of having "been there, done that." They had met with the Bilys months before. It had been a single session with a bit of wisdom that seemed like too much work: Be more like Christ.

"We've tried counseling," Craig finally said.

"Robert and Pamela last year," Annette added.

Nick didn't dismiss Robert's efforts, but he did indicate that maybe he could do better.

"Let's see what we can do together," he said. "I have another approach."

They had too much to lose by not working things out.

Annette and Craig nodded, neither knowing just what Nick had in mind or where he'd lead them.

PASTOR BOB SMITH HAD GONE ALONG WITH THE CHANGES to his church, but he was unsure about his own future. Although it had yet to be put up for a church vote, it was obvious that he was no longer in charge. Robert Bily was. At forty-nine, PB had to make a personal and professional change. So he and Adele discussed going to Africa, where their eldest daughter, Kim, twenty-one, lived with her husband, a Tanzanian named Godwin Selembo. Once there, he would pray about his future.

"We'll listen to what God tells us to do," he said.

PB would later tell friends that he sensed a "dark cloud" hanging over the church, but he was unable to see the truth at the time.

5

WHEN NICK AND DAWN HACHENEY RAN SHORT on remodeling funds, they applied for a second mortgage on the house on Jensen Avenue. The influx of cash, however, did little to stave off their spiraling debt in the spring of 1997. Many knew why. Although some didn't care much for Nick, considering him a blowhard and a spotlight seeker, none could call him a selfish tightwad. He gave funds freely to those who needed help. Where other guys might have stopped off at a tavern for beer after work, Nick pulled over at any number of ATMs.

He also put his money into another pursuit. Nick's big dream since he was a teen was to own and operate a Christian youth camp. He envisioned a cluster of cabins or tents along a lakeshore or riverside. As a test structure, he'd purchased a yurt, a circular tent favored by Central Asia nomads that was gaining popularity in America with hipsters and the practical alike. In March, Nick invited a young church member named Michael DeLashmutt to drive up north to take a look at some acreage in Jefferson County, west of Kitsap County across the Hood Canal Bridge. Nick was convinced it was the perfect spot to make his dream a reality. The property had a small lake, a meadow, and towering second-growth firs. Seeing the land Nick had his eye on, Michael agreed. It *was* perfect.

On the way back to Kitsap, Nick ended his incessant up-beat chatter about the youth camp so swiftly that Michael might have veered off the highway had he not been such a focused driver.

"I think when you go to heaven," Nick said, "you can have sex with whoever you want to."

Michael, a thoughtful young man of twenty-one, sat in awkward silence. *Where did that come from?* he thought. He recalled a time at a youth camp when Nick's persona changed from merciful counselor to dirty old man—when Michael had confessed that he and his then-fiancée had fooled around a little. When he got home to Kitsap after their drive, Michael told his wife, Julia, about his exchange with Nick.

"If that's his view of heaven, then what's his view of *this* life?" he asked.

Julia shook her head. She didn't have a clue.

At about the same time, a church member had a vision of the same property Nick planned to buy in Jefferson County, not far from his old stomping grounds at the church camp at Fort Flagler, where as a teenager he'd first grown close to Bob Smith. She—Sandy Glass—saw herself as part of Nick's vision.

"I got a Word," Sandy told a friend. "God will move me and my boys someplace beautiful and serene and we'll all serve Him from there."

She described how that property would become the location of a new church ministry, one in which she and Pastor Nick would play important roles. Her boys would be part of it too.

Notably absent from the "vision" was any mention of Sandy's husband, Jimmy, or Nick's wife, Dawn.

Whenever Sandy uttered one of her messages from God, those within earshot listened carefully. Married to carpenter Jimmy Glass and the mother of four boys—the youngest born in October of the previous year—Sandy had been through so much in her tumultuous life that her messages carried a lot of weight at Christ Community, the name most still called the church even after its split from the Assemblies. Her first serious boyfriend died in her arms of an unspecified viral disease. Her father was killed in a construction accident. Her brother was a drug addict. She'd been around the block a time or two and hadn't lived a perfect life, but she made no excuses for any of her own choices. Sandy lifted herself out of the abyss through God's love. In her midthirties, she was thin, almost frail, with a pleasant face and narrow brown eyes.

If there was anyone closer to God at that particular church, no one could name him or her. Longtime church secretary Sandy Glass was gifted with the prophetic Word.

Everybody said so.

MOST WHO KNEW NICK AND DAWN CONSIDERED THEIR union ideal. Nick was a pastor, called to serve God, and Dawn was his wife, called to serve *him*. She did everything she could for her husband, and did so gladly. When he needed something, she found a way to get it, even if it meant dipping into overextended MasterCard or Visa accounts.

Dawn's childhood friend Eunice Zeitner never liked Nick, however, and never made any pretense about her feelings. When Eunice returned to Kitsap County after living in Seattle for a time, she was broke, bitter, and forced to move back in with her parents.

"You know," Dawn told her during a dinner out, "if Nick and I ended up splitting up, I would never, ever want to live with my parents."

Just the mention of a hypothetical split fueled a little hope in Eunice.

"Then move in with me," she said, suggesting the two of them could get a place together and both avoid living with their parents.

Dawn took it in. "Okay," she said. "That might happen."

Eunice didn't press for further details. Maybe it was that she just didn't want to jinx the hope that Dawn would someday come to her senses and see Nick for the boob that Eunice was convinced he was. Ultimately, she figured it was almost too much to hope for.

IT WAS AT THE CHURCH LEADERSHIP'S URGING THAT NICK threw himself into counseling other married couples. However, it was immediately apparent that Nick was focusing his attention on the wives. In many ways, that was a prudent strategic move. Among many Christ Community families, the women held the balance of power in their relationships. That on its surface was troubling to Robert and PB and those who ascribed themselves to a more literal interpretation of the Bible: Submission is a gift from a wife to her husband. Jesus wants a woman to submit to a man's authority. In some churches, the familial chain of command worked as written. Not at Christ Community. Some of the men seemed weak and unassuming, kowtowing to their stronger, more driven women. And so, strategically, Robert knew that if he could capture the hearts, minds, and spirits of the women, the men would follow.

It was during that time that Nick was counseling three married church members—Sandy Glass, Nicole Matheson, and Annette Anderson—in private.

Annette, for one, saw Nick's push to get Craig out of the way as a means for her to move deeper into the spiritual life she desperately sought. Craig *wanted* to be involved in the counseling, but it seemed that Nick saw something more in Annette. By May 1997, Nick was focused solely on her. Craig became an afterthought, scarcely an aside in their deep conversations.

Nick's constant affirmation that her happiness would be restored and that something big would happen was like the promise of a healing drug. Whatever problems Annette endured, God was right next to her and He would save her.

"Your life will be happy. You are blessed and loved by God. Stand next to Him," Nick told her over and over.

Standing next to God meant separating from those who didn't see the truth of the Bible. Annette was reticent about opening up and truly embracing that. She wanted to, but if it meant denouncing old relationships, she was reluctant to do so. Nick told her she had to give up some things in order to gain the true glory of knowing God.

One afternoon in his office, Nick told her to stand up with her back toward him.

"I need you to trust me, to have faith."

"What do you want me to do?" she asked.

"Fall backwards."

She turned to see him behind her. He had a gentle smile.

"No, no," he said. "Without looking at me. Just fall."

Annette tightened her body. She knew Nick was there, that he would catch her. Even so, it was hard to let go.

"Go ahead, *fall*. God will be here. I'll be here."

Annette fell backward.

"I'm here for you. God's here for you," he said, catching her.

6

ALTHOUGH HOLLY KLOVEN WAS SLIGHTLY OLDER, AT the age of forty, she and Sandy Glass were at the same stage in life. When Holly and Sandy first met at Sandy's mother-in-law's Bible study in the mid-1980s, it was easy for the other women to see they'd become good friends. They both had been born in Bremerton, both felt their Christian faith completely and deeply, and both had suffered personal indignities not of their own doing. If Holly was a prettier woman—with lovely dark eyes, shoulder-length wavy brown hair, and a petite frame—Sandy was by no means unattractive. Her teeth may not have been perfectly straight, but when she smiled, she lit up a room.

Holly admired Sandy's take-charge attitude. She noticed that Sandy didn't rely on her husband, Jimmy, for everything. She couldn't imagine such independence for herself. She checked with Einar, also forty, on everything. A stoic Norwegian with an abundance of good sense, Einar didn't control Holly; she just felt safer running things past him.

Sandy, however, thought nothing of taking on a project and running with it. Sandy was fun, silly, and warm. She had horses and a vegetable garden, and she could use a Skilsaw like a carpenter. In time, Holly felt a genuine bond grow between the two of them.

This is what it must feel like to have a sister, she thought, coming from a family in which she was the only girl.

When in the mid-1980s Holly cooked up the idea to open a new Christian day care at Christ Community, she had turned to Sandy for help. Those were busy but satisfying times. Einar worked days in construction, and he'd come home ready to take the next shift caring for their daughters and son. Holly would head off to her job at the bank in the island's commercial district and do data processing throughout the night. Sandy pitched in where she could by watching the kids or doing whatever Holly needed.

If Holly knew that Sandy had something of a past—that she smoked and partied hard when she was younger, and had suffered the tragic loss of a boyfriend—it was because Sandy never made a big secret of any of it. Nor did she let any of that define her. If her marriage to Jimmy was unsatisfying in those early days of their union, Holly really didn't see it.

No matter what life gives her, Holly thought, *Sandy takes it all in stride.*

THE PROMISE OF CHRIST COMMUNITY CHURCH WAS NOT only heavenly salvation but the very speed in which all good things could materialize. If other churches promoted the idea that prosperity came with perseverance, it seemed that Christ Community Church leaders believed that better things came quickly to those who believed. God would provide, and he would do so lickety-split. Deliverance counseling sessions—whether three hours or ten—were a high-speed method for erasing years of sin. Desire and ambition were spun equally fast. If somebody wanted a hot tub or a new car, he or she was encouraged to go out and get it right away. If the charge cards maxed out, who cared? God wasn't about to let anyone down. Most believed that abundance was not only possible but guaranteed. Sandy Glass, in particular, held that view.

Framed by enormous evergreens, the Glass family compound was just off Arrow Point Drive, facing Bainbridge Island's Battle Point Park. Calling it a compound was a stretch by Rockefeller or Kennedy standards, of course, but the property was home to three generations in two dwellings. The acreage was divided by a gravel driveway, with Jimmy and Sandy's manufactured home on the left, along with a single-wide trailer that had been the family's first home but was now being used as a rental. Jimmy's parents, James and Mary, put in a smaller manufactured home on the other side of the property. A rolling pasture, a barn, outbuildings, vegetable gardens, and rosebushes that somehow survived nightly assaults by hungry deer made the place a gentleman farmer's modest dream. It was mostly Sandy's vision that created the farm milieu: She wanted the chickens and horses. It was Sandy who tilled the vegetable garden and fertilized and watered the sunflowers every day so they'd grow taller than her husband.

Sandy not only worked hard but spent hard. For a woman on a tradesman's tight budget, she'd been swiping her credit card to such a degree that it worried not only James and Mary Glass but also Holly Kloven, who often accompanied her on shopping trips to Poulsbo and Bremerton. Holly wasn't the type to say much about her friend's wanton spending, but it did cross her mind that Sandy was overdoing it. She mentioned it to Sandy once.

"I have insurance on these cards," Sandy shot back. "When Jimmy dies, the cards will be paid off."

Sandy's offhand comment was a reference to a Word from God that she had received on more than one occasion: Jimmy was going to die soon. Holly knew that Sandy walked closely with God, so the idea that God would tell her in a dream that her husband was going to die wasn't out of the realm of real possibility. It wasn't that Sandy was happy that Jimmy was about to meet his Maker; she took it as fate and was resigned to God's plan.

Sandy told Holly that she'd increased the life insurance on Jimmy too. She was getting her finances in order because she was convinced she'd be on her own with the boys. Holly found herself wondering who would take Jimmy's place when he did get called home to Jesus. She hated when those thoughts came: They seemed disloyal and wrong.

One time when they were out running errands, Sandy said that she had bought a new chain saw.

"A smaller one that a woman can handle easier," she said. "When Jimmy's gone, I'll still need to do things around here."

Several others knew of Sandy's premonition about Jimmy. But one person absolutely did not: Jimmy himself.

AT FIRST NICK APPEARED TO ACCEPT THE RESPONSIBILITY of providing marital counseling, although with a shrug that suggested he wasn't really ready for it. However, his marriage to Dawn gave the impression that he understood how to make a relationship work. Why not share advice with others? After a few weeks of being swept up in the positive feedback of what he was able to accomplish, Nick's feigned self-confidence appeared to turn into genuine assuredness.

"Helping these couples is my calling," he told a church member.

One day while waiting for Robert Bily, who was holed up in his home office, Nick chatted with Pamela in the foyer of the Bilys' spacious Bainbridge Island rental. Pamela, forty-five, never cared much for Nick, but she wasn't the type to show her true feelings. The wives of ministers seldom do. But when it came to Nick and his marriage-counseling acumen, Pamela's facade cracked.

Nick said the women he was helping were taking full advantage of his expertise.

"I'm basically on call," he said. "I'm available any time during the day or night."

Pamela bristled. It was too much involvement. And more than that, Nick was bragging. It wasn't what her husband or Bob Smith had wanted when Nick was enlisted to help the fractured couples of the church. And what about his own marriage?

"This is marital abuse," Pamela said. "You need to focus on Dawn. You need to comfort *her*, and Dawn needs to know that she's number one in your life."

Later, when Nick recalled the conversation with Pamela, he just shrugged it off.

"I guess she just didn't like me anymore," he said.

SOMETIMES THINGS SNOWBALL IN WAYS THAT ARE IMPOS-sible to foresee. In the spring of 1997, Holly and Einar

Kloven found themselves on the wrong side of Robert Bily when the Klovens let the Bily children watch the sequel to Jim Carrey's *Ace Ventura: Pet Detective*. Nick was among the onlookers when the Bilys' youngest started quoting some of the movie's gross-out humor at church.

"Someone's going to be in big trouble," he said. "No one better tell the Bilys."

Nick's remark bothered Holly. She'd been entrusted to keep an eye on things when Robert and Pamela were out of town. She figured she'd tell Pamela what happened.

I'd want her to tell me, she thought. *It was an innocent lapse, but the little girl has picked up some things that she probably shouldn't have.*

Pamela exploded at the news. The Klovens—certainly among the most decent and upstanding members of the congregation—were in need of major corrective action and repentance, Pamela decided. When Holly tried to defend herself, it only made matters worse. It quickly moved away from concerns about a girl watching a silly, vulgar movie to an unintended referendum on the Klovens, their family, and their parenting sensibilities.

Robert and Pamela kept pushing Einar and Holly. There were phone calls and confrontations at church. And when those didn't work, the cold shoulder was applied. The Bilys kept pressuring the Klovens to repent; the Klovens felt bad about the video but believed that the transgression hardly deserved the rebuke coming from their friends and leaders of the church.

One church member would later point to that time and say that "the devil creates his share of distractions and dissention. That's *his* job."

EMOTIONS CAME WITH FAITH. NICK SEEMED TO UNDER-stand that better than anyone. He thrived on it. Samuel Pennoyer, barely in his twenties, was one who felt the power of what Nick offered. Sam had been brought up in Burien, Washington, in the Community Chapel and Bible Training Center led by a charismatic and controversial pastor who twisted the scripture until it allowed adultery and near orgies among its three thousand members. Years later—after rehab and institutionalization for a crippled psyche—he'd married Carol McClung's sister, Julie Strum. They met at the Bible college that Nick and Dawn had attended.

In a way, Sam was an ideal fit for an evolving church under the triumvirate of Bob Smith, Robert Bily, and Nick Hacheney. His marriage was failing, despite the birth of a daughter. He was a young man with a broken spirit and a deep need to reconnect with God. In all his life, Sam would later say, he'd never experienced the kind of convincing, dynamic power that flowed from Nick. It went far beyond all the counseling, prayers, and intervention that had shaped his life up to that point. He moved in to a trailer in the driveway outside the Hacheneys' house on Jensen Avenue in April 1997. The next month Julie and their new baby joined him. Nick had brought a miracle.

"I tend to be dramatic, but I'm not exaggerating," Sam, a cook at a Poulsbo restaurant, said several years later. "He was amazing. He was able to make [Julie and me] feel valued, equipped, inspired for hope, and reconciled. Nick was like my hero. He single-handedly saved the day."

But not everything was perfect. That spring, Sam also remembered how the phone rang for Nick day and night. When he answered, it was Nicole Matheson on the line.

"I thought it was interesting in a way. *Interesting*, not good. We didn't chat. [She] never asked for Dawn. No one ever called for Dawn."

7

SUNLIGHT POURED IN THROUGH THE WINDOWS, ILLU-minating the Anderson family's living room. A view of Puget Sound filtered through the shaggy boughs of Douglas firs. Craig was off selling advertising, and the kids were napping. For Annette, the quiet of the afternoon was the best time of the day. No matter how frazzled her life, she was able to latch on to some clarity in those moments.

Not that May afternoon.

Nick had called with the urgent need to see her: He had something very important to say. Something was seriously wrong. Within minutes of his call, he was on her couch, distraught and on the verge of tears. Annette tried to comfort him, urging him very gently to let out whatever it was that he was trying to tell her.

Nick started to cry. "No one knows about this," he began. "Some bad things happened to me as a kid."

Annette could see the animated anguish on his face. She almost knew what he was going to say before he disclosed it. Nick had been through a lot with his brother's drug addiction, imprisonment, and death. His idea of "bad things" had to be dire.

"What?" she asked, a prompt that she knew would unleash something ominous.

The words came slowly, sputtering before ultimately mixing with a torrent of tears.

"I was molested as a boy," he said.

For a second, Annette flashed on Dan and Sandra Hacheney, with whom she'd become close through home group church meetings and the ladies' Bible study hosted at the Hacheney home. She wondered for a second if Nick had been abused by a family member: a brother, an uncle, maybe even his own parents. She could feel her own defenses rise as she pictured a little boy being messed with by some sick adult.

As he seemed to try to pull himself together, she leaned close to him. Her eyes were full of concern. "Who? What happened?"

Nick looked away, taking a moment to pull the words from his memory. "A school worker," he said. He offered the name of a Bainbridge Island elementary school he'd attended, and indicated that it had happened repeatedly.

Annette's eyes filled with tears too. She put her arm around his shoulders.

"What about Dawn? How's she with all of this?"

"There are some things Dawn doesn't know. She couldn't handle it."

Annette couldn't understand Nick not telling Dawn something so crucial. They had the ultimate marriage, and if they couldn't share something so intimate and so important, who could? Her heart went out to Nick, her pastor, her friend. He smiled at her in a way that was meant to convey appreciation and trust. Maybe even to cheer her up because of the burden he had just laid on her.

"I'm so sorry, Nick."

Nick turned off his tears. "You are my friend, Annette. Do you get that? You are my true friend. You can't tell anyone about this," he said. "Not even Craig."

Annette understood perfectly. It was a strange mix of emotions, but where Nick was concerned, it seemed almost typical. His personality, problems, and dreams always seemed amplified compared to those of others. In this instance, Annette had been the perfect person to whom to make such a disclosure. She'd shared her own past, which included both abuse and victimization that haunted her through her twenties. She knew what it was like to carry a burden. Maybe Nick understood that about her. He'd had that terrible secret bottled up inside with absolutely no one to share it with.

He can't even tell Dawn. But he can share it with me, she thought, feeling a bit honored.

IN THE BEGINNING, DAWN WAS A PART OF THE COUNSELING effort to save Jimmy and Sandy Glass's teetering marriage. It wasn't that she was there during the counseling itself, but when Nick needed to wheedle some time with Sandy—away from the kids—Dawn would gladly step in to babysit. She did the same thing for Nicole Matheson and her kids. Those who knew her knew that Dawn's participation had as much to do with her love of children as her desire to help her husband.

James and Mary Glass felt it was odd that the focus during counseling sessions was on Sandy, not their son, Jimmy. As far as they could see, Jimmy needed more help in getting his act together than Sandy did. He drank a little. He raised his voice. Sometimes he slammed his fist into the tabletop. Sandy wasn't exactly a saint, but she'd been through a lot and lived a perfect example of the power of God's spirit to change one's life.

Nick's attention on Sandy, however, began to grate on the Glasses. When they visited Jimmy and Sandy's place, Sandy would frequently get on the phone with Nick and retreat to a back room. It seemed more important to her to talk to Nick than to interact with her visitors, her family, or even her young sons. Sandy was on the phone all the time.

James Glass, a no-nonsense type, didn't really know what to make of Nick. He was too young to be all that wise, but Pastor Bob liked him and trusted him enough to put him in the position of being a leader and counselor.

Okay, I trust PB, James Glass thought. *Nick's probably all right.*

THE ENTIRE CONGREGATION KNEW THAT NICOLE MATHE-son was a fighter. She could be called erratic, immature, and even petulant, but no one could utter her name and "quitter" in the same breath. In her midtwenties, she had lovely gray-blue eyes, chestnut hair, and a slender figure that was the envy of any woman who'd had a baby. A light dusting of freckles cut a swath across the bridge of her perfect nose. As lovely as she was, as easily as she could have attracted another man, Nicole desired only one right then, and he was missing. She wanted, above everything, for her drug-addicted husband, Ed, to clean himself up and realize what he had waiting for him in their three-bedroom house up the hill from Puget Sound in Suquamish.

Ed was living somewhere in the southern part of the county, in Port Orchard, and Nicole let the word out that she wanted him home. It had been almost a year since he'd lived with her and the children. He'd never once said whether he'd return or stay away forever. His vagueness only gave her hope.

As the spring of 1997 blossomed into summer, even the calendar was conspiring with Nicole to get her man back. Father's Day, she felt, was the perfect time for Ed to snap out of his self-destructive behavior and come home. She made cookies, bought chocolate-and-caramel turtles, and cleared a space in the top drawer of their dresser.

He's gotta see what he's missing, she thought.

When Ed finally came to visit on June 15, it was painfully apparent in his eyes and attitude that he hadn't given up drugs. Nicole looked past all of that and gathered the children around him. They gave him key rings they'd made in day care. To Nicole, he seemed elated.

"So when are you coming back?" she asked.

"I don't see it in the stars," he said, breaking her heart once more.

Later, after Ed drove off, Nicole put pen to paper and wrote in her journal:

So we were sitting on the couch. He said, they're really great kids. You've done a great job with them. I said, it was God. He said it tears him up to say goodbye to the kids. I

want [him] to know that when [he] comes back this won't
be something that will be held over [his] head, it will be
done.

She cried into the telephone as she spoke to Pastor Nick
that same day.

"I'm so sick of waiting. Ed will never change."

"Let's pray on that," Nick said. As he led her in prayer,
Nicole tried to focus on what had gone wrong with her plan,
her own prayers. She later wrote:

Here are the things that Satan is trying to use against me.
Mostly, you're so stupid and you're a dork. But Nick says,
you're not a dork, you're a rock.

SALLY LAGRANDEUR, ED'S MOTHER, BEGAN TO WORRY
about all the attention Nick was lavishing on her daughter-
in-law. Nick was trying to be helpful, but his omnipresent
support of Nicole had shut out her son.

*If Nick is always there, why would Ed need to pull him-
self together to be a good father?*

Sally also began to have concerns about Sandy Glass. It
seemed a little peculiar that she was showing up for the
Thursday-evening service for youths. Sally, forty-one, came
occasionally because her teenage daughter Sara was attending
and sometimes needed a ride home. As the music played—
drums, guitars, voices rising together in song—Sandy would
hover in the back of the room, arms held high.

"Praise the Lord! Sweet Jesus!"

The showiness of Sandy's worship was a distraction for
Sally.

*Why is she here? Her kids aren't even old enough to at-
tend!*

Nick would frequently catch Sandy's eye, and a few times
he moved closer to be near her. Another time, at a regular service, Sandy broke down and Nick put his arms around her.

Sally was bothered by the intimacy between Nick and
Sandy, but she dismissed it.

That's not right, she thought. *But that's just Nick. He's a touchy-feely guy.*

THE FALLING-OUT BETWEEN THE KLOVENS AND THE BILYS continued to gnaw at Holly, but not so much that she couldn't try to summon the courage to do what was right. It was an open sore. Every time she saw Nick, Annette, and an increasingly distant Sandy huddled together around the sanctuary or in the church offices, it only served to remind her that she had suddenly been cast as an outsider. She'd been Sandy's best friend for years, and now she barely had a moment alone with her.

It seemed that Sandy had time for everyone but her.

Holly talked to Robert Bily about it, but since their friendship had iced over with the incident of the Jim Carrey video, it seemed that he was no longer a loving sounding board for her concern.

"Yes," Robert said, "Nick *is* spending too much time alone with these women. I agree: It is improper. I'll handle it."

As far as Holly could see, however, Robert was not handling it at all. Nobody was. In a blast of unexpected courage, she decided she'd confront Nick herself. She saw him in the church office and felt strong enough to bring up her concerns. Nick treated her as if she didn't really "get" what was happening and what he was trying to do for Sandy, Annette, and Nicole.

"I know I'm spending a lot of time with them," he said, his tone surprisingly glib. "I'm doing what God has told me to do. What I must do."

"But they're getting too close to you, Nick. It could cause problems."

Nick nearly rolled his eyes, his annoyance transparent.

"Look, Holly, these ladies need to know that God's love is forgiving and perfect and accepting of them, no matter what they've done. You should know that."

She felt a twinge of her past coming back: She'd confided in Sandy about her abusive stepfather, and the way he had made her feel until she came to understand she'd done nothing wrong. She now knew that Sandy had likely shared her secret with Nick.

"God loves Sandy without restrictions. God wants me to get this message to her. That's what I'm doing."

"It doesn't look right," Holly said.

Nick locked his eyes on Holly. "I know you're uncomfortable with it. God wants this. God wants this even if it looks wrong. God is all-powerful and He can do whatever He wants."

"God would *never* be contradictory to the Bible," she said.

Nick shrugged. "Even if it seemed wrong and outside the parameters of what you would expect, He can do it. He's all-powerful."

For a second, Holly thought Nick was talking about himself.

"Even if Sandy loved me like a woman loves a man, that would be all right in His eyes because she might need it right now," Nick went on. "It might help her really understand the power of God's love for her."

Holly had never heard such a thing in her life. Nick had corrupted God's word. He couldn't have been more off base.

8

EVEN TO A WOMAN JUST EDGING OUT OF HER TEENS, the worrisome pattern was apparent. Several times a week, Pastor Bob Smith's nineteen-year-old daughter, Lindsey, would find Nick and Sandy huddled somewhere in the church, whispering, praying. It had become so routine that it was almost irritating. Lindsey was known at the church as one of Nick's "little disciples." She was the member of the congregation closest to Nick—more so than Sandy, she felt. She considered approaching Nick about it, but to do so seemed petty.

Although she was young, Lindsey had a sense of caring and respect that didn't match the clichéd persona of the rebellious pastor's daughter. She had been a bit of a tomboy growing up, loving sports and hunting with her dad. She favored sweaters and loafers and wore her light brown hair in a short cut that suited a girl more concerned with practicality than looking like the pop star of the moment. She was humble but not shy when it came to getting a point across or stepping up to serve others who were in need.

Every now and then, however, she stewed about Nick and Sandy and the time they were spending together.

One sunny day in 1997, Lindsey arrived at the church and immediately observed Nick's and Sandy's cars parked out front. No one else was there. As she walked toward Nick's office, she noticed that his door was slightly ajar. All of a sudden it snapped shut.

What the—? she asked herself. It was uncharacteristic of

her to be so bold, but with all the time Nick was spending sequestered with Sandy, her curiosity got the best of her. She knocked.

A beat later, the door opened a sliver. Nick peered through the slit, looking angry and irritated. It was as if Lindsey's knock had interrupted something very important.

"There's a sleeping baby in here. You'll have to leave us alone," he said.

Lindsey mouthed that she was sorry. Over Nick's shoulder, she caught a quick glimpse of Sandy Glass curled up on the sofa. The room was dim; a single lamp sent a soft spray of radiance to the ceiling. Nick put his fingers to his lips and shut the door.

Lindsey stood outside, confused and upset. It was no secret that Sandy was unhappy in her marriage to Jimmy, but was something improper going on? *Was Sandy tempting Nick?* she wondered.

She held the thought only for the briefest of moments. Then it was gone.

SANDY GLASS, THE CHURCH SECRETARY FOR ALMOST A DEcade, was stoic as she sat across from Nick in his office for one of their one-on-one sessions in the early summer of 1997. Robert Bily had warned the young pastor of a disturbing prophecy that Sandy had recently shared. According to Sandy, the fact that Jimmy was no longer coming for counseling was of no matter. There was no need to save their marriage, she told Nick. Its fate was out of their hands.

"Jimmy is going to die," she said.

Nick pressed her. "How do you know that?"

"God told me."

As they talked about it, then and later, they accepted the prophecy as unqualified fact. The when and the how were not specified, but Jimmy was going to die. Sandy was a prophetess nearly without peer. Her messages from God—sometimes a little convoluted and difficult to fully understand—were typed up and disseminated at church services with almost the regularity of a weekly newsletter. Before one of her sons was born, God told Sandy that he'd be three months early—which he was. God also told her not to worry: Despite his preemie status, the boy would survive. He was right.

If God told her something, it was likely to be true.

The particular prophecy about Jimmy, however, wasn't sent out. It was just too sad to share.

Nick later asked Robert for his opinion. The apostle agreed that he "could see it happening."

No one seized on the most obvious disconnect between Sandy's dire prophecy and reality: Jimmy, at a strapping six feet two inches, was in apparent good health and only thirty-one years old.

IT HAD BEEN OPENLY PRAYED FOR FROM THE PULPIT THAT God would be with Pastor Bob as he embarked on his important spiritual and reflective journey to Africa that summer. Certainly there was important work—God's work—to be done there. But there was also a push coming from Robert Bily.

"Once I'm fully in charge," Robert had said to PB around that time, "you'll start seeing some things really happen."

Implicit was that PB was in the way. His old-fashioned method of doing things had become a stumbling block to the great apostolic vision that Robert had promoted since coming to Christ Community Church. They were going to grow churches in places that needed them: Silverdale, Bremerton, and beyond.

PB had grown weary of the endless meetings, the constant maneuvering of board members, the obligation to work as hard as Robert Bily. PB felt that seventy hours a week in the office and visiting members of the congregation was more than enough service. After all, he had a wife and kids too.

Although Robert had a family, he thought nothing of working until the day was completely gone and the sun was threatening to rise.

Bob Smith's defining problem with the church wasn't the hours; he had begun to take serious issue with the deliverance sessions, Robert's fast-track-to-redemption, church-basement counseling meetings based on probing personal questions. Robert had turned them into such a refined script and process that they now seemed more about methodology than actually helping anyone. The questions were exceedingly personal. PB didn't think there was a spiritual need to know specifically how many abortions a woman had. Just saying that one had terminated a pregnancy was enough. The detail, all written down, seemed intrusive, perhaps reckless.

Yet PB didn't speak up. For the most part, he permitted much of what happened to unfold. He just didn't like discord.

Robert Bily, on the other hand, *sought* confrontation. As PB saw it, Robert was so determined to move forward and act, he didn't always see what was right in front of him.

In time, Robert laid the blame for the congregation's dissension and the subsequent stagnancy of his apostolic vision at PB's feet. Pastor Bob was letting Robert's good intentions stall. They needed to drop the Assemblies of God affiliation and get on with their important work. He was ready personally, scripturally, and legally, having already set up a Nevada nonprofit for his food venture, Life Staff Ministries. The new church could be registered under Life Staff.

Pamela's dream, Robert's plan, and PB's acceptance—all of it was adding up to confirmation that something special was happening on Bainbridge Island.

Bylaws for the new church were completed that summer, making Robert the senior leader, answerable to an appointed or elected board. PB would remain a pastor but would no longer be the man in charge. Nick Hacheney would serve primarily as a youth pastor and a zone pastor, overseeing the home groups led by the Glasses, the Andersons, the DeLashmutts, and the Mathesons. Another Christ Community pastor, Ron McClung, who had sought a return to the pulpit after a scandalous divorce and subsequent remarriage, would be on board too.

More than a few longtime church members were uncomfortable with the influx of new pastors and proposed changes. However, those who questioned the new setup were told they

needed to submit to God's plan. Congregants who complained about seceding from the Assemblies of God were
reminded that spiritual denominations, no matter how well-
meaning, were a yoke that restricted man's service to God.

In the end, only one person dissented when the congregation voted in August 1997.

Robert Bily viewed the near-unanimous approval as a
supernatural event.

And yet, as everyone prepared to move on to achieve
some kind of spiritual greatness—as pastors or as a spiritual
fellowship—none saw at the time that their church had been
built upon a crumbling foundation. There was no greater clue
that something wicked was taking place among key players
in the church membership than what happened at Camp
Ghormley in the later part of August 1997.

According to one person who was there, "That camp was
the beginning of the end. Certain people were getting too
close."

9

THE FAITHFUL HAD BEEN GATHERING AT GHORMLEY Meadow Christian Camp, in the Wenatchee National Forest on the east side of the Cascades, since 1939. It had the vibe of one of those old-timey camps popularized in movies like *The Parent Trap*—a cluster of cabins under the pines with several large buildings for meals and worship activities. It had always been a Christian camp. Some seven thousand people visited each summer; it would have been impossible to count how many came to the Lord and were dunked in nearby Rimrock Lake.

Church members packed up their Bibles, sleeping bags, and toothbrushes, with Nick, as the program director, promising an "amazing" few days. For many, however, this trip was not seen as a completely joyous gathering. For one thing, the Smiths were not going to be there. In their absence, the status quo had dramatically shifted: Robert and Nick had become a kind of dynamic duo for Christ, Sandy seemed to be at Nick's beck and call, and Nicole Matheson appeared to lean on Nick more than ever.

There just didn't seem to be enough Nick to go around.

Sandy unconvincingly told friends that a change of scenery might inspire her to find something about her husband, Jimmy, that she still loved—or at least *liked*. Tension in the Glass house was unbearable.

Separately, Jimmy, one of his sons, and cowboy Phil Martini, twenty-four, loaded their gear into Jimmy's GMC pickup for the drive to Camp Ghormley. Jimmy had been through the wringer with Sandy, but if she'd wanted him to drive with her, he'd have been thrilled—even if that had meant sitting with the radio playing while she stared out the window. Instead, that year the plan called for Sandy to take the other three boys and meet them at the campgrounds the following morning.

Since Phil Martini had never seen Mount St. Helens, the landmark volcano in the southwestern part of the state, he and Jimmy planned to stop there for some sightseeing and spend the night at a friend's place in nearby Toledo, Washington.

The next afternoon, Robert received a breathless call from Nick, who was already at the camp. The call wasn't unusual: Nick and Robert talked several times a day about church business. This phone call, however, was dramatically different.

"Jimmy Glass is late," Nick said. "We're worried about him."

Robert tried to calm Nick; he was sure Jimmy was fine. But Nick was adamant that something terrible had happened. By the time Robert hung up, he shared Nick's concern. He'd heard both Nick and Sandy prophesy that Jimmy was going home to Jesus. He wondered if the prediction had come to pass.

When Jimmy and company finally arrived at the campgrounds some six hours after Sandy and the other Glass boys, Jimmy was met with the strangest of greetings.

"Oh, thank God, you're all right! We thought you'd been killed in a car wreck."

"No car wreck," Jimmy said, shaking off the bizarre and misplaced concern. Why would anyone think that?

The rest of the weekend was a complete nightmare for Jimmy. He was holed up in a tiny cabin with his boys, and Phil was packed in with a trio of kids on Ritalin. Sandy stayed by herself in a cabin next to Nick's. Jimmy attempted to be supportive of her desire to play a major role in the goings-on at the camp, and tried to prove to her that he was an engaged husband and father. Nonetheless, every time he tried to reach out, she slapped him down.

"I have to minister to Nick right now," she said.

Jimmy tried to shrug off her indifference by immersing himself in camp activities like waterskiing and boating, but her rebuffs still hurt. When he looked around, he could see one other person who seemed like a third wheel: Dawn Hacheney. Nick was always off with Sandy or Nicole.

WHILE NICOLE AND SANDY AND OTHERS WERE FIGHTING for Nick's attention, Holly Kloven was exiled to the shores of Rimrock Lake, away from the rest of the group. Someone had to stay there to keep an eye on the youths, and it was decided by Nick and his entourage that Holly was right for the task. The isolation stung. Holly wondered if it was payback for voicing her concerns over Sandy and Nick spending too much time together.

She talked to Einar about feeling separated from her church family. Her husband didn't like it one bit. He knew Holly was offended by some of Nick's comments—and that she was standing her ground.

"God loves us passionately," Nick told Holly one time, "like a man and his virgin bride."

It seemed that with Nick, even God's love was warped into something sexual.

Holly couldn't help but give him a disapproving look. Nick would laugh at her, make a joke about how she didn't "get" him and how God really loved everyone in a deep, almost physical way.

Holly had grown up in a home where a stepfather used humor to make her look foolish when she registered resistance to his too-familiar comments and suggestions. She knew that Nick's joking could be used as a weapon. It ate at her.

BACK HOME, OVER COFFEE, A PISSED-OFF JIMMY GLASS told a church buddy what he thought about what happened at camp.

"It is a groupie-fest," he said. "The whole thing is a big freaking Nick groupie-fest."

While not acknowledging her role in any of it, Sandy would later add her own take on Dawn's awareness that something was awry that weekend: "She came to me at the end of the camp crying. . . . She didn't get to spend much time with [Nick], and she was upset about it."

HOLLY TRIED TO REKINDLE HER EBBING FRIENDSHIP WITH Sandy. With Pastor Bob and Adele away in Africa, and Robert and Pamela Bily shunning her over the Jim Carrey videotape incident, she'd never felt more alone. Of course, that meant putting up with Nick, who, Holly felt, considered her "old school" and completely out of touch with the direction in which God wanted to take their church.

Sandy told Holly that she doubted PB would return to oversee the church. "Nick is the chosen one to lead our body," she said, her tone matter-of-fact. "Robert's going to help him."

It was such an outlandish remark that Holly couldn't think of a single thing to say. *What are you getting at, Sandy?* she thought.

Sandy skipped over Holly's worried look and related how everything had been foretold in the Bible. Nick was David and PB was a "mean king" who was trying to stop him from taking his rightful leadership role. It sounded delusional to Holly, but she didn't tell Sandy that. By then Holly could see that her once dearest friend had an agenda.

"Once Nick's in power, we're going to do a youth ministry together," Sandy said.

"What about Dawn?"

"Oh," Sandy said, measuring her words and looking off into space, "she'll be involved too."

LISTENING TO NICK RANT ABOUT WHAT HAD TRANSPIRED at Camp Ghormley made Annette Anderson all the more grateful that she, Craig, and their children hadn't attended. It seemed to be nonstop drama.

"Everyone's ticked off at someone," Nick said. "Nicole's mad at Sandy for taking up all my time. Nicole's mad at me.

Sandy's angry. Dawn's upset because she was stuck all weekend taking care of [Nicole's children]."

Nick was on a roll, nearly frothing at the mouth. He said Nicole was "freaking out" and was calling him nonstop. She needed help with her car. Her brake fluid was low.

"I'm not going to chase her down," he said.

"Aren't you worried about her?" Annette couldn't understand why Nick didn't rush to Nicole's rescue.

"I'm afraid of going over there." He rolled his eyes skyward. "She's probably waiting for me in a negligee."

The comment would have killed Nicole, had she heard it. The young mother of two had serious trust issues. It wasn't that she didn't want to trust, but she had been frequently betrayed and hurt by the men in her life. One time, shortly after camp, she met with Nick and Sandy, and Nick openly shared personal, sexual details in front of Sandy that Nicole had told him in strictest confidence. It stunned her, but she kept her mouth clamped shut.

Sandy looked on, and it was apparent that she already knew what Nick was talking about. It was a violation of Nicole's privacy. Nicole knew that whatever she'd tell Nick would probably be passed on to Dawn, and she was all right with that. Dawn was his wife. But Sandy?

Why are you sharing that with her? Nicole thought. These thoughts occurred to her a few times, and although she set them aside, they wouldn't go away. Something was up with Nick and Sandy.

That same summer, when Nicole couldn't get her hair to do anything she wanted it to, the only answer was a home permanent kit. She turned to Sandy Glass, because she knew Sandy had done perms for other women church members, like Holly. Sandy agreed to do her perm and Nicole drove across the Agate Pass Bridge. When she arrived, Nicole noticed that Sandy was wearing a pretty new dress.

Sandy said Nick was coming over to help Jimmy with their well's sputtering pump.

"Do you care if he sees you like this?" she asked, rolling up Nicole's chemical-soaked brown hair.

"No, I don't," Nicole said, surprised by the question. She couldn't care less what Pastor Nick thought of her hair. At times she considered Nick to be an obnoxious know-it-all.

Why should I care what Nick thinks of how I look? she wondered. *And why is Sandy all dolled up in that new dress?*

10

To most of those outside Robert and Nick's circle, things were moving along smoothly and happily while Bob and Adele Smith were out of the country. Nick preached a couple of times that summer, looking every bit the up-and-comer. He was young and enthusiastic. He'd counseled a couple of troubled marriages—most notably Samuel and Julie Pennoyer's—and had earned respect among some doubters. While Nick took up the slack, Robert had immersed himself in the arduous task of ensuring that the church's changing bylaws met his standards.

Even among the church members who'd embraced Robert's new vision, there were some doubts about the personal authority the apostle seemed to build into the bylaws. "We used to call them the 'Bily-laws' behind his back," one member recalled.

During PB's African sabbatical, a mini-coup was being planned in the downstairs offices of Life Staff Ministries. Some felt that the impetus was Robert's need to control the church coffers. PB had the largest salary, albeit modest by anyone's standards. With PB away, there was discussion among the board members that his salary be redistributed between Nick and Robert.

"PB isn't the senior pastor anymore," a board member said. "He doesn't work as hard as Robert and Nick. He should not get paid more than they do."

Robert would later say that he alone had been the one to stand up for PB.

"Wait a minute," he said. "I'm senior pastor now, he's *under* me, he's in Africa, and he's fasting and praying. He's coming back with a new fire, so let's see what he's like."

Others, according to Robert, were less willing to wait. They wanted to move the church forward, which meant getting rid of PB. Surprisingly, it was Nick, PB's former protégé, who led the charge. He did so with Robert's tacit consent, assuming an even greater role in the church. He was leading an evening youth group service, gathering goods for another shipping container bound for Africa, running several home groups, and counseling Sandy and Jimmy.

"You're ready for this," Robert told him. "Use your gifts."

SHORTLY AFTER CAMP, HOLLY KLOVEN FOUND ROBERT IN his office at the church. She drew in a deep breath.

"I'm worried that Nick and Sandy are getting too attached to each other," she said.

Robert focused his laserlike eyes on Holly. "Have you seen anything inappropriate?"

"No. Just hugs that seemed, you know, a little too squishy."

Robert nodded. "I'm on top of this. You don't need to worry."

He told Holly that he'd heard concerns from James and Mary Glass and was watching the situation very carefully. He didn't think anything improper was going on. In fact, he said he'd sent Nick to counsel Sandy to "see what would happen." He went on to say that Sandy had given him an improper hug at one point and, knowing Nick's penchant for being an effusive guy, he'd put him in charge of Sandy and Jimmy's case.

"I wanted to see if sparks would fly," he said.

Holly didn't understand what Robert hoped to achieve, but she didn't question him. She was glad that Robert listened to her at all. It was a step toward healing the rift between their families.

The next day, Holly opened her door to find an irritated Nick standing outside.

"Well, I guess we have to have a talk. You sure got me into trouble, Holly."

She knew immediately that Robert had finally talked to him.

"What were you thinking?" he asked.

"I was worried about Sandy. Is there anything going on with you two?"

Nick looked right at her. "Absolutely not!"

He proceeded to tell Holly that she'd been mistaken, that whatever cues she thought she'd observed had been misconstrued. He told her that younger people were more demonstrative in their affection for each other.

Sandy isn't that much younger than me, she thought. *Barely a few years.*

"You really don't understand," Nick said. "Our generation is different than yours."

Nick was making her out to be some old fuddy-duddy church lady with a Bible in one hand and a macaroni casserole in the other. She started to feel embarrassed and self-conscious.

"God has asked me to go out on a limb to show love to the people that weren't getting it in other ways in a way that they could understand it," he said. "Sometimes that might mean not doing things the prim and proper way to make sure people get what they need."

Nick took a gulp of air and went on.

"You really need to back off, Holly. You're just jealous that Sandy is giving all her attention to me and not *you*. All this time she's been trying to be just like you and she needs to be her own person. Let her be who she is. You've been overshadowing her."

MEANWHILE, NICK AND NICOLE CONTINUED TO DRAW closer as he suddenly turned to her for support—over what, it wasn't clear. Sometimes he'd call and they'd pray over the phone. Other times he'd show up at her house. At first it was hard for Nicole to wrap her brain around the idea that the man with all the answers, the man so close to God, could be troubled at all.

This is Nick! He's always blessed! she thought.

"I'm going through something that I can't talk about," Nick said. "I'm really confused. I don't understand it. I don't understand what God's doing."

In time, they developed a scale that indicated just how bad things were. Ten was bliss. One was somewhere close to rock bottom.

"How are you doing today?" Nick would ask.

"I'm a three," she would say.

"Well, your pastor is a two."

And once more they'd pray.

She wrote to God on August 11, 1997:

I need to pray for Nick. I need to help you help him to win.

11

THE SUMMER SUN WAS MAKING ITS SLOW DESCENT behind the Olympic Mountains, leaving them slightly blushed before the final dip of a dazzling sunset. The glory of the evening was lost on Mary and James Glass, who were torn up by what was taking place around the family compound: Sandy was on the verge of ordering her husband out of their home and was announcing that she ultimately planned to serve him with legal separation papers, the first step toward a divorce.

If they didn't side with Jimmy, they'd further hurt their son, so obviously wounded by Sandy's cool dismissal. Standing by Sandy was necessary, though, to ensure a close and continued relationship with their grandsons.

It wasn't exactly a tough call, given how Jimmy had disappointed them over the years. To be fair, Jimmy didn't do anything to shame his family; he wasn't a druggie or a drunk. He was just an amiable, directionless fellow. His younger brother, Kelby, a West Pointer, was the ambitious one. Jimmy was always in the shadow of the other men in the family.

Mary and James had also seen signs all summer that something was amiss with Sandy, Nicole, and Nick. There was too much togetherness, a closeness that went beyond counseling. Nick always seemed to be in the company of another man's wife. When out mowing the lawn, Mary would wave at the always-visiting women sunbathing and drinking ice tea as Nick drove up in his Jeep for an extended stopover of his own. Each moment that Sandy spent time with Nick meant less time for Sandy to reconcile with her son.

It worried Mary so much that she talked to Holly about it on more than one occasion. She wanted Holly to pressure her daughter-in-law into resuming marital counseling. Holly said she'd try. Despite her best efforts, it seemed that with each passing week the couple's estrangement grew.

"She won't call me back," Holly said, visibly upset.

And yet the Glasses, with their ringside view, couldn't just sit there and watch their world implode. Nick's omnipresence made Mary's and James's blood pressure rise. They liked him all right, but it seemed that he'd been a failure at marital counseling. Nicole and Ed were more divided than ever. Craig and Annette's marriage was being propped up by church counseling. Sandy and Jimmy were on the brink of total collapse.

It was the dinner hour when Mary and James were heading out the door for the Bargain Boutique, a high-end thrift store that benefited Seattle Children's Hospital, where Mary volunteered. Out in the yard, next to Jimmy and Sandy's double-wide, was Nick's all-too-familiar grungy, faux-wood-paneled Jeep. *Again.* Jimmy was gone, and Sandy had sent the boys off to God knew where.

"He's got a wife that's worked all day long to support him, and here he is over here with this other man's wife, counseling at night by themselves. It just isn't right," James said. He was a man who hated confrontation more than anything, but he'd been pushed to the precipice. "Let's stop by the church and see Robert," he said.

Mary agreed. With PB still out of the country, there was no one else to help but the apostle Robert. The Glasses got off the highway in Winslow, the commercial center of the island, and drove the switchback to the church parking lot. Robert Bily's Mercedes gleamed in his usual parking spot.

"Do you think it's right that Nick's over at Sandy's at this hour?" James Glass asked. Before Robert could answer, Mary piped up.

"When his wife is working all day? Shouldn't he be home with her?"

"Yes," Robert said. "He absolutely shouldn't be there with Sandy."

"What can we do about it?" James asked.

Robert thought for a second. "Let me know if he's still there when you get back home."

They promised they would. James and Mary felt somewhat better as they headed down the highway to Bargain Boutique. Three hours later they returned to the compound.

James could barely believe his eyes.

"Nick's still here!"

Mary sat silent, her mouth open. *Three hours!*

They could ignore it or call Robert. The hour was pretty late, and calling Robert seemed like a bit much.

"If we wait and call him in a couple of days," James said, "Nick will deny it. He'll say he wasn't here all that late."

With Mary looking on, James strode up the driveway to Sandy's front door. Leaning his frame toward the sidelight along the door, he glimpsed Sandy and Nick sitting on the couch. Shoes off. Feet tucked under their thighs, Indian-style.

James took a breath and knocked.

Sandy opened the door. "Oh, James, hi," she said.

"Can I use your phone?" He had no smile on his face.

"Of course," she said, handing it to her father-in-law.

James dialed Robert Bily's home number. "Robert?" he asked. Upon confirmation, he held out the receiver, staring at the youth pastor on his son's sofa. "Nick, someone wants to talk to you."

With that, James turned and went back home. It was all in Robert's hands now. He doubted anything inappropriate was going on—at least, not on Sandy's side of things. She wasn't that kind of a woman, period. She was driven only by a deep love for God.

WHENEVER THEY COULD, THE GLASSES TRIED TO GENTLY impede Nick and Sandy's relationship, and they weren't alone in that endeavor. They had Robert Bily to take up the cause too. Robert was the kind of hard-nosed pastor who'd have questioned Mother Teresa if he had the slightest provocation to do so. *Anyone can fall. Satan is always on the hunt for another soul.* Nick, with his occasional puffery and touchy-feely personality, was an easy target. He'd made no attempts, as far as Robert could see, to distance himself from Sandy.

Even after the phone incident at the house, Nick's limpet-like attachment to Sandy went unhindered.

Robert went ballistic when he heard that the pair had been seen alone together in downtown Seattle. He confronted Nick in the office about it a few days later.

"Have you formed an emotional attachment to this woman? Are you in some kind of relationship you're not telling me about?"

Nick didn't flinch.

"The Holy Spirit has instructed me not to answer you," he said.

12

A FEW CHURCH MEMBERS HEARD OF THE ALTERCA-
tions between Robert and Nick—first at the Glasses'
and then later at the church offices—and understood
that an unbridgeable rift had occurred. Those who didn't know
of the heated and bizarre exchange could still clearly see a
change in their relationship. It was swift. Missing was the
mentor-protégé camaraderie that had carried them through
the summer of PB's absence. No longer was Nick imploring
people to get behind the great apostolic vision of Robert Bily.

The catalyst of the transformation was a tiny wisp of a
prophetess, Sandy Glass.

During that time, Nick increased his visits to the Anderson place in Suquamish. He'd claimed Craig and Annette as
"his people," and had made it a crusade to get them up to
speed with the running of their own home group so that they
could be a major force in expanding the apostolic network.
Sometimes Nick only visited to shoot the breeze for a little
while before heading to another church member's home on
his endless route of door-to-door salvation.

One fall afternoon Nick stopped by the Andersons' when
Craig was at work. Annette answered the door and was met
with that conspiratorial look on his face, the one that said,
*I'm about to tell you something that you might not under-
stand, but you should.*

"Gabriel visits Sandy," he said.

Annette searched Nick's eyes. He was serious, but she
was unsure how to respond. By then everything seemed to

be some kind of test of her faith, her understanding of what God was all about.

"Well, what do you think of that?" he asked.

Annette couldn't accept what he was saying at face value. It seemed too fantastic. If he'd said Sandy had prayed to an angel, that would have been believable. But as far as she knew, the last time anyone had seen Gabriel, the messenger of God, for sure was the Virgin Mary on the occasion of the impending birth of Jesus Christ.

Gabriel appeared to Sandy in her mobile home on Bainbridge Island?

"What did Gabriel tell her?" she finally asked.

"Things that God wants her to know. Pretty amazing, huh?"

"I guess so" was all Annette could manage.

A little while later Nick left, leaving Annette even more confused. She had no doubt that Nick seriously believed that Sandy had a tangible connection to God either directly or through Gabriel. She'd seen Sandy deliver her prophetic words before the church or transcribed on little slips of paper. And she knew that Sandy was admired as a deeply spiritual woman.

HOLLY KLOVEN SPENT ANOTHER SLEEPLESS NIGHT IN HER island home. In her whole life, she never would have imagined that something as small as a videotape could be a wedge that would push her farther and farther from the church she loved so much. Einar was more direct: He'd have been perfectly happy telling Robert and Pamela to drop it all and behave. Yet he held it back. He figured that when PB returned, the status quo would be restored and the loving church would return to what it had been. The toxic summer of 1997 would find its antidote when the Smiths came home.

With each passing week, Holly found her position within the church eroding even more. As a member of the choir—known as the worship team—singing had been her greatest joy, after her children. But after PB and Adele left for Africa, she'd found herself excluded from singing. Pamela Bily convincingly and sweetly told her that others "needed a chance" to share the joy of the Holy Spirit.

An exceptionally polite woman, Holly didn't argue about it. Robert and Pamela doled out a number of verses from the Bible that would provide her with what she needed to know in order to repent. Holly loved the Bible, but she resisted the Bilys' recommendations. All of a sudden it felt as if something sweet and pure had morphed into something very dark, very ugly. All Holly had to do was look around the island to see the faces of those who had crossed Robert and Pamela Bily and now found themselves cast out from the church.

When she tried to talk to Sandy about it, her former best friend was too busy. That compounded the pain. She wondered why Sandy never seemed available. She wondered why Sandy was always with Nick.

While visiting at the Glass compound—a rare event in those days—a speechless Holly listened, openmouthed, as Sandy herself described how Gabriel had appeared to her. God wanted her to know that this time Jimmy was going to die. There were no tears, just a calm acceptance when she spoke.

"Amazing things are coming," Sandy said.

A prophecy from God was one thing. Holly believed that people heard from God. She felt that God touched her directly too, but not in audible words and certainly not by sending an angel to her Bainbridge Island kitchen. Holly didn't know what to say. By then the sisterlike bond between her and Sandy was completely gone. While they still saw each other on occasion, Sandy was tight-lipped about her personal life.

Holly confronted her point-blank.

"Are you and Nick having some kind of affair?"

Sandy held her gaze. "No, of course not."

"But what about an emotional bond?" Holly asked.

The wheels seemed to twirl.

"Maybe," Sandy said, digging for the right words. "Maybe Nick and I have become more emotionally involved. It is totally on my part. Nothing improper is going on."

13

EVEN BEFORE HER SON AND DAUGHTER WERE BORN, there had always been another entity in Nicole Matheson's marriage to Ed: his serious drug addiction. It manifested itself in ways that the young mother would later consider demonic. And yet, her faith was such that she stayed true to the idea that things would improve and the beast could be vanquished. What she likely didn't know was that there were others involved in the background of her life, pulling strings: Ed's latest girlfriend and their pastor, Nick Hacheney.

As Nicole fell deeper into her defiant dream of reconciliation with Ed, Nick stepped in to assure her that reality would match her prayers. He told her repeatedly that God would intervene, that her hope for a united family was worth believing in.

In the fall of 1997, things took a sudden and irrevocable turn with the Mathesons: Ed, then twenty-five, had gotten his girlfriend pregnant.

Nick came over to the Anderson place on his way to break the news to Nicole. It was as if he wanted to try it out on Annette first, almost rehearsing how he'd tell Nicole. As a pastor, it was his duty, he said.

"She needs to hear it from me," he said. "This won't break her. She has so much faith that God will intercede and make things right between her and Ed. He still can."

"This pregnancy will kill Nicole," Annette said. "It will

be the last straw. She's hung on to hope so long that Ed would come back to her. This baby will ruin that chance."

Annette offered to accompany Nick, but he insisted on going alone. She marveled at his sense of responsibility. How was it that Nick was so sure he was the right one to bring such devastating news to a woman who'd spent all summer in front of the altar, praying that her husband would pull himself out of his drug-induced haze and do the right thing? Annette knew Nick was willing to do anything for anyone in the congregation. He'd put himself on the front lines of human hurt and would take the bullet without a second thought.

A little while later, Nick dramatically reappeared on the Andersons' doorstep. His body was limp with a heaving sadness that seemed to shrink him before Annette's eyes.

"I just held her while she cried," he said of Nicole. "She was devastated. Then she got angry at Ed, at God, at the world. I stopped her from doing anything she'd regret. I stopped her."

IT SEEMED SO MONUMENTALLY UNFAIR. JUST DOWN THE road from the Mathesons' little house, Nicole's estranged husband had been romancing another woman, with the worst possible outcome. Nicole phoned Annette in tears. "How will our marriage be restored now?" she asked. "How will God fulfill my hope?"

As Annette struggled with her response, the familiar clicking sound of a call waiting came in on her line.

"Just a minute," Nicole said, taking the other call. She came back on a second later. "It was Nick. He was making sure that I was calling you like I was supposed to."

Annette told Nicole to hang in there. "God will take care of you and your babies," she said.

Nick phoned Annette later that same day and urged her to go to Nicole.

"As soon as you can," he said.

After her children were tucked in and asleep, Annette drove up the hill, past the lineup of grim little houses built on tribal land, to Nicole's place. Nicole was an emotional wreck, and Annette put her arms around her before the front door shut behind them. For the next couple of hours they sat on the couch and Nicole read from her diary, sharing the dreams she had for a future with Ed.

On the other side of the Agate Pass Bridge, another church couple was finding their future crumbling.

Nick Hacheney had climbed into the center of that storm too.

SUNDAY MORNING, SEPTEMBER 14, 1997, SAW JIMMY AND Sandy Glass's mobile home wrought with the kind of tension that comes when a marriage is stretched to the breaking point. They barely spoke, but there was no doubt who was master of their fate. If Jimmy and Sandy were at war, it was Sandy who was leading the charge. At his wit's end, Jimmy drank coffee in the living room. He was angry at the world and he most certainly was not going to church.

"Are you coming or not?" Sandy asked, although her brittle tone was hardly inviting.

Jimmy stayed planted where he sat as the TV blared.

"Does it look like it?" he shot back.

They had been like that for weeks. Sandy told Jimmy that she considered the church under Robert Bily to be leading her in a new and wonderful spiritual direction, fulfilling her hopes for giving more to God than she'd ever been able to before. If she loved Bob Smith, she admired and respected Robert Bily. He'd anointed her and embraced her gifts. He referred to her as a prophetess.

Yet, as far as Jimmy could make out, Sandy spent every moment she could with Nick.

That morning, as Jimmy's defiance and anger swelled, Sandy was cold as ice. She barely gave him the courtesy of a response.

"What is going on here?" he pleaded for the umpteenth time. "This church is a charade. What are you doing?"

"I'm going to church and so are the boys."

With that, he heard his voice rise. Expletives flew. He

wasn't proud of the words that came out and what his boys might think of him at that moment. He was a man completely at a loss for a way to fix his family.

Sandy left without another word. She didn't tell Jimmy to cool off. She didn't say that she'd be back later to talk things over. Her attitude was implicit and spoke loudly of how she felt.

He was nothing to her.

Jimmy climbed into his truck and drove the circuitous route around Hood Canal, Washington's dazzling fjord, carved by the glaciers that had shaped much of the Olympic Peninsula. Despite the perfect summer day, Jimmy barely noticed the scenery. He'd never felt so powerless in his life. His leaving, he believed, would be the wake-up call that Sandy needed to hear. Jimmy was the kind of man who thought that sometimes a man had to blow something up in order to fix it. He thought of how he'd yelled at her. He'd used the *F* word. He'd pounded his fist on the table. And he'd gotten no response, just more ice.

Sandy and the boys are everything to me, he thought. *Whatever it is that's tearing us apart is beyond what I can fix. If she doesn't want me anymore, I don't want to live.*

Seven hours later he returned home. The compound was oddly quiet. The dogs barked. There was no one home when he went inside. He could see signs that Sandy and the boys had been back after church, but they hadn't stayed home long.

Five or ten minutes later, Nick's Jeep was in the driveway.

"What's going on with you, Jimmy?" Nick asked as Jimmy let him inside.

"Sandy doesn't want to be a wife to me," Jimmy said. "I don't know if I can live without her. I don't know if I want to."

Nick nodded sympathetically.

"I feel like jumping off the Tacoma Narrows Bridge," Jimmy said.

"You've got to do what you need to do," Nick said.

The words shocked Jimmy. Was Nick telling him to go

ahead and jump? Jimmy's anger exploded. While Nick looked on, Jimmy tossed furniture and ranted about how the church had messed up his marriage. He balled up his fist and punched a hole in the wall.

"Sandy wants you more than she wants me," Jimmy said. Nick shrugged.

A coffee table flew and a minute or two later Jimmy was gone. He was so angry, so hurt, that he could barely turn the key in the truck's ignition. The vehicle lurched down the gravel driveway, down Arrow Point Drive, to the highway that bisected Bainbridge Island. Then he caught a glimpse of Sandy and the boys in the light blue Suburban, a vehicle that Sandy had told Jimmy that God wanted her to buy, although they could barely afford it.

There they go. There's my family.

Jimmy looked at his watch as he went across the Tacoma Narrows Bridge, toward a friend's house near Tacoma. It was too late to pop in unannounced, even though he was crushed and needed the company. He found a midrange motel just off I-5, but when he went to use his credit card, it was refused.

"Sorry," the clerk said.

Sorry? How in the hell did that happen? That card wasn't anywhere near maxed out.

Jimmy wondered what Sandy had been doing with their finances. He checked his wallet. He had some cash, but only enough for a dump near Lakewood, a town notorious for both the best and worst the Northwest had to offer—stunning waterfront homes and the squalor of military housing gone to seed. That night in his room at the Colonial Motel, in a sleep interrupted by police sirens, Jimmy tossed and turned.

His thoughts stayed fixed on his wife, his sons, and Pastor Nick.

Why did he want to let me kill myself?

WITHIN HOURS OF HER HUSBAND'S DEPARTURE, SANDY WAS on the phone with church members. She wasn't upset. She was more matter-of-fact than might be expected when a marriage takes its last breath. Among those she dialed were Annette and another church member, Julie Conner, age thirty-one.

"God told me to separate from Jimmy," she said to Annette. "I asked him to leave."

Annette, who did not consider herself an especially close friend of Sandy's at the time, was somewhat mystified by the personal nature of the disclosure. She knew Sandy and Jimmy were in counseling with Nick, but she had no idea that the situation had become so dire that they couldn't work things out. She didn't know what to say.

An upset Julie phoned Annette.

"God doesn't tell people with four children to separate," Julie said. "This is wrong."

Although she hadn't said so, Julie doubted Sandy's prophecies at times. One time Sandy flaunted some expensive jewelry. "God told me to go out and buy myself a pair of diamond earrings," she said. "He knows I don't have the money but He wants me to have a special gift."

Annette felt compelled to back up Sandy. "We don't know what's going on," she said to Julie. "And if God tells Sandy something, I think she should listen to Him. You're being too judgmental, Julie."

After a little give-and-take, an exasperated Julie hung up. The next time the Andersons' phone rang, it was Nick. It had made its way back to him that Annette had defended Sandy. He was very pleased.

"I'm really proud of you, Annette. You're amazing."

His words were so heartfelt, Annette felt a flush of embarrassment. She'd only told Julie to back off. It wasn't as if she'd rushed over with a casserole and an offer to babysit while Sandy cried her eyes out.

"You are so open to accepting what God's doing, things that others like Julie and [her husband] Gary can't see," Nick went on. "I love you."

The next day, a dead-tired and baffled Jimmy Glass found himself at a friend's place near Tacoma. As much as he'd blasted his buddy with what had been going on at home, he still had enough pride to take a cordless phone outside when he found the courage to call his wife to patch things up.

Sandy barely said hello. She didn't seem worried about him. In fact, it was evident she'd already moved on.

"I want to come back home," he said. "I want to work things out, Sandy."

"It's over," she said. She was terse and final. "You can't come back home."

Jimmy could feel his blood pressure skyrocket. He was talking to a wall.

"What about my boys?" he finally asked.

Sandy, who was given to long pauses as she searched for the right words, didn't miss a beat this time.

"They don't need you. They've already got somebody."

With those words, like a knife flung at his heart with precision, it was over. Sandy hung up.

Jimmy knew immediately who Sandy was talking about. She and the boys already had Pastor Nick.

14

NICOLE MATHESON COULDN'T PUT HER FINGER ON IT. Nick seemed agitated but unwilling to really say what was bothering him. He told Nicole his focus was on helping her, not using her as a sounding board for his own problems—even though he had increasingly begun to unload on her in that way. And she was fine with that: By then she had developed feelings for Nick, not romantic feelings as much as an attachment born of his kindness toward her.

One late-summer afternoon Nick came to Nicole's house, but instead of smiling his face was awash with worry. Not quite on the verge of tears, but very close to it.

"What is it?" she asked, letting him inside and ushering him to the couch.

"I need you to pray for me, Nicole."

"Can you tell me?"

"No, I can't talk about it," he said.

It seemed important. Deep. She wondered if it had something to do with the goings-on at the church. She'd heard that there was a little tension between Nick and Robert. It had to be that, she thought. It couldn't have been anything about his marriage. Nick and Dawn were the couple the others wanted to emulate. He was devoted to her; she loved him enough to give him the leeway to be the kind of caring man that he'd been called into being.

Around that same time, Nick paid a visit to the Andersons. His reason for coming over had nothing to do with how he and Annette might coax Craig into more of a leadership role in the home group—a frequent subject of their sessions. It had nothing to do with how "proud" he was of the Andersons' progress, or what approach might work best for the next home group meeting. This time Nick was noticeably anxious.

"Things are going to hit the fan around here," he said.

"What is it?" Annette asked.

"You'll see. Everyone will see. I think PB's coming home to a big mess when he gets back from Africa."

Annette had no clue what he was talking about. Nick seemed to prefer hinting at troubles to come. Annette knew that there had been growing problems between the Bilys and the Klovens, and wondered for a second if it was that. Jimmy and Sandy's estrangement also weighed on her.

Those scenarios went by the wayside with Nick's last words.

"Robert's starting to come after me too."

The idea of Robert and Nick not getting along was painful. It was like hearing that seemingly loving parents wanted a divorce. Yet, as much as Annette loved and respected Robert Bily, it was Nick who had gone out of his way to cultivate a deep friendship with the Andersons. She knew Nick well enough to know that he tended toward the dramatic. Moreover, she was sure things would work out. Robert needed Nick and Nick needed Robert. Robert was the brains; Nick, the heart. The symbiotic relationship they shared was what made their church all that it was.

"Don't tell anyone about this, Annette," he said. "Not even Craig. I don't want anyone to worry. But we're in a war here."

IT WAS AROUND THAT TIME THAT NICK TOLD ANNETTE about a book that he considered a near blueprint of what he was facing with Robert Bily. It was Rick Joyner's prophetic tome *The Final Quest*, about the author's personal battle against evil within established churches and the Christians who just sat idly by while Satan took over. Nick handed out copies to several people, including Sandy, Annette, Nicole, and Lindsey Smith. He told them the book would change their lives, their perspective on things, and, ultimately, the world in which they were living.

"You'll see that the people we had once trusted are actually doing the work of Satan," Nick said.

The women pored over the pages of *The Final Quest*. A few struggled to get through it, failing to see what role the story played in the future of their lives or the church. Nick cast himself as the martyr and Robert Bily as Satan—or, in author Joyner's vernacular, "the accuser of the brethren." The "hordes of hell" were marching toward the faithful, tearing them down with gossip, slander, and murmuring.

Furthermore, "Sandy had a prophecy," Nick said. "I don't know if I will survive this—if any of us will—but we're going to be ready for battle."

Nick highlighted a passage in Annette's copy of Joyner's book:

> I also knew that the battle that was about to begin was going to be viewed as The Great Christian Civil War because very few would understand the powers that were behind the impending conflict.

Whenever they talked that fall and into the winter, Nick referred to Joyner's book, the civil war, and how there would be casualties.

The first, he told several people, would be his wife, Dawn.

SANDY GLASS SCURRIED OUT OF PASTOR BOB SMITH'S OF-fice as if she had some urgent place to get to. It was late fall and the air was cool. She had no time for a sweater, just a sprint to the Suburban. She didn't say anything to anyone. Nick had commandeered PB's office while he was away, and Annette happened by just as Sandy departed. Nick looked upset and Annette immediately wanted to do whatever she could to help him.

"Annette, I need to talk to you. There are not a lot of people I can trust around here. Some things are happening and you need to know."

She sat down and Nick told her how he was sure he was "David" and that a scenario was playing out from the Old Testament. Robert Bily was "King Saul." Nick said the Bible story was a direct parallel with what was going on with the church. As David, he saw himself chosen specifically by God to combat a jealous Robert Bily—a man who could never win the hearts of the congregation. A man, Nick said, who would have him destroyed.

"He wants me dead. He knows that I know who he is," he said. Nick's words were deliberate. He was serious and Annette struggled to believe it.

"I don't understand," she said.

"You *will*. And don't worry. This is all God's plan and God is overseeing all of this. We'll be okay. This is going to be hard and spiritually bloody, but I'll prevail. What happens to me will be scary, but have faith and trust that it is all God's plan."

"What do you want me to do?" she asked.

"You can pray for me. Get ready for what's going to happen. But don't interfere. Trust that God is taking care of everything."

PASTOR BOB AND ADELE SMITH MIGHT HAVE FOUND A SENSE of peace in their Africa mission, but when their plane touched down at Seattle-Tacoma International Airport (Sea-Tac) in October 1997, they landed in the midst of turmoil. Nick and a scaled-down entourage arrived at the airport to greet them. Somehow Nick was able to stay ahead of the pack. He was on overdrive, hurrying as fast as he could. Dawn, Craig and Annette Anderson, and their three kids hung back.

There was good reason to keep their distance. It looked as if Nick was about to have some kind of a breakdown.

"I'm so glad you're home," he said. "And I'm so sorry. I messed up pretty bad when you were gone. I need your help, your forgiveness."

PB was taken aback. "Nick, what are you talking about?"

Adele looked on, saying nothing as tears fell from Nick's eyes.

"I made a lot of mistakes."

PB was unsure where Nick was going with this. A lot of mistakes? He knew it had to be deeper than that.

"Nothing's so bad that it can't be fixed," PB said. There at the baggage claim, impatient travelers lurched forward to collect their suitcases. The Smiths, however, were glued to the spot. Nick wouldn't budge.

"You don't understand," he said. "I betrayed you. We felt—*Robert felt*—we were going the wrong direction under your leadership, and I agreed with Robert. I'm sorry. I can't believe I did this. Please forgive me."

PB didn't let on that he understood how persuasive Robert could be. He didn't tell Nick about guidance the Lord had given him in Africa to free himself of the "spirit" of Robert Bily. Instead, he wrapped his arms around the young man.

"It'll be okay," he said. "I forgive you."

As Nick relayed the story, PB could imagine the conversation:

"Bob's lazy," Robert would have said. "We're not. It will take action to do the things we need to do. Bob's out. But can I count you as in?"

"Yes, you can!"

When the Smiths got home, Holly Kloven called to inform them about the impasse between her family and the Bilys.

"They won't let go of this. They just *won't*," she said.

The Smiths didn't tell Holly that they'd already made the hardest decision of their lives. Leaving the church they had built with their own hands would be as devastating as it was inevitable. It was what God wanted. PB had known Holly since she was a girl; the Smiths knew that she and Einar would go with them.

PB hung up and let out a deep sigh. Then the Smiths did what they always did when they needed help. They turned to God and prayed.

PAMELA BILY HAD ANOTHER DREAM. GOD HAD GIVEN HER an indisputable message that PB and Nick were in collusion against her husband. Robert listened very carefully. With the exception of the earthquake, she'd been so accurate that he had no reason to doubt her latest message from the Lord.

"They are going to try to usurp your authority and come against us," she told her husband. Her tone was certain. Her messages from God were always delivered with absolute confidence.

A short time later, Robert attended a church meeting with both Nick and PB in attendance. He knew from the instant that he saw Nick's face—smug and cool—that Pamela had been correct.

Nick looks like the cat that swallowed the canary, Robert thought.

15

THE CONVERSATIONS BETWEEN BOB SMITH AND ROBert Bily in the church office grew increasingly heated after the African sabbatical. It seemed that half the congregation had a complaint about the way things were going. Some were upset by the goings-on between Nick and Sandy. Others suggested that Robert had been too strict with members who needed love, and not more discipline. The Klovens informed PB about how cold the Bilys had been all summer.

PB confronted Robert about the charges, but Robert was unmoved.

Robert knew about Nick's interaction with the women of the church. Calls made from Nick's church-provided cellular phone gave further fuel for concern: Nick used hundreds upon hundreds of minutes to talk with Sandy, Nicole, and Annette. Although PB had alternated between leaving the church outright and trying to gently rein things back under his own control, he just couldn't get any traction. Robert refused to be pushed aside.

"You know, you're a little too harsh on people," PB said. "Maybe pastoring has gotten to the place where you need a break. You need to go to Bremerton and write. Nick and I will run the congregation."

That evening, an irate Robert told Pamela what PB had proposed.

"A womanizer and a lazybones are going to run this?" he said. "And I'm just going to go and do all this writing. . . .

I'm not going to fall for that. Bob's been buffaloed by Nick, and I have to figure out how to convince him that something isn't right."

Robert asked PB to keep a ledger that accounted for how he spent his time, the unspoken implication being that PB didn't hold up his end of the workload. PB agreed, filled out the ledger for a week, and handed it back to Robert. The apostle studied it, set it down, and said nothing.

One day Robert indicated yet again that PB was an unmotivated pastor and a slow-moving man. Weeks of growing frustration triggered an explosion of emotion and rage. PB scooped up all his papers off his desk and flung them at Robert. They stood within inches of each other, red-faced and bug-eyed.

"You want to take this outside?" PB asked.

Robert shook his head. He most certainly did not.

For his part, PB just couldn't get back in the groove. Part of it was the turmoil surrounding Nick, of course. All the rumors about his carrying on with Nicole or spending too much time with Sandy or others didn't help matters. PB was ready for a change. He'd tired of the endless board meetings and the deliverance sessions.

As THE SEASON PROGRESSED. TOWARD THE SNAP OF A Northwest autumn, there was growing chatter among Sandy, Nick, and Annette that Dawn Hacheney was troubled. It deeply upset Annette that Dawn could be so unhappy. She had the perfect husband, the perfect marriage. If she was discontented, what hope was there for any of them? Annette and Craig's marriage had been on a firmer footing since Nick's intervention, but it teetered every now and then. But Dawn? Why would she be so upset?

Only once did Nick explicitly state his belief that part of the coming turmoil might affect his wife. He was matter-of-fact as he talked over the phone with Annette.

"Dawn seems so down," Annette said. "Something's wrong. What's going on with Dawn?"

"God's plan for her means she'll suffer," he said. "The

misery she's experiencing right now is just part of it. This is
what God has ordained for her."

When Annette hung up, she felt like crying. *Why in the
world would God make someone so kind, so sweet as Dawn
suffer?*

She tried to put it out of her mind. Dawn was being tested
right now—they all were—but she would be all right. Still,
Nick's belief that Dawn was in harm's way seemed such a
heavy burden. She wondered how he could be so composed,
so straightforward.

Annette sought insight by rereading *The Final Quest.*
Nick quoted from it all the time; so did Sandy Glass.

> You, too, received some wounds, but your authority in
> the kingdom has come more from acts of faith than by
> suffering. Because you have been faithful in a few things
> you will now be given the great honor of going back to
> suffer, that you may be made a ruler over many more.

Annette braced herself. Nick's latest message could not
have been more disturbing.

"God told me not to listen to Robert anymore," he said
over coffee at her house. "I'm not to defend myself. I'm not
going to answer his questions."

DAHLQUIST'S FINE JEWELRY WAS A NICE LITTLE FAMILY-
owned jewelry store on the edges of a Poulsbo strip mall. In
October 1997, Nick and Sandy made several independent
visits there to put down money on custom rings. Sandy ordered a man's gold band with a Celtic-inspired design of a
braided rope. Nick's purchase was also gold but more elabo-
rate, a sword design with four small gemstones: a diamond, a
sapphire, an emerald, and a ruby. If there was any significance to the design of the woman's ring or the stones selected
by Nick, it was never mentioned to the jeweler.

WORD OF JIMMY AND SANDY'S BREAKUP TOOK ITS TIME TO
reach Kenny Goans, Mary Glass's half brother, who lived in

northeastern Oregon, where he was a corrections officer. He'd been in contact with Mary and the family throughout 1997, but no one mentioned an ensuing rift between his nephew and Sandy. He and Jimmy were relatively close. In late October, Sandy phoned Kenny with news she said she wanted him to hear directly from her.

"We've separated," she said. "He's lost his temper one too many times, and I told him he can't come and live here again."

"You're going to work things out, right?" Kenny asked.

"I don't know. I don't know," she said. She said she was afraid Jimmy might explode again. "I think it's better for everyone that he doesn't live here anymore."

Kenny offered to help, but Sandy said there was nothing he could do. She was still in counseling with Nick. Whatever happened, she was sure, was in God's hands. Kenny hung up the phone thinking that his nephew had better get his act together. Jimmy could be volatile. He could be a screwup.

JIMMY WASN'T AROUND MUCH AFTER SANDY TOLD HIM TO move out. His work as a carpenter frequently took him out of the area. He didn't mind being away from Sandy, who'd been colder than ever, but his heart ached for his boys. One weekend when he was back on the compound, he gathered up his sons and drove out to Island Lake for an afternoon on the shore. Everyone was in great spirits, and for a minute it felt like old times. The spell was broken, however, when one of the boys started to cry.

"Mom said that you're going to die and we're never going to see you again," he said.

The other boys began to weep too. It was like a dam had burst.

Jimmy put his hands on his son's bony shoulders. "No, honey," he said. "I'm always going to be right here. I'm not going to die."

His words soothed the boy, and soon everyone was having a good time again. Yet Jimmy was left to wonder: What kind of prophecy had Sandy had now?

What Jimmy didn't know at the time—and what only

Nick and Sandy knew—was that he was not the sole subject of Sandy's most recent and dire prophetic words. Sandy had had another prophecy that had come directly from God when she was at one of Nick's youth group gatherings. This time, it was about Dawn Hacheney's death. Furthermore, it had a specific date.

> God told me Dawn is going to die on December 18. He showed me that Nick and I will be together.

Sandy was so sure that God's words would come to pass that she would later say she and Nick talked about how they'd spend Christmas with her boys the week after Dawn died. She planned to give Nick a rifle and a small teddy bear.

THE HACHENEYS WERE ALWAYS RUNNING TO THE ATM for one reason or another. Usually it was because Nick needed something for someone. It wasn't that either Dawn or Nick lived lavishly; far from it. He was earning only six hundred dollars a month from the church and that, added to her annual salary at the credit union, barely covered their expenses— especially when remodeling was tapping their resources. Nick complained that he needed electrical work done, but they didn't have the cash for it.

He had other priorities.

Nick made two trips to the ATM at the end of October. He withdrew a $700 cash advance against the Hacheneys' MasterCard on October 20. The next day he took out a $1,520 cash advance on the same card. On October 22 Sandy showed up at Dahlquist's Fine Jewelry to pay $700 cash toward her custom-designed gold ring. A week later Nick and Sandy each returned to the jeweler to pay off their balances.

In Nick and Sandy's circle, commissioning rings was an extravagance that they would have remarked on or even boasted about. Neither Sandy nor Nick mentioned the purchase to anyone.

Not a single word.

16

S HE MIGHT HAVE LOOKED DELICATE, BUT SANDY GLASS was formidably strong inside. With all that was happening with Jimmy and Nick and Robert and PB, she felt compelled to write a letter to Robert explaining her take on things. The impetus for the letter had been a meeting between Sandy and Robert on November 4. He'd urged her to mend her differences with Jimmy and reunite her family. He'd restated his concern that she and Nick were inappropriately close.

That wasn't what Sandy wanted to hear at all. The next day she wrote:

> I feel judged by you, though I accept your place to judge me.
> I feel you have questioned my character, but again, that you
> have the right to do so. My conflict is this: the judgment I
> feel from you makes it hard for me to believe that you accept my giftings at all, or that you have any confidence in
> my ability to hear God and use this help to help anyone.

It must have been very difficult for Sandy to write those words. She wanted nothing more than to be accepted as a prophetess and a church leader. Yet, as Robert and Nick colluded over the summer to oust PB, she'd fallen out of Robert's favor. She had defiantly refused to take Jimmy back, despite the urgings of others. Jimmy and Sandy's separation divided the church as people sided with one or the other.

There is a difference in believing in me and believing me. I never asked them to believe what I was doing was right. They just chose to believe in me and stand with me. . . . [I] did not mean that they were not standing with Jimmy. There was never a moment of taking sides.

Both had their heels firmly planted. Robert felt Sandy's emotional connection with Nick was not only wrong, it was fraught with grave danger. Sandy felt that God had told her what was right and Robert—apostle or not—was not going to stop her from sharing her gift.

JIMMY KNEW NOTHING OF SANDY'S CONFLICT WITH ROBert. Sandy barely spoke to her alienated husband. In fact, she'd successfully frozen him out of every aspect of her life. If it weren't for their boys, Jimmy wouldn't have had much of a clue about anything that was going on. One weekend afternoon, one of Jimmy's sons came barreling across the yard to talk to him while he was outside working. The boy's blond head bobbed over the still-green field grass. He was crying.

"What is it?" Jimmy stooped down to embrace his son.

"Mom and Nick told us that after you die, he's going to be our new dad."

Again the suggestion of Jimmy's untimely death.

Nick their new dad? Jimmy just didn't want to think that for one second. And of course there was another hitch to such a plan.

What about Dawn? he thought.

For the second time that year, Jimmy assured his son that all would be okay.

"I'm not dying," he said.

THE ANNUAL SUNDAY OF SACRED ASSEMBLY AT THE CHURCH was supposed to be unifying, but in 1997 it brought more discord than togetherness. Julie and Gary Conner wanted all children to be with their parents for the assembly. Annette Anderson thought that was fine for those parents—like the

Conners—who had children who understood the importance of the event and the solemnity needed in the sanctuary.

"Some kids can't handle it," she told Julie a few days before the service. "We need to keep the nursery open and we need to staff it."

"The Sacred Assembly is for all of us," Julie insisted. "That includes our children." She added: "And Robert agrees with us."

Julie's remark and alliance with Robert bothered Annette.

Later, when Annette told Nick about her argument with Julie, he aligned himself with Annette. It was the validation that she craved.

During the service Nick approached Annette and said he wanted to help her with her conflict with Julie. Sandy emerged from the pews and met them at the altar. Annette caught a peculiar look in Sandy's eyes.

Has Nick told her about my argument with Julie? she wondered.

Then Nick started to pray aloud as Sandy swayed slightly and nodded in agreement.

Nick finished and turned his eyes back to Annette. He leaned closer and pressed his mouth to her ear.

"I'm so drawn to you," he said.

Annette tilted her head slightly as if to acknowledge it, although she really didn't understand what he meant. She looked over at Sandy, who had a knowing smile on her face; she had stepped closer too.

ALTHOUGH DAWN WAS CLOSE TO HER FAMILY—HER mother, Diana, in particular—she elected to spend Thanksgiving alone with Nick. Since the death of Nick's brother Todd years ago, Nick's family hadn't really been able to focus on holidays. In fact, those closest to Dan and Sandra Hacheney thought the already-frayed family bonds had all but disintegrated after the accident. Nick and Dawn spent many holiday weekends by themselves. It just worked out better that way. On Thanksgiving 1997, they drove down to a motel along the

Oregon coast, where they had dinner out and did some shopping. Dawn charged a man's flannel shirt to her credit card: a Christmas gift for Nick.

Shortly after the Oregon trip, Nick zipped over to the Andersons' place. He noticed a balloon with a big 30 trumpeting Annette's birthday from the day before and wished her a belated happy birthday. But that wasn't the reason he had come over. In fact, if Annette's kitchen had been on fire, it's doubtful that he'd have noticed it. He'd come from a pastor's meeting with his latest lament, this time about Nicole. He was irritated by her.

"I can't even get a weekend away without her calling or needing me for something. I have to go see what Nicole needs now," he said, checking his pager. "It's always something."

WHILE NICK WAS LAMENTING THE WOMEN IN HIS LIFE, Dawn applied to increase her life insurance at the credit union from ten thousand to forty thousand dollars. She did it the way she did everything: quietly and privately. If anything ever happened to her, she knew that Nick would need the money.

She was, after all, the primary breadwinner.

17

YOUNG CONGREGATION MEANT THERE WERE LOTS of babies, and a lot of baby showers. In the final months of 1997, at least four had made it onto the kitchen calendars kept so scrupulously up-to-date by the women of the church. Among the celebrations was a gathering to celebrate Travis and Susanna Pine's baby girl. A tall, good-looking, and outgoing couple, the Pines lived in an apartment on Wyatt Way, on Bainbridge.

Annette Anderson and fellow church member Tanna Martin brought Dawn Hacheney to Susanna's shower. Having Dawn come along was a little unusual. She was usually busy with work, for one, but there was something else at play. Several women felt that Nick liked to keep his wife on the sidelines. It wasn't because he didn't love her, the women told each other. It was because he wanted to keep her to himself.

Holly Kloven was also there, and although she would normally be in the center of the mix, on this day she was quiet, almost disengaged. It was obvious that she was still in turmoil over her estrangement from Robert and Pamela. Pamela, on the other hand, turned up her megawatt halo and beatific smile and carried on as if nothing were amiss.

Doesn't she see how Holly is hurting? one of the ladies wondered.

During the shower, Annette and Tanna noticed a crack in Dawn's shy but upbeat facade. She seemed on the verge of tears.

"Are you doing okay?" Tanna asked, direct as always.

Dawn bowed her head. Tears started to well in her green eyes.

Annette and Tanna went to comfort Nick's wife.

This time Annette tried to get at the source of Dawn's pain. "Dawn, what is it?"

"I don't know," she said.

"There must be something," Tanna pushed gently. It was only the mildest urging, but it seemed to work.

"Things are not so good right now," Dawn finally said. "I'm overwhelmed by everything. Our finances are a mess. But mostly I'm worried about Nick. I don't think I make him happy. He's never home. He's gone all the time. I don't know if he wants me anymore."

"Of course he wants you," Annette said.

"I'm trying to be a better wife. I know I let myself go a little, but I'm dieting. I'm going to lose this extra weight."

Neither Tanna nor Annette thought Dawn was fat. Not by anyone's standards.

"You look *great*," Annette said. "Nick is lucky to have a wife like you."

Dawn had more to let out. "I've been taking walks, exercising, trying to eat low cal. Keep the house cleaner. I'm trying to make him special dinners, you know, to show him that I love him."

Annette thought that the decidedly pudgy Nick ought to be dieting, not Dawn. Yet, something else troubled her even more. Whenever Nick had talked about his marriage to Dawn, he implied that *she* was the dutiful breadwinner and *he* was doing the housekeeping and cooking for her. It rankled Annette that the church preached "Women, stay home!," and here Dawn was working outside the home *and* cleaning the house and fixing dinner.

"My life isn't what I thought it would be," Dawn said.

Tanna saw something more in the sadness of her friend's story. Dawn had mentioned several times that she had looked forward to being a mother. She was disappointed when Nick kept putting her off, saying that his responsibility to the church and God superseded her dreams for a family.

When she returned home, Tanna told her husband about the encounter with Dawn. John, who knew Nick from childhood, figured that Nick was being Nick: a harmless braggart who took credit for everything. It would be hard for any woman to be married to him—except perhaps Dawn.

"Do you think we should talk to Nick?" Tanna asked.

John didn't think so, although the idea of Dawn breaking down at the baby shower was so out of character it alarmed him. He knew Nick and how such a conversation would go down.

"He wouldn't listen," he said. "He's always right."

Tanna considered it. Everything Dawn was doing sounded like a woman trying to win back her husband.

"You don't think Nick's having an affair?" she asked.

"Are you kidding?" John asked, almost laughing. "Cheat on Dawn? Never." As far as John saw him, Nick was a lot of things, but not a cheat.

When Annette asked Nick about Dawn's sad demeanor at the shower the next day, he coolly dismissed her concerns.

"I can't do anything about it," he said. "Dawn's sorrow is between her and God."

THE OLD NICK—A YOUNG MAN OF BOUNDLESS ENTHUSIASM and energy—was gone during the month of December. Insiders who knew about his troubles with Robert and his previous betrayal of PB pegged those as reasons enough to mope around or engage in the kind of glum theatrics he was displaying. He was dropping in on Nicole, Sandy, and Annette with such frequency as to suggest the women were on some kind of visitation rotation.

If it is 2:00 p.m., it must be Sandy; 3:00 p.m., Annette; 3:30 p.m., Nicole.

Nick arrived at the Anderson place on the afternoon of December 21. He'd been out shopping. He'd been out driving. He'd been to the church. He'd made rounds with Sara

LaGrandeur, who along with Lindsey Smith was considered one of his interns or, in Nick's vernacular, "little disciples." Both young women were scheduled to leave the country for missionary work in the New Year. Lindsey was going to Africa, where her sister lived, and Sara was headed for Belize. Nick slumped on the couch and Annette sat next to him. After he'd whispered to her that he was "drawn to her," Annette wondered if maybe he was seeking a confidante, a real friend.

"You can tell me," she said.

Nick's eyes fastened on her. "I know." He took a deep breath. "There is so much happening now. Things that are so big, so huge. Lindsey's leaving; Sara's leaving," he said, alluding to the two church interns.

"I know; it's really hard."

"It is," he said, "but maybe it's for the best."

"What do you mean?"

"Maybe it's God's plan that both Lindsey and Sara are gone when everything happens."

"You mean to keep them safe?"

He nodded.

Annette didn't understand what it was that was about to happen, except that Nick and Sandy had referred to "when *it* happens" constantly. Both seemed to have an awareness that God was going to do something big.

Is it the earthquake?

"Are you still going to be my pastor?" she asked.

"Quit asking questions, Annette. I'm not able to tell you anything else."

A WORD FROM GOD OR THE DELUSION OF A DESPERATE woman? Only God knew. The day after the December 18 prophecy failed to manifest itself, God spoke to Sandy Glass another time: *Don't do anything. You're being watched. Your hands are tied.*

At church after that message, another missive from God came to her. It was a chilling communiqué, but she accepted it without apprehension. She had no choice. She had to share it too.

Your hands are no longer tied.

Later, she would claim she phoned Nick to relay God's latest memo. The message was for him alone.

18

CHRISTMAS IN THE PACIFIC NORTHWEST ALMOST never matches the greeting-card nostalgia of white patches over evergreen boughs. Certainly, temperatures drop enough for a snowfall, but in a mild marine climate, snow rarely coats the towns and cities on the very edges of Puget Sound. The morning of Christmas Eve 1997 brought cool, wet air. There would be no white Christmas that year, just green and damp vistas. Like Nicole Matheson and Sandy Glass, Annette Anderson focused on her children and tried to take in the excitement of the holidays. It was hard to do that year, as the past weeks had pounded her relentlessly: *Something's going to happen. God is going to do something.*

All of it had been coming from Nick. He'd been in a dither since Pastor Bob had returned from his African sabbatical. He'd continued to be vague, telling Annette that the answers she was seeking could be found in any number of books. That day Nick stopped over at the Andersons to drop off a gift basket Dawn had made. Tucked inside was one of her charming handmade cards.

Annette asked Nick about a New Year's Eve party she had heard through Tanna Martin that he and Dawn were hosting. She, Craig, and the kids were heading down to Portland for Christmas, but they'd make sure they'd be back in time for the party.

"Oh," he said, "yes, we are. Come on over."

She wondered why Nick hadn't asked her to come in the first place. It was almost as if he didn't want her there.

At James and Mary Glass's house across from Battle Point Park, the holidays were in full swing throughout the day and into the evening. The tree glittered with ornaments, many of which were handmade by Mary. Their son Kelby was home from West Point with his fiancée. Absent were their oldest son, Jimmy, and his wife, Sandy. Sandy had come over earlier that day and left some gifts for friends of the family, Robin and Jan Mueller. Jimmy was driving home from a job in British Columbia with a stop at Bellevue Square, one of the region's toniest shopping malls. He was on the late-season hunt for a video game for his sons.

With the Glasses looking on, Jan Mueller carefully opened a small package from Sandy wrapped in red and green paper. Jan peeled back the open edge to reveal a stuffed teddy bear, small and cute, the kind a mother might buy a child.

As Jan read the card accompanying the bear, her face became devoid of color. It was like a white curtain falling over her features.

"Mary," she said, "I don't think this was meant for me." She passed the card quickly to Mary, who in turn glanced at it and handed it to James. It read:

> To Nick, my big hearted, huggable, holdable, hunk of a man.
> I love you so very much . . . Sandy.

"I'll keep this," James said of the note.

IT BEING CHRISTMAS DAY, THE LOAD ON THE SEATTLE-bound ferry from Bremerton was relatively light. Some passengers' cars were close to overflowing with wrapped packages for family members on the other side of Puget Sound. The crossing took about an hour. Nick and Dawn met Dawn's family on the boat for the ride to Diana's parents' house in West Seattle.

"Dawn's fighting a cold," Nick said when he met the Tienhaaras on the car deck. "She took some medication and she's curled up in the car trying to get some rest. She wants us to go up without her."

Donald, Diana, their sons Dennis, Daron, and Daric, and Nick trudged up the flight of stairs and scoped out a place to sit in the passenger area. Diana hoped that Dawn would get the rest she needed. *With all the obligations, nothing's worse than a cold during the holidays*, she thought. After sharing most of the day with Dawn's family, Nick and Dawn planned on returning to Kitsap County for a get-together at the Smiths' home on the Rolling Bay side of the island.

Nick sat next to his mother-in-law and, as always, taunted her throughout the day. He kept blowing in her ear.

Nick's such a tease, Diana thought. It was one of the reasons why she loved him so much.

ON CHRISTMAS NIGHT, NICK AND DAWN SHOWED UP AT the Smiths', as planned, and stayed until almost midnight. Among those gathered were the Smiths' daughters Lindsey and Kim, and Kim's husband, Godwin, and their one-month-old baby, Jasmine; Michael and Julia DeLashmutt and Phil Martini. They played board games, ate more than they should have, and exchanged gifts. The Smiths presented Dawn with a card with three hundred dollars and gave Nick an antique cork decoy. The Hacheneys gave the Smiths tickets for the touring production of *Riverdance*.

At the end of the night, Nick, Lindsey, and Phil Martini made plans to meet early the next morning for some holiday duck hunting on Indian Island in Jefferson County.

"Just before first light," Nick said as he and Dawn left for the ride home to Bremerton. "See you on the Kitsap side of the bridge."

That was the last time any of the others would see Dawn.

IT WAS A HUNTING TRIP THAT WOULD BE REMEMBERED IN small flashes, not for what happened during the hunt, but for the events that unfolded later that day. After meeting Nick at the Hood Canal Bridge in the early morning of December 26, Phil and Lindsey followed his Jeep to the hunting grounds. It was still dark, so they used flashlights as they made their way to duck blinds on a windswept stretch of Indian Island beach. When shooting light came, Phil and his dog went off alone and Nick and Lindsey stayed close to the blinds. They waited a short time without making a single shot, which all agreed was especially disappointing. When it was time to leave, they caravanned to Mitzel's American Kitchen restaurant in Poulsbo for breakfast, arriving a little after 9:00 A.M.

No one would later say anything had been particularly concerning or worrisome at the hunting grounds or the restaurant. Only one thing seemed even a little remarkable. Without so much as a warning, Nick jumped up from the restaurant table after their food arrived and said he had to get home. "Dawn and I still haven't had time to open our Christmas presents," he said. He paid the check and left Lindsey and Phil sitting there to make awkward small talk.

His Visa card receipt was time-stamped 9:27 A.M. It was an eighteen-mile, twenty-five-minute drive home. It was creeping up on three hours since neighbor Amy Pitts; her husband, Tim; and his boss, Jeff Richardson, had tried without success to save Dawn Hacheney.

19

IT WAS 10:15 A.M. WHEN CHIEF DEPUTY CORONER JANE Jermy, forty, approached Nick Hacheney as he started toward the smoldering house. Someone called out that he was the victim's husband, and there was no way the deputy coroner was going to let him inside to see his wife's charred body. No one should ever have to see that. There was some urgency in his pace, and Jane hurried down the steps. A kind woman who often identified with the victims and their families, she let her heart go out to the young man in hunting garb.

She'd already seen the death scene in the master bedroom and made note of the abundance of newspapers and wrapping paper, a collection of mini propane containers near the headboard on one side of the bed and the fact that the young woman apparently had not tried to escape the burning bedroom. A firefighter told her that it appeared that a faulty space heater had been the likely culprit.

There was nothing in Nick's demeanor that suggested anything other than a tragic accident had occurred. The deputy coroner led him to the back of a fire truck where he could sit. He was almost inconsolable, barely able to get out what had happened the night before, the hours before he went hunting. He told her that Dawn had been ill and was taking Benadryl; in fact, she'd crawled out of bed at 2:00 A.M. to take another dose. He wondered out loud if she had no tolerance for it, as she was not much of a medicine taker.

Jane made a note to have Dawn's remains screened by the toxicologist for diphenhydramine.

Maybe she took too much, Jane wondered as she stood on the steps, slick from the spray of the fire hoses. *It is so strange that she slept through the fire. Only suicides do that.*

A DARK MERCEDES PULLED ONTO THE WATER-SOAKED street and parked as Nick remained on the back of the Bremerton Fire Department fire truck, his palms pressed against his face. With Pamela just behind him, Robert Bily approached Nick and put his hand on the youth pastor's shoulder.

"Nick, I'm so sorry," Robert said.

Nick nodded, tears streaming down his face.

"Dawn's gone," Nick said.

Robert stared into Nick's dark eyes.

"We can raise her," he said.

Robert had often spoken of holy men who'd raised the dead in other countries. "Let's go up to the house and pray over her. Let's ask God to raise her from the dead."

"No," Nick said, jumping from the back of the truck. "We can't do that to her. She's been so badly burned. She'd be in terrible pain. It would be awful."

Robert backed down. He wondered why Nick would say such a thing. The apostle knew God would return Dawn in all her youth and beauty. He would never restore her to life as a horrific burn victim.

"Robert, you can help with something else," Nick finally said.

"What?"

"Can you go tell Dawn's family? I just can't do it."

DONALD TIENHAARA, FIFTY-ONE, WAS JUST GETTING OUT of bed when he heard a knock at the door of the Tienhaaras' home on Rimrock Avenue. With Diana and the boys still at her folks' place on the other side of Puget Sound, he begrudgingly put on a robe to answer the door. The faces that met him as he swung it open belonged to Robert and Pamela Bily. He'd met the apostle and his wife when Nick was ordained at Christ Community Church a couple of years before; Robert's severe manner and gaunt countenance left a lasting impression.

"We have some bad news," Robert said as he stepped inside. "Is the rest of your family here?"

"No," Donald said. It was obvious by the look on Robert's face that whatever he had to say, it was not pleasant. "They're at Diana's parents' house."

"There's been an accident," Robert said.

Donald slid into the rocker that faced the picture window and the Christmas tree. The tree, which Diana kept lit nearly 24/7, was now dark. Rain fell outside.

"Nick was out hunting and there was a fire at the house," Robert began. "Dawn's gone."

"A hunting accident?" Donald was confused. He'd experienced three or four instances when members of his combat unit in Vietnam had been injured or killed in friendly fire, and his mind immediately went there. "Nick was shot?"

"No, there was a fire at the house when Nick was gone. Dawn died in the fire."

Donald started to cry. He'd always considered himself an emotional man, quick to tears, and as the apostle's words began to compute, a deluge poured from his eyes. He needed to tell Diana and the boys the devastating news.

"Do you want us to go with you to West Seattle?" Robert asked.

Donald shook his head, nearly unable to speak. "No, I'll go," he said.

FROM THE FRONT WINDOW OF HIS GRANDPARENTS' WEST Seattle home, Daron Tienhaara saw his father come slowly toward the door.

"Dad's here," the teenager said, his voice full of surprise.

Everyone in the living room turned to look.

"What's he doing back here?" Diana said, wondering out loud. They hadn't planned on seeing Donald until he came to pick them up that weekend. Her mother went to the door and let him in.

It was obvious that Donald was in bad shape. His eyes were red and he appeared to tremble as he came inside. The room went silent. A TV played in the background. All eyes were on him.

"Something very bad has happened," he said, fumbling for words that would make what he had to say easier to understand. It was a futile consideration. Nothing, he knew, could make any of this easy.

Diana went to her husband. "What is it?"

"It's about Dawn."

Diana's mind flashed to a car accident that might have injured Nick and Dawn.

"Are they okay?"

"There was a fire," he said.

Still the words didn't register.

Donald started to cry. "It was Dawn," he said. "She's gone to heaven."

Diana felt her legs give way and her stomach lurch, then drop. She could feel herself falling into a dark, empty space. She started to scream and ran to the back of the house, then outside on the deck. She was going to vomit. *Not Dawn!* Her sobs blended with the cacophony of grief inside the home.

OTHERS WERE GETTING THE SAD NEWS TOO. WITH CHURCH member Debbie Gelbach, forty-five, manning the prayer chain, each person in the tight-knit congregation was learning the terrible details of how young Pastor Nick's wife, Dawn, had perished in a fire. One of the first people Debbie phoned was Mary Glass, who thanked Debbie before hanging up and facing her husband. Her face was white.

"Dawn's dead," Mary told James. "*He* killed her."

"He," of course, was Nick.

James, who could be a man of few words, called it as he saw it. "If that's so, the authorities will figure it out."

Back at the Gelbachs' island home adjacent to Meigs Park, Debbie, a homemaker and mother of four, finished her calls and started doing the dishes. She looked out her window at the nature preserve and barely noticed the tall, old-growth spruce shivering in the winter wind. Racked with grief, she turned off the faucet. Something was sounding in her mind. A thought began to form, and she shook her head to stop it. Instead, it grew louder.

This was murder.

The very whisper of something so violent in her mind startled her. Debbie had never been a suspicious person. Mary Glass could be, but never Debbie. She was an openhearted woman who only wanted to serve God and be a good mother and wife to her naval engineer husband, Roger.

She talked to Roger about what had come to her mind. Like James Glass, Roger figured the cops would settle the whole thing "one way or another in about sixty minutes."

And yet, in the hours following the fire, hearts all over Bremerton went out to the young pastor who'd tragically lost his lovely wife. He was a victim of a terrible accident. Robert Bily, Mary Glass, and the Gelbachs, however, were among a handful of those who were suspicious that something sinister had transpired. But the authorities didn't think so. Bremerton police left the forensic investigation in the hands of the fire department. The fire department abdicated much of its responsibility to the investigators at Safeco Insurance.

No one seemed to notice what was going on right before their eyes.

20

LINDSEY SMITH MADE HER GETAWAY FROM THE STILTED conversation with Phil Martini, returned home, and started unloading her hunting gear. Still in her soggy boots and heavy jacket, she stomped up to the French doors that looked out at the wooded backyard. She saw her mother through the windowpanes. Adele Smith had the phone pressed to her ear, her face pinched in anguish.

Lindsey opened the door.

"Lindsey's here," she said into the phone. "Just a second. She's here now."

"Mom, what is it?" It was merely a reaction to a situation, not really a desire for an explanation, because Lindsey knew the minute she saw her mother that whatever was being said on the other end of the line was devastating.

"Lindsey," Adele said, "where's Nick?"

"He should be home by now. What happened? What's going on?"

Adele was ready to cry. "There's been a fire," she said. "Dawn died."

Lindsey fell into her mother's arms. "Not our Dawn!" she said.

There would be no telling how much time had passed. Lindsey, like her mother and father, was so overwhelmed by the shock of the news, she lost any real sense of what time it was. When Nick finally contacted them a little while later, it was Lindsey who told him to stay where he was, that she'd go to him.

"I'm leaving now," she said.

"No," Nick answered, his voice soft with emotion. Yet he didn't cry. He too was in utter shock. A couple of hours earlier, he and Lindsey had been creeping around the duck blinds on the shores of Indian Island. It was the day after Christmas. He'd been headed home to unwrap presents with Dawn.

And now the unthinkable had transpired. A fire. It occurred to Lindsey that maybe on some level, supernatural or spiritual, Nick had known something was wrong. He had bolted from the restaurant.

God had told him to go, she thought.

NICK SHOWED UP AT THE CENTRAL OFFICE OF THE BREMERton Police Department, as investigators at the fire scene had requested, at about noon. He was a blubbering mass of grief, still wearing his hunting clothes and looking as though he were held together by grime and tears. He met with Scott Rappleye of the fire department and Bremerton police detective Dan Trudeau. Both men told the youth pastor that his visit there was a formality, that they thought that what had happened on Jensen Avenue had been a tragic accident.

"I do have one question I need to ask," the detective said. "I need to ask as a matter of course so that I can close out this investigation. You didn't kill your wife, did you?"

Nick's face went a shade redder. "No, I did not."

That satisfied both investigators, and they asked him to detail what had happened the night before and earlier that morning. Nick told them Dawn was sick, they'd stayed up late, and he'd had a hunting trip planned for the early morning.

"Hunting wasn't good, the weather wasn't good, so we gave up and went to breakfast. I remembered I forgot something at home, so I came back."

Neither man asked what he'd forgotten. Neither thought it necessary to talk to Lindsey Smith or Phil Martini.

A few minutes later, Nick left. He was on his way to Nicole's.

*   *   *

SHORTLY AFTER DEBBIE GELBACH CALLED HOLLY KLOVEN with the heartbreaking news, Nick phoned Holly. She barely knew what to say, beyond how shocked and sorry she was. She asked the young pastor how he was doing.

"I'm okay. This turned out to be such a hard year," he said. "I'm sorry if this messes up Stewart's birthday. But how are you?"

His response seemed so bizarre. Dawn had just died and Nick was worried about her son's upcoming party. He was worried about how *she* was doing. She figured he must be so deep into his grief that it hadn't sunk in yet.

That same day Holly went to see Sandy. She expected Sandy to be an emotional wreck, but she was relatively calm. Sandy seemed concerned when Holly talked about going over to Pastor Bob's, where some members of the church had planned to meet to comfort Nick.

"I really want to see him," Sandy said, "but I don't want it to look wrong."

To Holly, the statement didn't make sense. How could it "look wrong" to support a friend?

They went over later. Holly cried most of the time. Curiously, Sandy seemed to be holding up pretty well.

In fact, nearly everyone who had even the thinnest of ties to Christ Community or Life Staff would either call or visit the Smiths' home on December 26. Some arrived with things they thought Nick might need: money, food, a jacket. Most came either crying or in stunned silence. It was Nick's own entrance that was the most memorable.

Adele found him on the front steps, stiff, hunched over. The tears were flowing. She reached out and he collapsed in her arms.

"It's my fault," he said, sobbing. "*All* my fault."

"It's not," Adele said.

"Yes, it is. I wasn't there to protect her."

When Annette and Craig arrived, Nick hurried toward Annette and gave her a hug. As he backed away, he glowered at Robert Bily, who was talking to others across the room. No words were said, but Annette got the message. Somehow Robert's war against Nick had caused all of this.

Annette said nothing, but one thought wouldn't leave her alone: Dawn, only twenty-eight, had died because of the battle between good and evil.

GOD, FIRE, AND TIMING—IT WOULD ALL COME DOWN TO that so many years later. Why had a cache of small propane containers been in the bedroom? Nick told people that they'd been a Christmas gift from Dawn. Long after the fire, he'd argue that the propane had been the source of a flash fire that sealed his wife's larynx, cutting off her air supply and killing her. The canisters had leaked, the space heater had arced, and a tragic accident had stolen the world from him.

"What happened was an accident," he said. "Nothing more and nothing less."

21

TWO DAYS AFTER THE FIRE, A KITSAP COUNTY weekly newspaper put Dawn's death on the front page with an impersonal headline:

WOMAN DIES IN EAST BREMERTON BLAZE

That same afternoon, Nick, now homeless and without anything but the clothes on his back, made the trek to Silverdale's Kitsap Mall, where he bought a suit, ties, and shirts. Adele and her daughters, Kim and Lindsey, came along, as did thirty-nine-year-old Ron McClung—the other pastor at the church, who had somehow managed to stay out of the political fray there—and his wife, Carol.

"Nice to have the attention of so many beautiful ladies," Nick said as the women hovered around to pick out the start of a new wardrobe.

The comment made Carol McClung, thirty-two, feel funny. *It's almost like he's enjoying this*, she thought.

ALTHOUGH NICK HAD MADE IT PLAIN THAT HE WANTED TO honor Dawn by giving her eulogy, several of those closest to him sought to spare him from the trauma. Bob Smith, who was a natural choice, offered to do it, but Nick explained that it was something God wanted him to do. PB backed off. One person who didn't was Robert Bily. He made a number of overtures right after the fire was extinguished, saying that he'd be honored to lead the service.

"I have a service prepared for Dawn," Robert said.

"I'm going to do it," Nick said.

"No, you're in shock. It will be better this way."

Nick shot him a determined look that was meant to shut Robert down once and for all.

"No. I'm doing it. Dawn would want me to."

Cast as "celebrations of life," funerals are often miserable affairs, recollections served up with a big scoop of pathos. In most cases, the person being interred is eulogized with such superlatives that many are left feeling disappointed, almost cheated, that they never really knew the deceased at all. Where's the part about how she left her children? What about the affair he had? How he cheated on his taxes? How she never repaid the money she borrowed from Aunt Hazel?

Dawn Marie Hacheney's funeral would have none of that. Her short life had not been marred by scandal, petty infractions of the human kind, or even a single utterance of harsh words directed at anyone. As everyone who convened at Poulsbo's Christ Memorial Church knew, even before her death, Dawn had been an angel.

Friends who attended the service on that crisp winter day were making new memories as they faced old ones. Dawn's mother, Diana Tienhaara, had scoured her Bremerton house to create what many considered a very touching tableau of her daughter's life. Photos of Dawn as a girl, as a sister, as a young bride—all the roles that she'd played with devotion— were placed on a table against a wall in the back of the church. No one could deny that she had been a lovely girl. Tears fell. Stories spilled forth. Memories whirled.

Among all that unfettered emotion stood Nick Hacheney. For many, the sight of Nick as he greeted guests with bear hugs and sloppy kisses was indelible and a little unnerving.

"He's acting like this is a wedding, not his wife's funeral," a friend said.

Said another church member: "He lingered just a little too long on some of those kisses and hugs."

Diana caught the strange vibe, but she tried to put it out of her mind.

That's just Nick being Nick, she thought.

NO ONE LEFT THE SERVICE UNMOVED BY NICK'S EULOGY. Some saw it as the greatest tribute to a woman that a man could ever give. Others wondered how it was that Nick could summon the strength to do it. No one—pastor, friend, family member—would say that they could have done it had they been in Nick's shoes.

He stood facing the mourners, a tissue in his hand and tears in his eyes.

"If somebody could please say, 'Do it, honey.' "

Julie Conner found her voice: "Do it, honey!"

Nick raised his arms. "Every time I preach, I look down there in that front pew, second pew, or wherever she found an inconspicuous little spot. Before I start, I make eye contact. She mouths the words, 'Do it, honey.' "

He told the mourners how much he loved Dawn, his angel. How much she loved all of them. How she was the gentlest and kindest person any would ever meet as long as they lived.

"We all know that Dawn was innocent and blameless as a lamb. . . ."

For the next hour, Nick took those gathered around him on a tour of Dawn's life and his. Those who'd heard Nick speak before knew that he was skilled at pulling in an audience, person by person, until he commanded everyone in the room. He was on fire that afternoon, giving the tribute that he'd promised Dawn's family. He praised Dawn's teachers and work friends, among others. Mostly, however, his words were about how he was feeling.

"I've never known pain like this," he said, tears pushing at the edges of his eyelids, "but somewhere beneath all the pain there is more joy than I can fathom. You just can't be truly sorry when someone you love that much gets to go home early. . . ."

A wave of sobbing had swept through the congregation as Nick touchingly told the world of Diana's only daughter, so good and so godly. Clarity came to the grieving mother at that moment. She knew that whatever loss she would experience in her life would seem a trifle compared to the loss of her daughter. Her own fraying marriage. Her shattered faith. Each word Nick uttered was like a razor to her wrist: the pain and hurt, draining like blood.

She knew exactly how Nick felt, because she felt the same way.

"I will miss my little angel more than I can fathom. I will hurt and I will cry and I will wait for the day when the Lord calls me home," he said. "My flesh has been totally and literally torn in two and I need to take the time to grieve and hurt."

Many considered Dawn's eulogy Nick's finest moment at the pulpit.

After the service, little clusters of weeping mourners began to disband as people made their way to their cars. Few wanted coffee or the sugar cookies that had obviously been left over from Christmas. Annette Anderson waited in the reception area just outside the sanctuary, where Nick found her. His eyes were deep, dark pools of sorrow and hurt. He reached out for her and gave her a very long hug.

Julie and Gary Conner were standing nearby and felt a flicker of awkwardness.

This is too long of an embrace, Gary thought. His eyes met Julie's. She seemed to be thinking the same thing.

At about that time, a small group of Sandra Hacheney's friends came up to Nick to offer their condolences. They'd known Nick since childhood and knew that of all the Hacheney children, he'd been the prize. It seemed so unfair that he had to suffer such a loss. Nick lowered his gaze and thanked them. He hooked his arm around Annette's shoulder and spoke.

"This is Dawn's best friend, Annette," he said.

Annette didn't say anything. *Best friend?* It was such a huge honor, and she really did love Dawn. But the statement didn't correspond to the reality of their relationship.

"I loved her very much," she said, although her words felt hollow. She didn't know Dawn as well as she knew the other women. Nick had kept Dawn away from the church as much as possible. Annette did recall several occasions when there was some backbiting among the church ladies that Dawn wasn't doing her fair share. That was unfair and Annette had called the women on it. Dawn wasn't around because Nick didn't want her there. Period.

If I'm really her best friend, that's really sad, she thought.

AND AS ALL THAT WAS GOING ON, SOMETHING ELSE WAS happening. Something no one would have expected. God was about to whisper in the ear of another woman.

The thought that came to Lindsey Smith's friend, Becky Burns, revolted her. Becky had watched Lindsey bolstering Nick's sagging frame as he prepared to give Dawn's eulogy. Lindsey was shattered, of course. She'd barely stopped crying since learning of Dawn's death. She'd been by Nick's side every minute since then. On New Year's Eve she'd be put on a plane headed toward Africa, for her own mission experience.

The disquieting notion occurred to Becky again.

Well, now maybe Lindsey can be his wife, she thought.

Lindsey was thinking the same thing. She had found herself drawn to Nick, closer than ever in the hours and days after Dawn's tragic death. She'd sat up with him on the couch as he cried his eyes out and told her how much he wanted to die, that losing Dawn was more than he could bear alone. He hinted that maybe there was something divine at work, that God had already found him the woman to be his next wife.

PB Smith's daughter held Nick—homeless, wifeless, tormented—as he cried, and she cried too. All of a sudden he was no longer the brother she never had; no longer the youth pastor who implored her to be all that God wanted her to be. She could feel stirrings of emotion that felt a little like love.

THE *CENTRAL KITSAP REPORTER* TRUMPETED THE CAUSE OF Dawn Hacheney's death on New Year's Eve:

SPACE HEATER LINKED TO FIRE DEATH

By then fire investigators had trampled through the smelly wreckage that was once Nick and Dawn's master bedroom. A web of extension cords went every which way, indicating what Nick had told them: The couple had been in the midst of a remodel. Even a layperson could tell that the fire had burned hot and fast, though in a relatively small space. The bed that had held Dawn's burned body was little more than a black outline of charred batting and box springs. A mesh of wires covered her body, the remains of an electric blanket: the possible cause? Not far from the bed, investigators recovered a space heater. Near the headboard on Dawn's side of the bed was a supply of mini propane containers that Nick said had been a Christmas gift from his wife. He used the propane to heat the yurt in the backyard and when he went hunting. Photos were taken of the space heater, an arced wire, burned wrapping paper, melted mini-blinds, and a stopped clock on a nightstand.

One fire investigator was concerned that the paper next to the space heater burst into flames after Nick went hunting and not during the long cold night when the heater was going nonstop.

A press release was issued by the Bremerton Fire Department detailing what investigators thought had transpired prior to their arrival around 7:20 A.M. It was a tragic accident, they said. Working smoke detectors could have saved Dawn's life. There were no smoke detectors anywhere in the house.

Nick talked to several people—friends, his family, insurance investigators, police officers—about the heater.

"The heater was on, but there was nothing in front of it that I recall," he said. "We were careful to push the papers from the presents the night before away from the heater."

PHOTOGRAPHS OF DAWN HACHENEY'S GROTESQUELY CONtorted body were tucked into a file that would go unexamined for years. It would nearly take a magnifying glass to ferret out a possible—and potentially damning—clue. Newspapers and wrapping paper cocooned her remains. Later, it would chill those who examined the image. All around the victim's torso were the remnants of burned pieces of paper.

It appeared in at least one photograph that there was paper *underneath* her remains too.

22

AFTER A PRIVATE GRAVESIDE SERVICE HELD IN DAWN'S memory at Poulsbo's Cherry Grove Memorial Park, Lindsey Smith caught a plane to Muizenberg, just outside of Cape Town, South Africa, to start her work with Youth with a Mission. Contrasts were sharp in Muizenberg, and the extremes of culture, race, and societal status didn't just abut each other, they collided. White-sand beaches beckoned well-heeled tourists, while poverty-stricken locals subsisted on squash and grains. Apartheid had been abolished four years before, and the air was charged with the struggle for change.

It was hard for PB's youngest daughter to reconcile or even focus on any of that. Nick tapped out an e-mail to her on Friday, January 2, one of several that had filled her inbox while she made her way to South Africa. He told her he already missed her.

I gotta find somebody who can give a great hug like you. . . .

Lindsey wrote back, lamenting that she was unsure what kept her on the plane, flying to Africa, far from him.

[E]verything is such a blur. There are so many things that I want to tell you . . . but God has told me to keep it to myself for at least a year. . . .

In his next e-mail, Nick said God's plan for him was unclear: "It seems to include keeping me in the dark the majority of the time. . . ." Whatever it was, however, he was certain that Lindsey was part of the plan: "I want to try to weasel every piece of info out of you I possibly can but I'll respect your ability to hear and let it be." He pressed her a little, suggesting that they could find an Internet chat room where they could speak more directly, more intimately.

Nick held some righteous disdain for the insurance investigators who questioned him about the fire. "They asked me all sorts of really hard questions including if I started the fire myself." He'd taken a long drive that day, sorting things out, thinking about what God's plans were for him.

Lindsey, he wrote, was his "lifeline."

About other messages from God, Nick was unambiguous. Ron McClung, who was probably as close to Nick as any other man aside from PB, asked Nick during a January 4 phone conversation if he had any idea that Dawn was going to die.

"Well, I knew that something like this was going to happen," Nick said. "I didn't know how or when or anything like that."

Ron wondered if God had warned Nick. Had this been a prophecy? Nick had indicated to others—Sandy, Annette, and even Ron—that big things had been coming to him.

One of those things, apparently, was Lindsey. Nick wrote:

You have stopped being a disciple and are just a sensual beautiful woman with feelings and emotions that I need. . . .
I close my eyes and I feel your lips on mine. . . .

SOMETHING NAGGED AT DIANA TIENHAARA IN THE DAYS following Dawn's funeral. Diana wondered if God had tried to warn her about the fire. Her thoughts returned to that fateful Christmas night as she slept in the back bedroom of her parents' home. The room, an addition to the original house, had no heat source. Sleeping there in the winter had always been akin to curling up in a Frigidaire. That night Diana woke up feeling as though desert heat had filled the room. She threw off all the covers save for the top sheet.

Why had it been so warm? Had God been cautioning her?

Donald Tienhaara also let thoughts of the Heavenly Father console him. The only thing that kept him from completely shattering was the fact that he knew his little girl was in heaven; he knew so because of an incident that took place barely two days before she died. It was the kind of moment that becomes fixed in a grieving parent's mind: a concrete memory.

Dawn and Nick had arrived with bags of gifts to exchange that Christmas Eve. Dawn lamented how much still had to be done: cookies yet to bake, gifts at home waiting to be wrapped and passed out. Dawn was very much a young woman who did things in an efficient, orderly manner. That year, for some reason, the season had gotten away from her. That evening in the Tienhaaras' kitchen, Dawn and her brothers crushed candy canes for a special cookie recipe. Diana and Nick chatted about things that were going on in their lives. Nick, as always, was an attentive listener. While everyone milled around and opened their gifts, Dawn and her dad sat around the Christmas tree.

"You know something?" she asked.

Donald cocked his head. "No, what?"

"If I were to die tomorrow, it would be all right. I know where I'm going."

THE UNPLEASANT BUT NECESSARY TASK OF HELPING TO sort out Nick's finances fell on the capable shoulders of three women: Carol McClung, Adele Smith, and Annette Anderson, who readily volunteered. Carol was adept with organizing finances, Adele was an insurance representative, and Annette agreed to help Nick document what possessions had been lost in the fire.

Carol had known Nick since he was about ten. Although they had had their difficult moments—one time he made an inappropriate comment about her breasts—she liked him and wanted to help. She worried that it would be hard to re-create the Hacheneys' finances since so much of the house had been damaged by the fire and water.

"I have most of our paperwork," Nick said as he settled into a chair. Carol looked on, perplexed, as he handed her a sheaf of papers and a checkbook retrieved from Dawn's purse. "Dawn left her purse in the car."

Wow, Carol thought, *how lucky Nick is to have all this available.*

As she started to review the documents, Carol felt a little wave of panic. The Hacheneys were Hell's Canyon deep into debt. Nick acknowledged they had some outstanding bills but indicated that Dawn was the money manager who kept the accounts current. Working at the credit union, she knew her way around a budget.

However, this was far from a managed budget. Carol started a tally: $2,500 to Shell MasterCard; $5,400 to Capital One; $5,700 to GM; $1,800 to AT&T; $2,100 to Bankcard Services; $3,600 to another company. . . . She totaled it up with a few odds and ends and came up with just under $30,000.

"I have some more," Nick said. "The bills came to our P.O. box."

Carol was not the type to comment on her shock at the credit card debt. Instead, she forged ahead, helping Nick work out a plan to make the minimum payments on all outstanding balances.

They also discussed insurance. Nick said that Dawn had a life insurance policy through her work; in fact, she had just increased its payout value in November.

It turned out to be a stroke of luck that was short-lived, as Carol noticed that the policy increase did not go into effect until January 1.

"Nick, this one won't pay out," she said.

"No?" He looked confused, then disappointed.

Carol nodded. "I'm sorry."

A day later, Adele was called on to help Nick with the homeowner's insurance claim he was making to Safeco.

Nick bristled at the process, no matter how many times Adele told him that it was standard procedure. He was offended by the adjuster's invasive questioning.

"I don't know what they are trying to imply," he said.

"This is how it always goes in an accidental death."

"Why are they questioning me about Dawn and what happened?" Nick asked, raising his voice.

Adele, who had some misgivings about Nick and the way he'd conspired against her husband the summer she and Bob were away, nevertheless reached out to calm him. "Look, they have to ask those questions," she said. "They can't pay out until the case is closed. That means they can't pay until the coroner has ruled."

MEANWHILE, NICK HAD OTHER PROBLEMS THAT COULDN'T wait. Things were heating up between the most important couples in the church: the Bilys, the Smiths, and the somewhat reluctant McClungs. Relationships had eroded into an all-out war. Nick was made the scapegoat by Robert for much of the dissension among the ranks of the congregation. PB was furious about it. As far as he could see, the one causing problems was the apostle Robert, not Nick.

Why don't they cut Nick a break? His wife just died! PB thought.

That January night, Nick stayed up into the wee hours e-mailing Lindsey. He hinted that trouble was brewing at the church, but mostly delved into more personal areas. He wrote that her messages were "starting to make me blush." He said he was frightened about what "God is doing especially with everything else He has told me, but I need you so much right now that I can't help but to just lean on you."

One omission should have been glaring, even to a young woman like Lindsey. In none of his e-mails did Nick mention Dawn. It was as if she had never existed.

For her part, Lindsey was sure God's hand was in everything happening between her and Nick. She wrote: "I love God using me in this way. I love loving you."

23

L OVING SOMEONE DURING A TIME OF SORROW CAN BE A full-time job. Adele Smith understood that completely. The pastor's wife had her own job to do at the insurance office where she worked, but in the initial days following Dawn's death, it was easy to decide what was more important. She was worried about Nick's state of mind, which she considered fragile.

How will he cope with Dawn being gone? What more can I do? she asked herself.

Adele found the display board of Dawn's life that had been central to her memorial service. Adele's girls, Lindsey and Kim, had stayed up half the night making sure that the photos depicted Dawn at all stages in her life: girl, teen, young woman, wife. After the service, Adele brought the display upstairs to Lindsey's room, where Nick had moved in.

"I thought this would be something you'd like to keep," she said.

Nick, slumped on the daybed, replied, "Oh, thank you."

Adele didn't get it. Nick was almost dismissive, as if she was burdening him with more things to deal with.

A day or so later, while putting some clothes away, Adele noticed that the photo collage had been shoved to the back of the closet.

It must be too much of a reminder of the life he's lost, she thought.

At the same time that Adele was wondering about Dawn's photos, investigators going through the Hacheney home were concerned about a box containing personal papers, photographs, and a case with a pistol that had been found tucked away by the front door. One cop worried that it could point to arson—an inside job—in which everything is burned but the truly irreplaceable.

Nick had an explanation at the ready. He said he was moving his office from Bainbridge to home to save on commuting. He didn't mention to investigators how lucky he'd been that Dawn had forgotten her purse in the car the night before the fire.

FOR SOMETHING THAT WAS MEANT TO BE KEPT SECRET, THE teddy bear story made the rounds among some members of the church. It wasn't just gossip; whenever Mary Glass breathed a word of it, it was out of concern that something terrible could be implied by the gift.

"It wasn't right of her to write that kind of note," she said of Sandy. She thought that it might indicate an affair, and, with Dawn's demise, it only made her worry that there could be a connection between Sandy, Nick, and Dawn's death.

One of the people she told about the note was her half brother, Kenny Goans, forty-three. Kenny didn't really know what to make of it. As a corrections officer in a women's prison, he'd seen women do horrible things to their men or, even worse, their children. Sandy didn't have an evil bone in her body. He dismissed all of Jimmy's bellyaching about the relationship between Sandy and Nick. It was pathetic, he thought. He recalled how the two men had been watching the Arnold Schwarzenegger film *True Lies* at the guesthouse when Jimmy first spoke up.

"You should have seen Nick at Camp Ghormley," Jimmy had said. "He had all his groupies running around doing stuff for him. Sandy never left his side for one minute. Nicole too. Sandy and I argued about Nick, but she said he needed her."

"Give it a break," Kenny said.

Jimmy shook his head. "I can't," he said. "Something's going on."

* * *

ON THE EVENING OF JANUARY 5, AFTER THE SMITHS HAD gone to bed, Nick wrote another note to Lindsey. As much as he liked attention, the days following the fire had been difficult. He told her, "Everywhere I am everybody is watching me. I am almost afraid at times to feel because of how everyone will react. . . ."

Most of all, however, he wanted Lindsey to know how he felt about her, and where he thought God was taking the two of them.

> God is putting you right in front of me. Somehow having you to lean on is sustaining me. . . . I am experiencing a kind of love for you that feels totally appropriate to me.

He cast Lindsey as the healer for his "brokenness."

> I am falling in love with you. I can feel your tears on my cheek and it touches deep into my heart.

Lindsey felt a rush of emotion so mixed with grief, love, and uncertainty that she scarcely knew how to process it. The idea that Nick was being watched didn't come off as paranoia: He was a martyr of sorts. The church, the world, all eyes were riveted on him because he'd been anointed to lead. He'd told her before she left for Africa that others would note his cues to see how he handled his grief over Dawn's death. He had to be strong.

"They'll be looking to me," he said.

With her primary relationship hindered by the miles between them, Lindsey found it hard to engage with others in Africa. She shared a Spartan but clean flat with four other missionaries. The flatmates, while welcoming to the young woman from Washington, had already bonded. Lindsey felt estranged and lonely. Each moment in her room, she stared at the ceiling and waited for Nick to contact her. No one could possibly understand.

The only one who really knows me is Nick, she thought, *and he's not here.*

That same night on the other side of the world, Nick arrived at the LaGrandeur place on Bainbridge Island. It was the eve of intern Sara's departure to Belize to fulfill her commitment to God as a member of the youth ministry. She was a pretty girl, wide-eyed but less trusting than Lindsey. That night Nick was in a depressed mood. He was in such a state that when he asked if he could spend the night, Sara didn't think twice. It was only later, as they sat on the couch, that Nick got too close for comfort. He started stroking her hair and drawing her closer. Sara felt as if Nick's obvious affection for her was too intimate, but given the circumstances she couldn't find the words to stop him. After a couple of awkward hours, the eighteen-year-old extricated herself and went to bed.

The next morning, a caravan of church folks left the island for Sea-Tac to see Sara off to Belize.

In some ways it was a repeat of Lindsey's Sea-Tac airport sendoff on New Year's Eve. Nick had been in a cudding mood. He had entwined himself with Sara in an embrace that suggested too much closeness. At one point his head was on her lap.

Those who viewed the scene didn't know what to say. Grief is strange, of course. Who knows how a man would handle losing his wife?

Always with a camera for events like these, Craig Anderson snapped a final photo of Nick and Sara. Nick stood next to the young woman, his hands pressed deep into his pockets, his face etched with longing. The image was held in the memories of all those who were there.

That night Nick wrote to Lindsey:

Just another gut-wrenching day in the life of Pastor Nick. Now all of my girls are gone.

PAMELA BILY HAD ANOTHER OMINOUS DREAM THAT INDIcated something inappropriate was transpiring between Nick Hacheney and a female member of the church.

Not Lindsey.

Not Sandy.

"I saw Nick driving Nicole Matheson's car," she said.

The image was clear. Robert couldn't dismiss it. First the Sandy Glass "emotional" affair, then Dawn's death. Now Nick was potentially involved with Nicole. By then it was plain to Robert that Pamela had been 100 percent right in her description of the alliance between PB and Nick against him. But a romance between Nick and Nicole seemed so out of line that Robert just couldn't fathom it. She was a vulnerable single mother; Nick was a leader of the church whose wife had just died.

He called Ron McClung and told him about his wife's prophetic dream; Ron agreed that it was time to find out just what Nick was up to.

The apostle decided on a stakeout of Nicole's house.

24

Nick Hacheney was on a kind of a circuit of sympathy as he drove from house to house visiting female church members in the days after Dawn's death in the fire. Sometimes he was tearful, sometimes just matter-of-fact. He often carried a calmness that seemed to come with understanding that what had really transpired was not some random act but divine intervention. Tucked under his arms was a stack of stapled photocopies from New Zealand youth minister Winkie Pratney's book *The Thomas Factor: The Key to Believing When You Cannot Find an Answer.* The pages were about "the dark night of the soul."

"The answer is on these pages," Nick told various hosts and comforters. "This will help all of us understand the spiritual journey I'm on."

As the new widower understood it, God would reveal the answer to him in time. Something good would happen from all the tragedy. Dawn's death had a necessary purpose.

It was the middle of the day when church member Tanna Martin, twenty-five, opened the door to find Nick Hacheney outside her Poulsbo home. He was looking forlorn and more unkempt than usual. Dawn had been gone a little more than a week and Tanna had no words to console him. When he asked her to sit next to him on the couch, she complied.

"I miss Dawn so much," he said, sobbing into his hands. "I miss her smile. Her touch."

Tanna patted Nick on the shoulder; her beautiful blue eyes glistened with tears. Even with her baby just home after a hospitalization, she knew her troubles paled in comparison. Dawn was gone forever.

Nick put his head on her shoulder. Tanna felt her muscles tense a little. Something didn't feel right.

"I miss having sex with her," he said, now sobbing into his hands.

It started quietly but grew louder. Alarm bells sounded in Tanna's mind. When one of her children stirred, she jumped to her feet.

"I better check on the baby," she said, leaving Nick on the couch.

Was Nick making a pass at me? she wondered. *Or am I just suspicious?*

NICOLE ALWAYS LEANED ON NICK WHENEVER THE SLIGHT-est thing went awry. If the kids were acting up, she'd call and Nick would zip over and take care of it. If her son refused to get dressed for school, Nick would somehow get to Suquamish in time to tell him that he had better get ready. They listened to Nick. Whenever Nick intervened, things around her house were happier. Life itself was better. In the days after Dawn's death, however, Nicole was feeling a kind of role reversal reshaping their relationship. Nick needed *her*. She found herself drawn to him for something other than what he could do for her.

All he wanted to talk about was Dawn. How much he missed her. How his life would never be the same. A fountain of tears flowed, and Nicole was right there on the sofa next to him, drying his eyes.

"It'll be all right," she promised.

"I don't know," he said. "I feel like I'm being punished. God is punishing me."

Nicole had no idea why God would seek retribution. Nick had always been a source of support for any member of the church who needed him. PB was too busy. Robert was too cold. Nick was the caring one. Nicole knew the kind of man

Nick was. He wasn't the type of fit, handsome man that she'd found herself attracted to in the past. He wasn't Ed—that was for sure. Yet Nicole was drawn to Nick.

When he leaned over and kissed her on the couch late one night in early January, Nicole knew that they were crossing a line. *But he needs to be touched*, she thought. *He's so lonely. He misses his wife. I'll help him through his grieving. God will understand.*

IF E-MAILS COULD STAMMER, THAT'S JUST WHAT LINDSEY Smith's would have done. After much rambling about God and what He was telling her, she wrote:

> While I was still there, I loved you deeply and I could see God using me like some supernatural thing . . . when I sat down on that plane it turned from loving you to being in love with you.

If she thought, as she wrote, that she might be "testing the waters," she wasn't going to be disappointed. Nick was getting what he'd wanted all along.

Hours after the incident with Tanna, Nick reacted to Lindsey's confession of love with another lengthy late-night missive. He told her that he was filled with so much joy, he couldn't believe it. And yet, he cautioned her that he didn't know where their love could take them, since God had told him his life would be going in another direction:

> God has given me some specifics on my life in the next few years. But my heart and my feelings scream out that I am desperately in love with you and want you by my side forever.

He let Lindsey know that her being in Africa might be a saving grace of sorts. If she were in Washington, he wrote, "I would be having a real problem."

What Lindsey didn't know, however, was that Nick was

casting a wider net. He sent an e-mail to Sara in Belize too, telling her that he wanted her in the way that "a man wants a woman."

Sara wasn't having any of it. She loved Nick too, but not in *that* way.

SOMETIMES THINGS JUST HAPPEN. ON JANUARY 9, THINGS dramatically changed between Nick and Nicole. When Nicole's two children were asleep, Nick tearfully told her that he needed love—*her* love. Although their relationship had grown, Nicole had never considered Nick a potential suitor. He wasn't the kind of man that she'd pick as a lover, either. Ed had been tall with handsome, chiseled features. Nick, in all fairness, was not.

That night she gave in to her feelings and they had sex. Nicole knew immediately that what they'd done was wrong.

"It's too soon after Dawn," she said. "You shouldn't be intimate with other women right now."

"I know," Nick told her, "but I think God will allow it."

He said he felt as if God had given him grace. That it was all right for her to help him through his devastating grief. That was something Nicole could understand. Her own love life had been a shambles for well over a year and a half. Ed, she feared, was never coming back.

Nick needs to be loved, she thought.

Over the next few nights, and for a short period into the winter, the sexual part of their relationship persisted. Nicole saw it as a gift to a man whom she admired.

Whenever she felt herself slipping toward the idea that she'd fallen in love with Nick, she put on the brakes.

I can't be in love with him; this is Pastor Nick!

Things were messy and Nicole was a woman who liked order. She'd wanted nothing like this. She knew that no matter how her emotions and loneliness persuaded her to spin it, the idea that she and Nick had been sexual could only be seen in the most tawdry and disrespectful of terms. Dawn had been gone for only sixteen days. *Sixteen days*. Nicole wanted God to come into the situation and make whatever was happening pure and worthy.

She made a journal entry the morning of January 10:

> I woke up with this feeling of knowledge that because of Nick's tragedy my response to him was out of love. It has to do with the deep love I carry in my heart for him. It's just coming out in a wacky way.

Nicole knew that if word got out that she and Nick had been having sex, it would be seen as wrong, shameful and embarrassing. Her relationship with Nick was nobody's business. Period. She never told her family or any friends that he'd been coming over at night. But as the weeks marched on, so did the innuendo.

"Pamela had a dream," Nick told Nicole during one of his late-night rendezvous at her house, "that you and I are together. Now they *all* think that we are."

"What should we do?" she asked.

"Maybe we should stop."

Nicole thought about it, and agreed. "Okay, this is the last time."

Nicole believed they could stop. There was no future in what they were doing. She didn't see it clearly just then, but her feelings were slowly shifting.

It wasn't the last time. Not even close.

DAWN HACHENEY HAD BEEN DEAD FOR TWO WEEKS, AND the memory of the morning she died lingered on Bremerton's Jensen Avenue. The Hacheneys' front door was boarded up with sheets of quarter-inch-thick plywood, as were the blown-out bedroom windows in the back of the house. Neighbor Tim Pitts couldn't shake the recollection that as the fire burned, he had overheard a neighbor tell Nick that Tim and his boss, Jeff Richardson, had "risked their lives" to try to save Dawn. Nick was in shock back then, Tim surmised, because all he had done was shrug his shoulders.

On January 11, 1998, Tim and his wife, Amy, watched as Nick marched up the front steps of the house and then quickly disappeared around to the backyard.

"Wonder what he's doing there," Tim mused aloud before deciding to go over. He met Nick outside. The air was like ice.

"I'm sorry about your wife, you know, passing away," he said.

Nick stared at Tim. Unexpectedly, without a word, he turned his back and walked down the steps, to his Jeep, and drove off. It was bizarre.

Tim told Amy about the encounter, and she too thought it was strange. The Pitts had been good neighbors. Friendly, even. They'd chatted up Dawn and Nick on the street about their remodeling, about their church. A building contractor, Tim had a certain amount of expertise and he was willing to share tips and advice. At times Dawn seemed interested in the Pitts' children, which made them wonder when the young couple would start a family of their own.

Something's not right here, Tim thought after Nick gave him the brush-off. *Something's strange with that dude.*

HOW LONG DID THE HOUSE FIRE BURN BEFORE THE PITTS called 911? In time, there would be arguments over when Nick Hacheney said he left home, how long he was gone, and how that timeline played into the events of December 26, 1997. If it had been a flash fire that had lasted only twenty minutes, would Dawn's body have been as charred as it was? How could Nick have set the fire to blaze at a slow burn? If he did, how was it possible that it burned undetected for hours?

Years later, at the same time of day his son said he left to hunt with Lindsey Smith and Phil Martini, 5:00 A.M., Dan Hacheney followed the route from Jensen Avenue to the duck blinds on Indian Island. He ticked off the miles, the minutes. It took him exactly an hour. When he got out of his truck, he looked at the murky waters of Puget Sound. *Just as Nick had told the investigators, his friends, members of the church, it was first light.*

"I *drove* it," he said several years after the fire, "I know for certain that he arrived to hunt at first light with Lindsey and Phil. The fire had to have started long after he left. He couldn't have set it. It wasn't arson. It was an accident."

25

BREMERTON WAS IN A GLUM MOOD IN JANUARY AS THE town prepared to see its greatest tourist attraction leave port for Hawaii. The USS *Missouri*, fondly known as the Mighty Mo, was being taken from Puget Sound Naval Shipyard, where it had been moored for decades. Thousands lined up to get one last look at the ship on which Japan had officially surrendered during World War II.

Away from the tourists, the Hacheney house was like a damp, fetid campground fire pit. Yellow police tape crisscrossed the front door. Craig and Annette Anderson stood breathless with Nick as he pushed it open to let them inside. The three had arrived, along with Ron and Carol McClung, to record more of the inventory needed by the insurance company. Of the group, Nick appeared to be the strongest and the most capable of dealing with the sad task at hand. The sight of a smoke-damaged Christmas tree met them as the three passed by the living room. Holiday decorations sat ruined on the kitchen counter. The half-melted microwave oven was Daliesque.

Power had yet to be restored, so the house was somewhat dark as they moved from the front door to the master bedroom. It was like a funeral march. Nick stopped short as he entered; he looked at the blackened rectangle that indicated the bed where Dawn had perished. He had a notebook in his hand, as did Craig. Nick started to call out some household items that had been damaged, and Craig started writing. Then Nick stopped and began to cry.

Annette glanced at Craig with a look of understanding. They were bearing witness to a man's deepest moment of sorrow. She put her hand on Nick's back. She wanted to console him, but she started to cry too.

"It's okay," Nick said. "I can do this." The tears stopped as quickly as they started, and the shout-outs of the inventory continued. Propane canisters, collectible duck stamps, clothing, bedding, a radio—even the space heater that all were certain had caused the fire—were recorded. His eyes glistened again when he came across a trunk that had held Dawn's collection of dolls.

"Dawn loved those," he said.

Drifts of ashes had collected in the corners of the room. The window had been busted and boarded. It was the kind of place in which no one wanted to linger. As quickly as they could, the three retreated to the living room. Once more, the singed Christmas tree caught their gaze.

"These presents were for your kids." Nick indicated the sodden packages under the tree. "Dawn got them. I'll have to claim them. Water damage."

When no one could take another minute, the McClungs and Andersons followed Nick outside, where Annette noticed a waterlogged mattress dumped in the yard. It was burned black except for a portion on one side. Had that been Dawn's side of the bed? She put it out of her mind and trailed Nick's Jeep over to his brother Ron's house on the other side of Bremerton for pizza and a chance to decompress from the heavy but necessary burden. Nick stayed only a short time, seemingly uncomfortable with the care and support of those who loved him.

"Maybe you can come over tomorrow after church?" Nick said to Annette on his way out the door.

"Of course," she said. "I'll be there."

Seeing the wreckage of Nick and Dawn's home was like seeing a real-life metaphor for a life ended, and one that might never recover. It shook Annette hard. She replayed the images of Nick standing in the bedroom, trying to be strong and breaking down, only to fight himself out of it. No matter how devastating it had been for her, the experience for Nick was a million times worse.

She wanted to reach out to him and let him know her faith in God was strong and it was clear that God had a plan for Nick. He had to—God would never have taken Dawn to heaven if there wasn't some meaning behind it.

After she and Craig put the kids down for the night, Annette sat at the kitchen table and wrote out a three-page letter to Nick. She thought about each word and whether or not she could find the right combination to inspire him, to comfort him:

> You aren't like most; you never took it for granted or mistreated Dawn. You knew your life was a fragile gift from your God.

She promised that she'd be there for him. God would see him through, and God wanted her to help him. He wasn't alone.

She showed Craig the letter before sealing it in an envelope.

"This is nice, Annette," he said, absorbing each word. "Nick will appreciate this."

NICOLE NOTICED A RING BOX ONE AFTERNOON WHEN PUTting things away in Nick's temporary bedroom at the Smiths'. Curiosity got the best of her and she opened it. Inside, she found a woman's wedding band. It was gold with a small diamond, sapphire, ruby, and emerald. It wasn't grand, but it was undeniably pretty.

"What's this?"

Nick looked over, caught off guard. "Oh, that's a ring I had made for Dawn. I never had the chance to go give it to her."

Nicole didn't ask any more about it. It didn't seem to her that he was defensive or agitated. Maybe it was just too painful for him to talk about. . . .

She put it away.

* * *

IT WAS JANUARY, COLD, SOPPING WET. BARE TREES FRAMED the views of the leaden Puget Sound, and the baseboard heating system in the Anderson house was working overtime to keep the place warm. Sometime after 10:00 P.M. there was an unexpected knock on the front door. Annette opened the door to find Nick Hacheney standing glumly on the front step. She invited him inside.

"I've been out driving around aimlessly," he said. "That's what I do now, drive around at night."

Grief was etched on Nick's face and Annette knew that her own sorrow paled next to his pain. She gave him a hug, feeling his grief transfer to her. He'd lost his soul mate: Dawn was an angel. It also struck her that Nick had somehow tried to prepare himself and others like her and Sandy for something major. Dawn's death had been ordained.

As they took a seat on the couch, Annette found the words. "You knew this was going to happen," she said. She stared hard into his eyes. "How did you know?"

Nick put his fingers to his lips. *Shhhh.*

Annette didn't let up. She'd spent the last four months reading the books Nick and Sandy had provided, poring over the Scripture with an acolyte's fire for learning. But she still didn't get it.

"This is exactly what you've been talking about for months, Nick. Isn't it?"

Nick brushed her off. "Don't ask me that again."

SOLIDLY ENSCONCED AS NICK HACHENEY'S CHIEF PROTECTOR, it pained Pastor Bob Smith to hear the constant murmurings of those among the board members who were sure that Nick was handling his grief in a manner unbecoming a man of God. PB shrugged off the possibility of Nick being unfaithful to Dawn. Robert Bily, of course, was the chief accuser.

Very indignantly—and rightly so, PB thought—Nick brought up two occasions when PB was in Africa that Robert had accosted Dawn with a question that shook her: "Do you think your husband is having an affair?"

As Nick related it to PB, the words had echoed like a thunderclap. Dawn was in tears for days. She could barely shake the hurt of the insulting question.

All PB could think about was how out of line Robert had been to suggest such a thing to Nick's wife. It was a knife in Nick's back too.

Nick worked his butt off while I was gone trying to hold the church together and you accuse him of this? he thought.

Fed up with Robert's political machinations, PB confronted him at a board meeting.

"Did you say that to Dawn? Did you ask her if she thought Nick was betraying her?"

Robert's face was emotionless. His eyes were unblinking. "I *never* said that."

YEARS LATER, NICK BRISTLED AT THE MENTION OF THE ENcounter between Robert Bily and his wife over his purported involvement with Sandy. "It upset Dawn. We went to one of her favorite restaurants and talked about it. She was a very forgiving woman."

26

SUNDAY AFTERNOON, CHURCH OVER, THE KIDS UNDER Craig's watchful eye, Annette Anderson returned to the Smiths' house. Nick met her at the door and embraced her. A hug from Nick was expected at most greetings, but immediately this one felt curious.

"Stop with the hug, already," she said, trying to defuse the awkwardness of the moment.

Nick cocked his head and smiled. Despite the grin, his dark eyes were sad and pleading.

"I have to tell you, Annette," he said, "I really like hugging you."

She held her tongue. She knew that he was lonely, heartbroken, and reaching out for the comfort of his friend.

"You have to stop hugging me like that," she said. "Let's get back to work."

Annette pulled out the notebook they were using to list what had been lost in the fire. After a while Nick wrapped himself in a blanket and was nearly supine as Annette reviewed the list.

Out of the blue, Nick said something that rattled her deeply.

"I want to run you upstairs and make mad, passionate love with you right now. What would you think of that, Annette?"

"Don't talk like that," she said.

He moved closer on the couch, and she found herself pulling back. The moment was supremely uncomfortable.

"Why?" he asked.

"Because it's not right. It's a sin."

Nick shrugged. "Fine." He kept his eyes riveted to her body—not her face, not her eyes. It was the look of a man trying to play some kind of seduction number.

We're not going there, she thought.

Annette finally found her voice. "It is a sin to even *think* that way," she said.

Nick laughed. "Whoops, I did it again."

The next day Nick made another remark about Annette's body being sexy. Nick sat on Lindsey's old bed and grinned as Annette shifted the contents of the bedroom for the influx of Nick's things. He was in his bizarre, playful mood and it bothered her. She was there to help, not flirt.

"You know," she said, "I don't really like the way you're talking to me."

"Oh, yes you do," Nick countered, doing his best approximation of coy.

He motioned for her to sit with him on the bed.

"We need to talk," he said. "Would it be so bad to touch me? How wrong would it be?"

"I'm married, for one thing," she said, now sitting.

He ignored her. It was the one thing he couldn't argue against.

"Feeling good isn't wrong, Annette. The Bible says that love is the most important thing. You love me, don't you?"

"You know I do," she said.

"Sometimes I forget how much you don't know about the Scripture," he said. "You're just a baby, a little lamb, when it comes to God. You have no idea what people have done for love. Christians are in the habit of being so narrow-minded that they are not even willing to risk *anything* for love."

Annette found herself understanding a little of what he was trying to say. His physical desires were out of a holy love, not some kind of lust that was dirty and immoral. It was a pure, God-like love.

"I've done things out of love that you wouldn't believe.

When [another church member] was going through his divorce, he was a broken man, a hurting man; he needed comfort and love. I was there for him."

Had Nick's past hinted at some kind of sexual encounter with a man? She didn't say anything, and Nick kept talking.

"The bottom line is that there are times when the rules are meant to be broken. Only those who are less in tune with God see this as wrong."

NICK WAS UNORGANIZED IN EVERY ASPECT OF HIS LIFE. Annette, going over the notes that she'd made of the inventory, felt stressed and frazzled. She felt that in his state of mind, Nick might not get everything he was entitled to when the insurance was settled. She knew Nick didn't care about the money, but she'd been called into his service and she felt she knew the reason.

He was lost without someone watching over him.

After the first Sunday when they worked at Pastor Bob's house and Nick made the sexual remark, she felt the beginning of a pattern. He hugged her another time, aggressively so, and she told him to stop. Then he made further remarks about wanting to get physical with her. They sprang from him like a barrage of non sequiturs.

It's the way he's grieving, she thought. *It has to be.*

Half the time she ignored him; other times she tried to shut him down. She told him he didn't know what he was saying. When her rebukes only served to egg him on, she tried a new approach.

"What you're saying, Nick, is a sin. You're sinning. Stop it." She was firm, like a mother to a son who begs for a chocolate bar before dinner. "Stop it. No!"

Nick would become sad once more.

"I can't help it," he said.

During the next week Annette showed up at the Smith house almost daily to re-create the inventory of what had been lost in the fire. Nick curled up on the couch, his eyes looking upward as he tried to visualize what was in each room.

"We had some toys for your kids, Annette. We better write those down."

Annette dutifully transcribed his recollections. Guns, furniture, duck stamps, decoys, clothing; it went on and on.

"Lingerie. Dawn had some really nice stuff."

Then he went quiet and Annette looked up from the notebook. "What is it?"

"Sorry. Can't remember. I'm completely distracted by the thought of your lips and what it would be like to kiss them."

Annette blushed. "Knock it off," she said.

Teasing innuendos were one thing. Annette thought they were harmless at first. When Nick started to really push an agenda that included a physical relationship, he did so with rationalization, not a leer.

"I keep thinking about this, little lamb," he said as they sat on the couch in the Smiths' basement. Nick was nearly supine again, with his legs over Annette's lap. "I keep thinking about God and what he wants, and things are becoming clearer."

"Clearer?" Annette wasn't buying any of it, but she needed to believe that there was some kind of order, a plan, in the literal ashes that surrounded her.

"Like King David in the Old Testament," he said. "He was a man after God's own heart, just like me."

Annette believed in Nick's closeness with God. After all, Nick had been given to God to raise when he was a baby. Dan and Sandra Hacheney had talked about that several times. Nick was God's son.

"Do you believe me? Trust me?"

She nodded.

"Our being together isn't wrong," he said. "There is no absolute wrong because God will use it all. God used David's sin and through it, he built the very lineage of Christ."

Nick searched her eyes. "I'm God's man," he said, his confidence growing. "I've been different since birth. Different from others. God has a plan for me. I don't know what it is, but you are a part of it. I know it."

Overcome, Annette started to cry, and Nick put his hand

on her shoulder. "It's all right," he said. "I've paid the ultimate price for God's plan." Annette knew he was referring to Dawn's death. "And I am ready to do whatever God asks of me."

Nick had the most understanding and accepting countenance. It was like looking into a mirror and seeing a part of herself in him. Within Nick, there was God.

"You have to be ready too," he said.

27

BLEAK WHITE WALLS LOOMED ALL AROUND LINDSEY Smith, and they were closing in. She had to talk to someone about what was going through her mind. Given that she was constantly checking her flatmate's computer for e-mails from Nick, she felt that she owed the woman an explanation. Lindsey was embarrassed about it. Nick's wife had just died. No matter how it was presented, it couldn't possibly be seen as appropriate. The internal stalemate was broken one afternoon when the flatmate, Colleen, read an e-mail that Lindsey had accidentally left open on her computer.

"Lindsey," she said, "I think we need to talk about this."

With Colleen's eyes drilling her own, Lindsey unleashed the flood of what had transpired in Washington. She told Colleen that she was in love with Nick, or thought she was.

"Be careful, Lindsey. Nick's not in his right mind. He's been through a devastating loss. This could end up hurting you."

Lindsey understood that Colleen's words were meant to protect her, but she couldn't dismiss her true feelings for Nick.

God wants this.

"I'll try to be careful," she said, although she knew it was a commitment she couldn't keep.

There was one person above all others with whom Lindsey wanted to confide her relationship with Nick: her father. Nick promised he'd say something to her dad when they went on a hunting trip. God, she believed, was directing all of this. He'd given her the Word that she and Nick would marry. She hoped her father would understand it was God doing this.

Lindsey never found the right time to tell him. Nick did.

THE WAITRESS AT THE PERKINS RESTAURANT IN MOSES Lake, Washington, had only just taken their breakfast order when Nick admitted to PB that he was carrying something inside that he had to get out. They'd left their motel before first light, spent the morning duck hunting, and had been talking about stacks of pancakes swimming in butter and maple syrup.

"I don't know what's going on," he said. "I don't know how you're going to feel about this. I don't understand it. I've just got feelings for Lindsey."

PB heard him right, but it seemed like such a bizarre comment that he almost did a double take.

"That's crazy," he finally said.

Nick got quiet. "I know," he said. "But it's happened all at once."

The kid is in deep grief, confused over Lindsey's kindness to him, and flat-out mixed up over what his feelings are, PB thought.

"Look, Nick," PB said, "I know you and Linds are close. But what you're feeling isn't what you think it is."

Nick looked up. "I don't know. My feelings are strong."

"You need to back off," PB said. "If God has something to work out, let God work it out."

PB looked for words that would soothe but were strong enough to show that Nick's feelings were way off base.

"If, down the road, God has a purpose for the two of you together—if that's God's will—I'm fine with that."

Nick appeared relieved, but that faded as PB continued.

"But I am not fine with you trying to work out your feelings about my daughter in your current state of mind. You just don't make a decision like this after you've just lost your wife."

The food came and Nick seemed ready to comply with PB's request. He started to eat.

"Okay, you're right," he said.

THE ONLY GYM ON BAINBRIDGE HAD ONCE BEEN A BOWL-ing alley. It was converted to a fitness center that quickly became home to the island's beautiful bodies. Nick had begun a regular routine there, joining Annette, who had been going for about a year.

Since Dawn's death, Nick had been overtly flirtatious with Annette, but out of pity for him, she persuaded herself that she was misreading him. He might have been more attentive because he required so much attention of his own. One afternoon, however, any doubts about what he was after vanished. At the gym, he pulled her into a tanning room and kissed her.

She kissed him back, stunned at her own reaction.

"It's just like I thought it would be," he said.

Annette didn't say anything. She couldn't even explain her response to herself. It was sudden, a bear hug of an embrace. It unnerved her, and she gathered her things and returned home to Suquamish.

Nick arrived a little while later. While the kids napped, he kissed her again.

"This isn't right," she said.

"But I need to. God wants us to. It's okay."

"I don't know."

"I *do*. I need this."

Annette could feel the world spinning. A force was carrying her into the sky. She couldn't see straight. She trusted Nick. She had to be strong for him. God wanted it and Nick knew better than she did.

"Don't question this," he said. "This is part of the plan."

"I don't know," she repeated.

"We need to take this further. We need a place where we can be together," he said. His eyes were fierce in their certainty.

"All right," she said. "But not here."

* * *

THE SMITH FAMILY'S DEN WAS A COMFY ROOM, MOST NOTED for its display of hunting photos that the family called its Wall of Fame. There were images of PB, Adele, and Kim and Lindsey at various ages posing with their prizes: ducks, doves, and bigger game. When Nick first became a kind of adopted son, he'd looked up at the wall and vowed he'd make it there too. In time, he did. Once, when he and PB were up hunting on the famed Dungeness Spit near Sequim, Nick's lucky shot brought down a European wigeon, so rare that seasoned Northwest hunter PB had to send a photograph off to a friend with ties to the Audubon Society to identify it.

"I've arrived," Nick said the day the photo of him, beaming alongside his dog Hope and holding the dead fowl, was hung with the others on the wall.

Later, there would be much discussion among members of the church over whether PB Smith had been blinded by the adulation of the son he never had. For his part, PB would insist the relationship was overstated.

If not a deep bond, what else could explain PB's lapse in letting Nick look him in the eyes and make promise after empty promise?

A few days after the Moses Lake trip, Nick wrote an e-mail to Lindsey. He said that he had been unsure of going hunting so soon after Dawn's death. He was glad that he did. It was fun. He'd been thinking of making that trip to Africa to see her, and "to seek God's heart on life, the future and what in the world is happening to me."

He just wanted to hold her, kiss her. This was more than something merely physical. Their love was ordained by God. "I prayed the other day that God would take my life if this wasn't Him and I'm still alive so I guess I'll just keep walking forward," he wrote. Nick said that God had spoken to him, saying that Lindsey was a gift, "an opened gift from Him."

He never mentioned the encounter with Annette. Nor did he tell Lindsey what her father had said about backing off from their relationship.

28

LINDSEY SMITH WASN'T ALONE IN HER CONFUSION over what was happening between her and the church's beleaguered youth pastor. Annette Anderson was dealing with a turbulent mix of loyalty and sorrow. So was Nicole Matheson. In fact, from the very moment they'd become sexually intimate, Nicole tried to rationalize the sex as a gift she'd given a good friend. He needed to be loved by a woman. She was there, able, and after some unconvincing internal dialogue, she found herself willing to do whatever he needed.

From the time he had shown up with a hammer and a carpenter's saw and his ever-present positive attitude to help build their Suquamish house long ago, he'd given both his body and heart to the Matheson family. Dawn had also been a true friend, almost an extension of Nick. Now it was Nicole's turn to give back.

On the morning of January 19, 1998, she gently opened the pages of a spiral-bound notebook and began to pour out her heart. When they'd first crossed the line, she'd told herself that it was a onetime thing. Except it hadn't been. Nick had been over several late evenings when the kids were asleep in their bedrooms down the hallway. She knew their sexual intimacy had distorted things:

Maybe Nick can never be my pastor again, even when he's back to being Pastor Nick, I still know that it was worth it. It was worth it because of who Nick will become. I'm thankful for the time of Pastor Nick and Dawn. I'm thankful for the time of Nick.

As Nick and Nicole's relationship moved tentatively forward, there were still moments when former congregants would broach the idea that something sinister had taken place at the Hacheney house on Christmas night. Whenever Mary Glass looked across the yard and saw Faith, the chocolate Labrador retriever that Nick had given Mary's grandson as an early Christmas gift that year, she shook her head about the timing of the gift.

It upset her and she prayed on it.

"Notice how no dogs died," Mary told Debbie Gelbach.

"He got the dog out of the house . . . *before* the fire," Debbie said.

Mary nodded. "Right. Faith just happened to be living over here when the place burned up."

By all rights, Nick *should* have taken Faith and not Hope hunting that morning. Hope was pregnant. Those who knew Nick well believed he would never have taken his prized yellow Lab out on a hunt in that condition. He was too picky about his dogs.

He took her from the house because he knew the place would burn down, Mary thought.

Mary also talked with Gary and Julie Conner about her concerns. The Conners told Sandy's mother-in-law that they'd heard that law enforcement had said there was no smoke in Dawn's lungs.

"How can that be?" Mary asked.

Gary, ever logical, knew of only one possible explanation. He hated to say it aloud but he did anyway: "She was already dead."

Later, when Mary was visiting with Sandy, she mentioned the autopsy report and how it seemed suspicious that Dawn died without taking in a puff of smoke.

Sandy disagreed vehemently. "They had a lot of propane canisters that exploded. That's what happened. A big explosion."

Mary didn't know it at the time, but Sandy had just shared with her mother-in-law a specific detail only known by the insurance company, the police, and Nick.

Had Nick kept Sandy in the loop?

That wasn't all Sandy knew. Dawn had been burned so badly her arms were gone. Her chest was nearly a solid lump of charcoal. But there was—just barely—enough blood to run toxicology screens. Besides a large dosage of Benadryl, the lab analysts were surprised to learn that no carbon monoxide or cyanide from burning plastics was found in her lungs. She had not breathed in any smoke. How could that be? The pathologist came up with an answer, concluding that Dawn was asphyxiated when her larynx reflexively shut in response to a catastrophic flash fire. The propane bottles and their explosive contents were key to this theory.

IT WAS COLD OUTSIDE IN THE GYM PARKING LOT AS NICK and Annette walked to their cars. He had been playfully flirting with Annette between stints on the cardio machines. She'd smiled back at him as he huffed and puffed through a workout. It was clear he wanted more than encouragement from his workout partner.

"Follow me," he said.

Against her better judgment, she agreed.

Annette and Nick got into their cars and Nick pulled onto the highway and started driving, Annette following. She had no idea where he was going. To the Smiths'? To her house? Over to Sandy's? Instead, he turned onto Moran Road.

He was going to the church.

The Jeep's brake lights pulsed, and Nick rolled his window down and indicated for Annette to pull around to the back of the church, a place they'd never parked since it was far from the main entrance. A moment later, he opened the basement door and they both went inside.

Without flipping on the lights and without saying a word, Nick unlocked Pastor Bob's office and went inside. Annette followed, thinking it was strange that Nick didn't go into his own office. He settled himself in the chair behind the desk.

"Sit there," he said, indicating the chair in front of the desk. "I know that I should be thinking about Dawn, but all I can think about is you."

Annette could sense where this was going. The kiss in the tanning room. The constant innuendos. She tried to cut him off.

"Nick, I've been missing Dawn so much too."

Nick wasn't listening.

"Dawn's only been dead a month," he said, "and I haven't even dealt with it yet because of you."

While there was a kind of trusting innocence in her character, Annette knew a line when she heard one. Yet somehow this didn't seem like one. She knew Nick, and he wasn't like some guy in a bar trying to get what he could from a half-drunk girl. Nick was a man of God, almost childlike at times, but cocky too. He was pouring his heart out in an authoritative tone that seemed thoroughly sincere.

"You're the first thought I have when I wake up in the morning and the last thought I have when I lie down at night."

He paused, as if to gauge how far he could go with her. "I don't know what it is, but I don't want to fight it. You know, I think God is directing this. It *has* to be God. How else could it be that someone like you would want someone like me? I know that I should be grieving for Dawn, but I can't even get there. All I can think about is you."

Annette was unsure how to respond, but it didn't matter. The conversation was over.

"I want you to go out into the hall and wait for me. I'll be there in a minute."

His manner was direct. Her heart raced and a sense of foreboding seized her. She was scared but sure of her love for this broken man who needed her.

In the hallway outside Pastor Bob's office, Nick put his hands on her, his body against hers. He told her what to do, what he wanted. She did not resist as he whispered in her ear, "God wants this."

When it was over, when Nick had gotten what he wanted

and Annette had given up a part of herself—for reasons even she couldn't comprehend—he told her to go home.

"I'll call you tomorrow," he said.

THOUSANDS OF MILES AWAY, LINDSEY WAS WIDE AWAKE. She wasn't in a trance. She wasn't a love-struck fool, either. She simply didn't have the strength to put Nick's constant barrage of love and lust away. She couldn't set him aside until the emotions had lessened. Nick wouldn't let her.

"You're inhibited," he told her during one late-night chat over the phone. The subject was sex.

"I don't feel comfortable about this," she countered. "I think we're going too far, too fast."

"It is difficult to understand true love for the first time. I'm giving you a great gift. Our love is a great gift from God."

Lindsey was torn. On several occasions following such phone calls, she cried herself to sleep. Whenever doubt crept into her voice, Nick attempted to persuade her. She was young, he said. She'd grow up. Maybe he was wrong about her.

The implication was clear: If she didn't take what he was offering, another woman would. There were plenty of other women.

"I think Nicole is in love with me," he told her.

He never uttered a word about Annette or Sandy.

29

ACH WOMAN—LINDSEY, ANNETTE, AND NICOLE—
had been compartmentalized by Nick. While Annette
knew that Nicole was interested in Nick, Nick never
indicated that he returned those feelings. If anything, he
acted as if it were Nicole's fantasy life that was propelling
her closer to him. None of it was his doing.

Lindsey, of course, was completely isolated from what
was happening back home. All she knew was what Nick and
her father told her. Certainly, Lindsey knew that Annette and
Nicole were helping Nick through a very bad patch, but that
was nothing more than the sisterly love of two women for
their pastor. They'd turned her childhood bedroom into Nick
Central. Lindsey was in another place completely. She'd
fallen in love. Those who didn't know her might have dismissed her feelings as a schoolgirl crush born of compassion.

The only hitch was Dawn. Lindsey had loved Dawn too. Her
sudden deep feelings for Nick felt like a strange kind of betrayal.

Nick told her repeatedly to release those doubts.

"Dawn *wanted* this. Dawn wanted us together. She loved
you too. You are the perfect one for me," he said.

Lindsey permitted herself to accept the incomprehensible; the dam around her common sense began to break.

"God wants it, so it will be so."

LINDSEY KNEW THAT HER FATHER DESERVED AN EXPLA-
nation, but this was complicated. Nick was like a member

of the family, and Dawn had only been dead a little over a month. In an e-mail to her dad, Lindsey acknowledged that she'd been doing a lot of talking to Nick. Everything needed to be out in the open. She was leaving it all in God's hands.

> God knows my heart's desire but that is always the will of God and I realize that. It does make it difficult at times to be here and also be in love with Nick.

PB recounted the conversation he'd had with Nick during their duck-hunting trip: how he'd told Nick that he only wanted God's will, and if God said it was all right, then that was good enough for him and Adele. He asked his daughter for details of what God had told her.

Lindsey divulged that several weeks before Dawn's death, God had spoken to her. In the first week of December, she was driving down the road and a "wild thought" came to her: She and Nick were going to be married. God said: *Nick is going to be a widower and [you are] going to marry him*.

She'd struggled with the Lord's message, even to the point of wondering if she'd lost her sanity. God's words kept coming: *Dawn will die and Lindsey will be the next Mrs. Nicholas Hacheney*. Following the fire, she spent every moment she could with Nick. "I loved him so much. . . . [But] I was not in love with Nick. . . ." Falling in love, she wrote, came after she arrived in Africa. She wanted God's guidance and told her father that she'd give the situation until the end of the year.

> Thanks for standing by me no matter what crazy things I do or that God asks me to do. . . .

It was Nick, however, who kept pushing. He told Lindsey in an e-mail about his desire to explore the depths of their passion.

I love the way you kiss me. I love the tender hesitant
beginning. The exploring brush of your lips against
mine and the spark of ignited passion . . .

Nick went on:

I love the way your head tilts back as your lips part . . . love
to run my tongue past your teeth and feel the softness . . .
still hungry for more.

Just as he probably hoped, Lindsey returned his love letter with her own:

I don't know how I got so blessed to be loved by a man like
you, but it is happening and I am loving it.

EVERY NOW AND THEN, THE NAGGING QUESTION WOULD
pass through the minds of Dawn's friends and family: Why
didn't Dawn make it out of bed at the time of the fire? She
had been young, able-bodied; she'd been sick the night before, certainly, but she wasn't so ill that she would have been
oblivious to the sounds and smells of a burning bedroom.
Both the investigators and Nick pointed to the space heater
and the propane canisters. Had they failed? Had they been
the source of an explosive flash fire? Each DOT 39 nonrefill-
able cylinder appeared intact, indicating that there had *not*
been an explosion. None was completely empty.

It was possible a slow leak had filled the bedroom with
the flammable gas after Nick left to go hunting.

YEARS LATER, NICK AND HIS SUPPORTERS MAINTAINED
that there was no arson and therefore no cover-up of a crime.
It had been a flash fire, and the cause was the leaky propane
canisters. They theorized that the room filled up with propane and when the outdated space heater cycled on and off,
it arced. A spark ignited the gas, and a fire exploded. The
problem with the theory, investigators insisted, was that the
heater never cycled off and on. It was too cold. The door

to the rest of the house was open. If it didn't cycle, it couldn't arc.

Moreover, of the millions of propane canisters of similar make and model sold in the United States and Canada, none had ever failed.

Not one.

30

ON MONDAY MORNING, JANUARY 26, NICK HACHENEY sauntered into the Bremerton Police Department. He'd told people that he'd been dreading the interview: Living through Dawn's death another time was too much to bear. He'd indicated to some friends that the meeting was a "formality" or "routine," parroting what Adele Smith conveyed about insurance company procedures. During the police interview, Nick said that he and Dawn had gotten home late from the Smiths' on Christmas night and opened a couple of presents, leaving wads of wrapping paper on the floor next to the space heater, the sole source of heat in the house. One of the gifts that he opened was a case of propane canisters used for hunting.

Nothing unusual happened that night except that Dawn got up to take more Benadryl for a cold she was fighting.

"Maybe she took too much. She was sensitive to it that way," he said. "Maybe that's why she didn't get up when the fire happened."

Before leaving, he said he turned on the space heater and kissed Dawn good-bye.

The detectives asked him all the pertinent questions, including, once more, the Big One.

"Did you kill your wife?" a detective asked.

Nick started to cry. "No. No, I did not. We had seven wonderful years. The best years of my life. I don't know how I'll go on without her."

Nick arrived at the Andersons' place shortly after the interview, and Annette ushered him into the living room while she went to the kitchen for something to drink. He said talking to the police had been hard, but he could handle anything God threw his way. At one point he seemed to brighten a little. He teased Annette about their sexual relationship and its origin just after the fire. He wondered out loud how the detectives might have reacted if they knew what was going on between the two of them.

"What do you mean?" she asked.

"Don't you think it would change how they looked at this whole thing if they knew? They might not think it was such an accident."

Annette had no clue how to respond. There was a menacing tone to his remark, and it bothered her.

Nick wore a strange smile. He appeared to be enjoying the conversation. "Think about it. They would never believe that this *just* started," he said, referring to their growing intimacy.

"Well, it *did*," Annette said, finally finding her voice. She didn't like what he was suggesting, but put it off to poor judgment skewed by a broken heart. She also wondered if he was just saying these things to shock her. Maybe it was a diversion from his pain. Whatever the case, the Nick she knew was first and foremost a Christlike man who'd suffered the devastating blow of widowhood at twenty-seven.

"Well, what would you think if they thought that we had started before the fire?"

His suggestion—an implicit threat—scared her. "It wouldn't be good, that's for sure," she said through the passthrough that opened onto the living room. Nick, ensconced on the couch, just grinned.

From the Andersons' house, he continued his route up to Nicole's. It was a different Nick from the one who had shown up on Annette's doorstep. With Nicole, he was more direct about what was really eating at him. There was no teasing, no innuendo.

"They think I killed her," he said, tears rolling down his cheeks. "How could anyone think that?"

Nicole put her arms around him; his big frame convulsed in tears. "I'm so sorry you went through that," she said. "You need a hug."

He's lost Dawn, they ransacked his house, and they've got some people thinking he killed Dawn, she thought. *The poor guy.*

On that same tumultuous day, Nicole's divorce from Ed was finalized, and for the first time she finally summoned the courage to tell everyone at her church group that she was a free woman. She wrote in her diary:

> Lord, I'm divorced. My marriage is over. I said it at home group last night and it sounded really weird. Help me today.

Almost simultaneously, Lindsey sent an e-mail to try to bolster Nick, who felt he had been decimated by the detective's interrogation. She wrote:

> I am so sorry that this all has to hurt so much. I wish I could do something to take all the pain away. . . .

Meanwhile, the adjusters at Safeco continued to document questions they had about the Hacheney fire. An internal e-mail exchange posed one other little concern: the hunting trip to Indian Island the morning of Dawn's death:

> One question I would follow up with the insured and his friend on is how long this trip had been planned (it was the day after Christmas, had it been planned for weeks, or did the insured call the day before, or is it a weekly thing, etc. I think you get the idea).

ON FEBRUARY 1, 1998, BOB SMITH JOSTLED THE MOUSE ON his computer and the screen saver turned off to reveal an e-mail from Nick to his daughter. It took only a second for the pastor to know that something very wrong was going on:

I am lonely for your arms and your touch. . . . I love
how sexy you are. . . .

The text was a sucker punch to his stomach. PB had
heard the comments from the Glasses about Nick being a
liar, how he'd colluded with Robert over the summer but had
begged for forgiveness. Nick, PB knew, was a pleaser. He
wanted everyone to like him. It was as if he didn't know how
to stand his ground and do the really tough things. He had
promised that he wouldn't carry on with Lindsey. It was not
only inappropriate, given Dawn's death, it was also dangerous territory. Lindsey was young and impressionable, and
her father didn't want to see her hurt.

PB steamed in the living room as he waited for Nick. In
the immediate weeks following Dawn's funeral, Nick had
been staying out late. There were times when the Smiths
would hear him park the Jeep and come inside well after
midnight. Once or twice it had been as late as 2:00 A.M. He'd
said he'd been out driving or had been visiting a friend. He
was a brokenhearted man and he had to work things out.

PB confronted him without even saying hello. "I want to
know what the hell is going on with you and my daughter."

Nick flinched. He had the kind of deer-in-the-headlights
look of a teenager caught smoking. PB almost never raised
his voice, not even a little. This time he was angry and hurt,
and he let his words fly. "I don't ever want to read anything
like that on my computer again."

Nick looked downward. "I'm sorry."

"It was way too familiar. Way too descriptive," PB said.
"You promised that you wouldn't do this to Lindsey."

Nick shrugged. "I know. I know. I just got carried away
in the e-mail."

"It's not right."

Nick locked his eyes on PB. "I promise it won't happen
again."

"You're right," PB said, hammering the point hard. "It
won't."

The emotional affair—or whatever it was—between Nick

and Lindsey was a complication that PB didn't need right then. Robert Bily had been claiming that Nick had carried on with Sandy before Dawn's death. There were growing whispers in the church that Nick was spending too much time alone with Nicole. Maybe even Annette.

Now Lindsey? he thought. *She's just a kid!*

EVEN BEFORE THE BREMERTON POLICE DETECTIVES ASKED Nick directly if he had killed his wife, the decision that the fire had been nothing more than an accident had already been made. In fact, for most it had been decided on December 26. Later there would be little to suggest otherwise. Very few photos were taken by any reporting agency. No evidence to speak of was collected; the mattress, the papers, and the heater were left behind. Even some propane canisters were left in the ashy mess. The supposition that Dawn had died in a flash fire that sealed her larynx, preventing any toxic gases from finding their way into her lungs, was also based on a suggestion from initial investigators who'd seen the propane canisters—not necessarily on forensic evidence.

Some murmured their suspicions, but if Nick had been a killer, he surely must have had a guardian angel. No alibi witnesses were interviewed.

But would an angel protect a murderer?

BOOK
TWO

Hellfire and Damnation

God spoke to me. He told me to stay and fight alone. Wait for Nick. God has promised me a new life.

—SANDY GLASS

While her husband was away hunting, Dawn Hacheney perished in this Bremerton, Washington, bedroom on the morning after Christmas, 1997. *Kitsap County Court Records*

The oldest sibling—and the sole girl in a family of boys—Dawn was co-valedictorian at Bremerton Christian High School before enrolling at Northwest College of the Assemblies of God in Kirkland, Washington. *Carole Zeitner*

Dawn Tienhaara and Nick Hacheney were all smiles in this engagement photograph taken in late 1990.
Carole Zeitner

Nick and Dawn were married on April 20, 1991, at Faith Fellowship Church in Silverdale, Washington.
Carole Zeitner

Jimmy Glass and two of his sons at a Seattle Mariners game in the mid-nineties. Jimmy had no idea at the time, but his wife, Sandy, was receiving messages from God that he was going to die.

Nick Hacheney and Craig Anderson were photographed holding the Hacheneys' puppy at Fort Flagler in 1995. Fort Flagler is the site of an Assemblies of God youth camp that first connected Bob Smith with Nick.

Nick and Dawn cradle a Christ Community Church member's newborn at a Seattle hospital. Dawn told friends that she wanted to have children, but was unsure how to fit motherhood in with a full-time job at the credit union and the responsibilities of being a pastor's wife.

Ed and Nicole Matheson, photographed in happier times, had a turbulent marriage marred by Ed's infidelity and drug use. Nicole sought counseling from Pastor Nick with hopes that her marriage could be saved.

Christ Community Church as it appeared in 2009. The Bainbridge Island, Washington, building has been for sale for several years.

Christ Community Church's Pastor Bob "PB" Smith and his wife, Adele, photographed on the beach at Fay Bainbridge State Park. It was the summer of 1997, a week before the Smiths left for Africa to seek God's guidance on their future with the church.

Pamela and Robert Bily at a restaurant on Bainbridge Island in 1997. The apostle Robert and his wife were left in charge of the congregation after a bitter dispute over the direction of the church in April 1998.

Smoke pouring through the master bedroom window alerted neighbors to a fire on Jensen Avenue in East Bremerton. The first responders arrived on the scene a little after seven A.M.
Kitsap County Court Records

Nick Hacheney blamed the fire on Christmas wrapping paper placed too close to a space heater.
Kitsap County Court Records

Next to the charred mattress where they found Dawn's remains, fire investigators discovered a cache of propane canisters used for camping. Nick said the propane was a Christmas present from his wife.   *Kitsap County Court Records*

Nick Hacheney at Sea-Tac airport in the autumn of 1998. By then, he'd distanced himself from Sandy Glass and was putting all his efforts into his relationship with Nicole Matheson.

Annette Anderson (left) and Sandy Glass (right) at Battle Point Park in the summer of 1999. Despite their close personal and spiritual bond, Annette had no idea what secrets church prophetess Sandy was holding inside.

Bremerton, Washington, home to Puget Sound Naval Shipyard, is a fifty-five-minute ferry ride from Seattle.

Dan Hacheney has never stopped believing in his son's innocence.

31

T HOSE CLOSEST TO HIM—ESPECIALLY HIS FAMILY— knew that Robert Bily's singular focus was something that could not be swayed. In both his home and church offices, Robert surrounded himself with neatly squared-up piles of paper. For the most part, he knew exactly where things were. No one dared to touch a single sheet. Both offices were the domain of a man on a literal mission from God. And no one messed with God.

Right then, his calling from God seemed to be in catching Nick doing something he shouldn't be. And proving that to PB Smith.

Nothing fueled Robert like an affront to the truth as he viewed it. He just wouldn't let it rest once he learned that PB's faction of the church's membership doubted the authenticity of his claim. It went beyond his personal pride, his need for being seen as right and righteous. Through more prophetic dreams, God was telling him over and over that Nick was embroiled in a potentially scandalous affair. Pamela's dreams were proof that Nick was involved with a church congregant.

EVEN THOUGH IT WAS MIDNIGHT, IT WAS AS CLEAR AS DAY. Nick's Jeep, with its dirty faux-wood paneling, was parked outside Nicole's tidy little rambler in Suquamish. When Nick and Dawn bought the Jeep, it had been pristine. Now, a Dumpster on wheels, it fit right in to the neighborhood of barking dogs, old RVs, and beaters alongside the cluttered yards of people with too little money and not enough time to take care of what they had. Yet the Matheson house was better maintained than most of its neighbors. Inside the fenced yard was a dormant flower garden, cut back for the season. There was not a spot of debris anywhere.

Robert parked his Mercedes, reached for his cell phone, and selected the number for Ron McClung. By then Ron had perceptibly distanced himself from Nick and PB. He was unmistakably in Robert Bily's camp—his "go-to" guy.

"He's over here at Nicole's," the apostle said.

"At this hour?" Ron was as disgusted as Robert. "Stick around. See what happens."

Robert dimmed his lights and slowly parked behind the Jeep. The living room lights were off, but he detected a flicker of light coming through the window.

The TV?

He sat in the car and waited. It was like some kind of moral surveillance, and Robert figured he could wait as long as it took. Condensation coated the windows of his car.

What's going on in there?

With each minute, the apostle grew more and more anxious. At one point, maybe an hour or so into his wait, Robert got out of his car and walked closer to the house. Silently, he leaned his lanky frame toward the windows and looked inside.

Candles. Not a TV. They were burning candles!

Robert was a suspicious man, but even the most naive could do the math. A man plus a woman plus flickering candles at 1:00 A.M. equals romance. He returned to the car, started the engine, and drove to a spot near the Agate Pass Bridge.

An hour or so later, the dirt-caked Jeep pulled out toward the highway, and Robert smiled.

Gotcha, he thought.

ANNETTE STOOD IN HER SUQUAMISH KITCHEN, A REPLICA Tiffany lamp fixture casting a sunny glow over the small, orderly space. She could see her youngest through the pass-through opening onto the living area. The window facing the yard was a splash of green, even though it was winter. The feeling of the scene didn't fit, because to Annette, it was as if the ceiling had cracked open and sent in a flood of cold air. She was stunned as she listened to Nicole on the phone.

"I have to tell you something." Nicole was tentative, but there was excitement in her voice too. "I *really* need to tell somebody. I think I'm falling in love with Nick."

Annette didn't know how to respond. Nick had asked her to keep tabs on Nicole, but this kind of confession wasn't something she'd expected, nor had she solicited it. The disclosure rocked Annette. Nick had been pursuing *her*, promising a godly connection of some kind. He'd been saying how lovely *she* was. How unworthy and needy he was for her affection. He told her over and over how blessed their special friendship had become. There was no room for Nicole in any of that.

About a half hour later, Annette was on the phone again, this time with Nick.

"Do you know what Nicole just told me?"

"What did she say?"

"She said she's in love with you now."

Nick let out an annoyed little sigh. "Yeah, I know."

"You *know*?"

He repeated that he did. He said that the whole idea of Nicole being in love with him was just one more burden he had to bear. Yes, he was fond of her. Her being in love with him, he insisted, took her feelings to a place he hadn't intended.

"I'll talk with her," he promised.

The call left Annette on edge. There was something not right in his distracted and annoyed tone. It passed through her mind that he wasn't being entirely truthful. If God was calling her to be with Nick, was Nicole getting the same message? What about Lindsey? Nick had told her that God told Lindsey that *she* was supposed to be with Nick as well.

DIVINE INTERVENTION OR INCOMPETENCE? BEFORE THE conclusion of the autopsy—even before it was initiated—the reporting agencies determined that the fire was accidental. The Kitsap County Coroner's Office's forensic pathologist,

Dr. Emmanuel Lacsina, found no soot or carbon monoxide in Dawn's body and determined that this was an indicator that she'd suffered a laryngospasm, a reflex that sealed off her airways in a flash fire. He ruled the death of Dawn Marie Hacheney an accident. A flash fire caught her unaware and instantly killed her.

> In consideration of the circumstances of death, the investigation, as well as this examination, the cause of death of this 28-year-old white female, is ascribed to asphyxia secondary to reflex closure of the upper airways, probably resulting from brief inhalation of a blast of hot air on the face damaging the upper airways. This can account for the absence of noxious gases such as carbon monoxide and cyanide in the blood.

The tox screen confirmed that Dawn had ten times the normal dosage of Benadryl in her system. But, the pathologist said, that could be explained by postmortem redistribution, since the blood collected for analysis had come from her heart.

LINDSEY SMITH ATTENDED A STAFF RETREAT EARLY IN THE month to do some team-building exercises for Frontier Missions, a program her organization supported. Ordinarily, Lindsey would have been front and center, doing whatever she could to help, but she was barely functional. Her heart and mind were on Nick, their future, and the possibility that later in the year he'd be able to come to Africa.

Nick fed her a steady stream of romantic suggestions over the phone and in e-mails, and Lindsey found herself responding in ways that she'd never have imagined in a million years. His fantasies became hers.

She recounted in a message how she walked home in the evening after they talked on the telephone. The air was warm with a nice breeze. "I went to bed without any clothes on and thought of you lying next to me. . . ." She followed that e-mail with another the same day: "I am lonely for your arms and your touch. . . . I love how sexy you are, and how handsome you are. . . ."

During one of their clandestine phone calls, Nick talked about the rigorous workouts he was doing to get in shape. He was at the gym almost every day.

"I'm going to get ripped before I come to Africa. I'm doing it for you," he said.

Lindsey was encouraging, but even she had doubts about Nick ever having a six-pack. He was always the type to go into some scheme or program with "110 percent," only to crash and burn after a couple of weeks. He'd fasted once for a month. He'd adopted a vegetarian meal plan for several weeks to break his addiction to junk foods. After crunching carrots and celery like a rabbit, he went back to Ho Hos and Ding Dongs.

"I'm doing the StairMaster at the max speed for forty-five minutes and people look at me like I'm crazy!"

Lindsey laughed. The remark was so Nick.

Later, during a lunch break, she typed out an e-mail to Nick, referencing his hard work: "I'm really not going to be able to keep my hands off you, think you can handle that?"

HOLLY KLOVEN COULD PLAINLY SEE THAT NICK WAS IN A desperate situation. He'd lost his wife, his home, his world. But she also heard alarm bells. One afternoon several weeks after Dawn's death, she found a pensive Nick alone in the church offices. He spoke with her about life without Dawn.

"You know how much I loved her," he said, his big eyes now melted chocolate. "I miss her every day."

"She was a very special girl," she said. For a second Holly expected that they both might grieve together, so she allowed herself to forget Nick's role in her ongoing estrangement with Sandy Glass. The conversation suddenly shifted.

"My biggest worry is that we had such a great sex life, and I just hope I don't just blow it and have sex with someone I'm not supposed to. I don't want to hurt any of the people around me."

Is he flirting or confessing or just musing? Holly wasn't sure. She knew she didn't like what he was saying.

"Well, you better surround yourself with people that are really solid and really strong and have good marriages," she said, stepping back.

Seeing her recoil, Nick backed off.

"I guess you're right," he said.

IT WAS EARLY SATURDAY MORNING WHEN THE ANDERSONS' phone rang. Annette was alone with the kids. It was Nick. After their encounter in the church hallway, he was pushing for more. She was his chosen one, he said. He had begun to suggest that they get a motel room, but not a local one. People wouldn't understand what was going on if they were seen together. Since Annette had family in Portland, Nick suggested maybe they could be together there.

"You and I can't deny that God is bringing us together, Annette."

Annette was not a passive woman, but for some reason she just let Nick say what he had to say. Part of what appealed to her was that Nick was a talker. He had so much to say. Craig, on the other hand, didn't have that trait. Handsome and physically fit, Craig Anderson was everything Nick wasn't on the physical side. He was the strong and silent type. It was hard to get him to dig into his feelings.

Nick was all about feelings.

"It's weird how of all the women who want me, you're the only one with an intact marriage. But God is directing this and we shouldn't question it. We need to get away from here. I'm thinking Portland could work."

"The kids and I haven't seen my family for a while," she said, thinking of the last visit with her parents and how it had been cut short by the devastating news that Dawn had died in the fire.

Implicit in her statement to Nick was that she was willing to go along with him, go along with God's plan.

"We could drive down together," she said.

"No way!" Nick said. "That wouldn't look right!" There

was nothing glib about what he was saying or how he was saying it. Each word was dark and enveloped in concern.

"Well, the kids love you, and if this is directed by God, who cares if we ride together?"

"Robert would just love that. You and I going down to Portland together. Forget it. I'll meet you," he said. "Besides, we're not doing anything, unless we're sure this is God. We have to be sure. I love you."

NICK AND NICOLE HAD A HEART-TO-HEART AROUND THE same time Nick was hearing from God that Annette was meant to be with him. As much as both enjoyed and needed the closeness that came with sexual intimacy, it just didn't feel right. Certainly they were old enough. And neither was married any longer. They were discreet around the children, of course. Besides, Nicole's son and daughter adored Nick. In many ways he really had become the father that Ed Matheson could never be. Nicole grieved over her decision to cut off Nick, because she could see that he was flailing around with the disintegrating church and his personal downward spiral, but she felt she had no choice.

"We just have to stop," she said.

"I agree" was Nick's solemn reply.

But the next time he came over, they'd be at it again, being as close as a man and a woman could be, then suddenly praying to the Lord that they wouldn't do it again. Nick was hardly in the frame of mind to be a boyfriend or a partner of any kind. He told her he was unsure he could ever be a pastor again. He didn't know what he wanted to do or if he wanted to live. He loved Nicole, he insisted over and over. Love, however, wasn't enough.

Nicole wanted to make things right.

"I just don't want to contribute to making you fall more than you have," she said.

"You don't even know," he said. "You're not making me fall."

"This is the last time," she said as they retreated to her bedroom.

* * *

NICK WOULD EVENTUALLY CONCEDE THAT HIS SEXUAL trysts immediately after Dawn's death were immoral. He saw them as an indicator more of grief and anger than of lust. Explaining it later, he chose his words carefully and directed them to God: "God, if this is how you're gonna behave, I can behave badly too. I don't care. I've been carrying around my Bible since I was ten years old. I was the kind of kid in school who didn't drink or chew or smoke. I make one big mistake and this is what you do?"

Though unsaid, there was no doubt Nick considered his greatest error in judgment to be getting caught up with Sandy. Sandy, who had been his disciple, lover, and confidante, would ultimately be his Judas.

32

THE TENSION IN THE CHURCH SANCTUARY WAS PAL-
pable. The division between the various factions had
intensified. Robert Bily openly expressed his concerns about Nick, remarking on his apparent philandering
and hinting that his wife's death ought to be investigated by
the police with more vigor. Bob "PB" Smith dug in and defended Nick, as any father would stand up for a son under
attack. Ron McClung sided with Robert against Nick, which
surprised some: Nick had been a tremendous support to Pastor Ron when the scandal of a divorce sent him packing
from Christ Memorial Church years before. It had been PB
who invited Ron to join their church.

Nick threw his thickset frame onto the floor of the sanctuary on Sunday, February 8. His sobs were nearly guttural.
Hearts went out to Nick.

Everyone but Annette Anderson was sure his tears were
for Dawn. As she sat with Craig, she wondered if he was crying because God was giving him another message, a message
that told him whether or not they were to go to Portland.

I don't want to go to a hotel room with Nick, she thought.
*But I want to honor God's plan and I want to comfort Nick.
I love him.*

Ken Linden, another church member known for prophetic
gifts, raised Nick up from the floor. Annette watched as the
two prayed at the altar. She couldn't hear what they were saying, but it appeared to comfort Nick, who quickly regained
his composure.

Later, Nick found Annette in the back of the church. His eyes were puffy and red. He had never looked worse. Despite the tears, he had a slight smile on his face. He put his arms around her.

"Ken had a Word," he said. "God wants us to go to Portland."

Annette let the words slip from her mouth. "All right. Okay. I guess we're going."

Craig and the kids appeared a few moments later. It was time to go home. Her heart was nearly bursting inside her chest.

If God wants this, why am I so scared? she lamented.

That same day Nick wrote to Lindsey, referencing the encounter at the church with Ken Linden.

"Ken had prophesied," he wrote, "that I would be going outside the boundaries that had previously been. That I would love beyond all."

He didn't mention Annette or Nicole. Lindsey was the sole focus:

> I would love to put you in front and slip behind you like a spoon. . . . I would also like to lie on my back with you on top of me . . .

ON VALENTINE'S DAY 1998, NICK HAD SOME JUGGLING TO do. He took a moment to send a note to Lindsey before driving down to Portland in his folks' big old boat of a car: "I just wanted to tell you how much I love you but there is really not enough room on this computer for that. . . ." It was more by convenience than romantic design that Nick had booked a room at the Ramada Inn near the airport for the day after Valentine's Day. Annette had driven her children to her mother's house the night before, telling Craig that a visit with Grandma would be good for the kids. She nearly choked on her lie, but Nick had been so insistent, and since the kiss in the tanning room it had been inevitable that they'd consummate their bond with intercourse.

Nick spoke of the whole thing in terms of a great romantic endeavor, heightened by the special relationship he—and by extension she—had with the Lord.

"He wants this," he told her. "I want it too. This is part of what is to be."

Annette had endured waves of nausea as Nick persisted about how they needed to take that crucial step. She wasn't a good liar. She hated deceiving her husband. He didn't deserve it. On some level, though, she thought Craig might even appreciate why she was doing it. He too loved Nick. To anyone who didn't or couldn't understand where Nick was coming from, it all would have seemed completely wrong. As she searched her heart and dug into her faith, Annette couldn't deny what Nick was telling her God had told him.

"Whatever God says," she said.

Nick refused to allow Annette's doubt to slow the momentum of what they were about to do.

"We're going back to the Garden of Eden, you and I," he told her.

Annette didn't put on a sexy outfit the morning she drove to the Ramada Inn. Instead, she wore her usual uniform of black on black: black jumper, black turtleneck, black clogs. It wasn't a funeral, but there was no need to carry on as if it were a honeymoon, either. When Annette entered the hotel room, she was greeted by two or three dozen flickering candles. Nick did his best to play the suave seducer, promising her an afternoon she'd never forget. He'd set out a spread of sandwiches and candy. If he had thought to bring champagne, Annette would have gladly downed a glass or two. Her nervousness was as obvious as Nick's paranoia. At one point he put his fingers to his lips and told her to be quiet while he sidled over to the slit in the drapery and peered out over the parking lot.

"He might be watching us," he said, snapping the fabric panels shut.

"Who?"

"Robert. He's been following me. I know it."

"All the way to Portland? Seems a little extreme, even for him," she said.

He narrowed his brow. "You don't know him. He'll do whatever he can to destroy me."

Annette felt a shudder. Nick was up against something very dark. He'd lost his wife, his house, everything. Robert was his attacker, an agent for something dark and evil. Nick needed her, and in that hotel room she gave herself to him. In doing so, she knew that everything she had known to be true and important had been irrevocably changed. She was Nick's and God's completely. She had to be. Because if it was anything else—an adulterous affair—she'd just squandered her marriage, her children, and her future for nothing.

"This is only going to be the one time," she said, getting undressed.

"Agreed. Just this once. That's all that God wants of us now."

Nick's pager went off and he glanced at the number and made a face. "Must be noon. Church is out and Nicole is already paging me!"

It was the first of several pages from Nicole. Each went ignored.

Throughout the afternoon, Nick talked about the church-women who wanted him. Sandy and Nicole, he said, were pining for him day and night. He didn't mention Lindsey, although he'd e-mailed her incessantly since she left for Africa. Dawn's name came up too.

"You," he said, crying. "God has given you to me to take away some of the pain of losing Dawn."

Annette tried to process it all. It wasn't a line from some lecher but the words of a holy man thanking her for her sacrifice. She knew the sex was a violation of her marital vows. She thought that if Craig knew the full story of Nick's struggles, Craig would understand.

Whatever suffering this causes Craig and the kids is nothing compared with what Nick is dealing with right now, she told herself.

ON FEBRUARY 17, LINDSEY SENT ANOTHER OF HER MASSIVE e-mails to Nick, peppering it with her thoughts about him and questions about where they were going. Nick complained that the barrage of questions "creates the illusion of having said a ton of stuff when in reality you have merely asked a lot of stuff . . ."

Nick told Lindsey he "loved her style" and that the questions provided a kind of insight into her soul: "I feel like I see the real you all the time. . . ."

Even as he was getting to know the "real" Lindsey, Nick was also working hard to show the other women in his life that they too were worthy of his love and attention.

No one would say that the women of the church were unattractive—far from it. In fact, many of them, Annette and Nicole included, were quite lovely. Sandy Glass, though older than the others, had her charms too. She had a sweet and loving countenance that drew people close. One common trait they all shared was the fact they'd all had children. For many women, childbirth alters a body; stretch marks and scarring are frequently part and parcel of the joy of motherhood, of course, but few would trade physical perfection for their children.

Nick seemed to focus on a woman's imperfections, but in a way that glorified rather than denigrated. He made mention several times of the evidence on Annette's body that she'd been blessed with three children.

"God loves you," he said one time. "He knows of your sacrifice. So do I. God has called me to love you. He wants me to show you that you are beautiful."

Annette didn't always feel beautiful. She doubted her husband—or any woman's husband—was delighted by some of the changes brought by pregnancy and childbirth.

"Sometimes I think that Dawn died so that I could be free to show women just how beautiful they are," Nick said. "I think that's what God wants me to do: share my gift with women who need love."

HAVING STAYED WITH HER FOLKS MOST OF THE WEEK, ANnette returned from Portland in time to attend Nick's Thursday-night youth group service with Craig and their children. Nick was the pastor, the ringmaster, the emcee of those services. Craig took the kids to the nursery and volunteered to stay there and preside over the boisterous brood. Annette went back upstairs and ran into Nick. He didn't say a word to her; he just stared. His eyes betrayed their secret and seemed to say, *We're connected now, Annette.*

"Where's Craig?" he asked.

"In the nursery watching all the kids."

Nick shrugged sheepishly. "Wow, that's like heaping burning coals on my head," he said, referring to Romans 12:20. ("If your enemy is hungry, feed him; if he is thirsty, give him something to drink. In doing this, you will heap burning coals on his head.") "Craig's doing me a favor by watching the kids so you and I can have some time together," he said.

Annette took a seat but could barely focus on Nick's sermon or any of the songs that were called for. Her mind raced with what she'd done with Nick and what it all meant. When he sought her out after most of the worshippers had left, she knew what he was going to say.

"I've been praying for another time with you. I think God wants us to."

"Okay," she said. "If God wants it."

Then the conversation took a menacing, threatening turn.

"I wonder if they are going to drag us to the front of the church now for what we've done." He patted her on the thigh. "For what *you've* done."

Annette didn't know what to make of the remark, and Nick went on.

"Who would ever believe that this was *me*, Annette? They'd all think it was *you*."

He laughed a little, a laugh that was supposed to convey that he in fact knew it was him and God that had ordained their tryst. But by outward appearances, he was the poor widower and she was a woman who used his wounded heart to get what she wanted.

Annette didn't think it was funny. Not at all.

On the way home, Craig mentioned how he'd seen Nick and Annette together and he didn't like how it appeared.

"He had his hand on your leg," Craig said. "It made me feel uncomfortable watching you two."

Annette tried to shrug it off. "He touches everyone. You know Nick!"

THE CAUSE OF THE JENSEN AVENUE FIRE WASN'T EVER IN major dispute during the inquiry, although one investigator thought an extension cord had arced and ignited the fire. Nick told investigators he'd turned on the old space heater and left Dawn sleeping while he departed for the Hood Canal Bridge. Dr. Emmanuel Lacsina of the Kitsap County's coroner's office understood that the bedroom where Dawn had died contained a case of mini propane canisters, a Christmas gift to her husband. The forensic pathologist ran with that information, concluding that it had been a flash fire that engulfed the Hacheneys' bedroom. There was no documentation from any investigative agency to support that, and there wouldn't be any to dispute it. No one seemed to think it was peculiar that the propane canisters were on the floor, five feet from Dawn's customary side of the bed.

After the county coroner's pathologist made his ruling, the Bremerton Police Department fell in line. Everyone else simply followed. Each agency posited that the other had built a strong foundation for whatever they reported.

33

THE PREVIOUS SUNDAY, SANDY GLASS PRESSED A SLIP of paper into Craig Anderson's outstretched hand. It was another of her prophecies. Sandy continued to have the direct channel to God, although her closeness with Nick seemed to be eroding. She practically lived in front of her computer by then—when she wasn't crying or praying.

Annette found the paper on the kitchen table.

"Sandy had a Word for you," Craig said, "while you were gone to your folks."

Annette sat down and read. The date held her attention: February 12—three days before she and Nick met in the Portland motel.

> My need is great, very great (vast)
> I desire to be intimate with My people (to make
>   love, know them)
> But My need is greater than this
> I have desire for them every day.
> I long with the greatest of longings to be with
>   them.
> As lovers long for the touch, the glance, even the
>   voice of their love,
> Even more than this am I not satisfied with My
>   relations with you.
> Even more than this do I long for your touch, your
>   glance, and your voice.

It went on, acknowledging her life was filled with distractions, that only He could bring her the kind of love, comfort, and joy that could end this suffering. The Word also challenged her, cajoled her in a way, asking if she really was ready for the kind of pure and holy love He was offering.

"Will you take a hold of my hand?" it read.

Annette had taken his hand, of course. She'd done what God had wanted, what Nick had needed.

Later, Nick called Annette about Sandy's prophecy. He was wildly animated.

"Can you believe that Word that Sandy had?"

Annette thought it was incredible that God would speak to someone like Sandy Glass about something so directly related to what she and Nick had done in Oregon.

"I don't know what God is doing around here," Nick said, "but I know that it's God."

Annette hung up, her pulse pounding. It seemed that God, Nick, Sandy, even Ken Linden's prophecy to Nick—they were all in sync. God wanted to express His love through her sex with Nick. She let go of whatever reservations were holding her back. She was reminded of what Nick had told her over and over, before and after Dawn's death.

You don't question God, she thought.

PHONE CALLS AND E-MAILS ESCALATED INTO A SEXUAL territory for the pastor's daughter and the youth pastor, despite the fact that Dawn Hacheney's fiery death was so recent. An e-mail to Lindsey in late February acknowledged that the two had engaged in phone sex.

> I think maybe we broke several rules . . . but I can't
> help feeling great. [I] can't wait to get to Africa to
> show you the real thing.

A couple days later, Nick became frustrated when he couldn't log on to his e-mail account. He told people that he was worried that he'd been cut off by Robert Bily because of budget constraints, or that maybe PB found "some weird e-mail" to his daughter and changed the password.

It took some time to get back online. Toward the end of the month, Nick bluntly acknowledged to Lindsey how much trouble was brewing between himself, Robert, and her father. The "pastors meetings were heating up," and the future of the church was in doubt. Once more, Nick cast himself as the victim. Robert and his group were tearing him apart, trying to squeeze the life from him. He was fearful that they wouldn't stop trying to run him down until he was dead.

Or until what had once been a happy little church on Bainbridge Island was reduced to rubble.

He was sure, he said, that either outcome was imminent.

AFTER THE FIRE, OUTSIDE OF THE MEMORIES HELD DEAR BY loved ones there was barely any tangible proof that Dawn had ever existed. Certainly, she left behind her parents, brothers, and friends. But there were no children. No youth camp, as she once dreamed of with her husband. There wasn't even a marker at the cemetery. Aside from the photographs that Adele Smith had seen shunted to the back of the closet, all that remained of Dawn was her brown leather purse left in her car the night of the fire.

"It was a miracle that her purse was in the car instead of the house," Nick told several people.

One afternoon, as Annette looked on, Nick announced it was time to get rid of the things that no longer mattered. He started tossing the contents from Dawn's purse into the trash can. Next was the purse itself.

"What are you doing?" Annette asked. "I mean, are you sure you want to do that?"

"I don't need this anymore," he said. He studied her face. "Do you want it?"

"Sure," Annette said, although she didn't really want Dawn's purse. It just didn't seem right that he should just throw it away. *Nick's in grief,* she thought. *I'll save it for him until later.*

* * *

WHEN NICK NEEDED A CONTRACTOR TO REPAIR THE HOUSE on Jensen Avenue, he naturally sought the help of the church. Several of the men who were members of the church were handy with their hands or, like Einar Kloven, were licensed contractors. It was Einar who agreed to work with Nick to get the house back in shape and ready to sell. The insurance company approved Einar for the work, and in turn Einar hired Nick. That way Nick could draw some income for work done to the house. Einar wrote his first check to Nick in the amount of $350 on March 3, 1998.

Another man who put on a tool belt was Eric Kruse, a thirty-seven-year-old South African who had been sheltered by the church when he left his home country and sought political asylum in the States. On two different occasions, Eric and Einar caught the glimmer of something dark in Nick's behavior.

Einar, a six-foot-four-inch-tall man who didn't say anything unless it was important, observed Nick move about the bedroom, the scene of his wife's terrible death, as if he were walking on the beach without a care in the world. He watched from the open doorway as Nick picked up a framed portrait of Dawn that had fallen to the floor along with other blackened debris.

Einar felt a lump in his throat as the youth pastor held the picture and looked at his wife's smudged visage.

This must be so hard for him, he thought.

Before Einar could get too choked up, however, Nick spun around and dropped the portrait into the trash. The glass broke. He looked over at Einar and grinned.

What was that all about? Einar thought.

Eric was working in the kitchen, pulling a melted and crumbling range out of the wall. It made him heartsick having Nick around. Eric thought that if his wife had perished in a fire, he'd never have been able to stand around with a ham sandwich and act as if nothing were wrong—which is what Nick seemed to be doing. He didn't appear to have any emotional attachment to his surroundings.

In the cinder-block basement, Eric found a box of books,

a handsomely bound set of childhood classics including *Treasure Island* and *The Count of Monte Cristo* that had been among Dawn's prized possessions.

"Where should we put these?" he asked.

"They belonged to Dawn," Nick said. "She won't be needing them anymore. Throw them away, or if you want, you can take them."

It seems so cold, Eric thought.

THE FAMILIAR PING OF MICROSOFT'S INSTANT MESSENGER alerted Annette that Nick was online. Whenever Nick IM'd her, he always had an agenda. It could be about Robert Bily's evil war against him, or about making plans to meet. Whatever the case, she'd found herself waiting for that tone night after night, the hours going longer and longer. Nick was huddled in the office he'd set up in the bedroom next to Lindsey's. Annette was ensconced in her bedroom. Craig was watching TV or dozing on the sofa.

> NHACHENEY: *I need u.*

> GRACE23619: *Thanks.*

> NHACHENEY: *I NEED you. U don't understand. I've needed you before, but not like this. I really need you. . . . Can u come over tomorrow a.m.?*

> GRACE23619: *I can't. The kids are in preschool, but I have the baby.*

> NHACHENEY: *No prob. Give her some Benadryl before you come over. She'll be asleep before you get here.*

> GRACE23619: *I don't know if we have any.*

NHacheney: *Look.*

Grace23619: *brb*

Passing the sleeping Craig, she found a bottle of grape-flavored Dimetapp—known by parents everywhere to make cranky and sick kids drowsy. She returned to the keyboard.

Grace23619: *No benadryl. Have dimetapp.*

NHacheney: *:)*

The next morning Annette gave the baby a little dose of Dimetapp and dropped off the older two at the church pre-school. By the time she arrived at the Smiths', the baby was asleep and she carried her inside. A moment later Nick got what he wanted. It was like being a waitress serving a meal to a starving man. It was quick and impersonal, and Annette felt nothing. She picked up her baby and returned to Suquamish.

ALL OF NICK'S NEEDS WERE BEING MET. FIRST SANDY, THEN Lindsey, then Nicole, and finally Annette. He must have needed a scorecard to keep track of all the women he was seeing, all the women who didn't know about one another.

With the exception of Sandy Glass. She knew about *all* the others.

34

A S PRESSURE AND SUSPICION OVER NICK'S BEHAVIOR
mounted, rallying the troops became essential. Nick
had already won the confidence of Annette, Sandy,
PB, and Lindsey; he needed to make sure that whatever
Robert tried to say about him was met with a united front.

He phoned Craig Anderson.

"I want to warn you," Nick said. "Robert's going to try to
throw me under the bus. He's going to try to tell you some
things that are not true. He's got me pinned to the wall, Craig.
I really need your support."

Craig, who had seen his wife's mental state and physical
health ebb before his eyes as she spent more and more time
with their beleaguered pastor, still saw Nick as a source of
hope for their teetering marriage and for Annette to recover
from the loss of her friend. Without hesitation, he promised
to back him up, no problem.

As predicted, Robert called saying he wanted to talk to
the Andersons about Nick's behavior. Craig, who wasn't the
confrontational type, resisted. He told Robert that he'd talk
to Annette about it and hung up.

*Robert is such a hardliner. Nick just lost his wife. Why
beat him up even more?*

ANY MISGIVINGS THAT LINDSEY HAD ABOUT NICK AND
their future—and what her father might have thought—
waned a little. PB had told his daughter to be careful, and
she had prayed on it often and long enough to believe that

she'd done her spiritual due diligence. Outside of her father's warnings and the caution of a few close friends in Africa, she based everything on what Nick told her.

She wrote in an e-mail on March 9 that Nick's love had reawakened a part of her that had been dormant, or might not ever have existed at all.

> I never knew what it felt like to be touched by people that loved you or even that you were to express love to in that way . . .

She referred to their most recent phone conversation and the subject of a trip they planned to take to Mount Kilimanjaro and Zanzibar when Nick flew to Africa later that year. She was excited about seeing him.

> I love & miss you so much, Nick. You have got me completely wrapped around your little finger.

THERE WERE SO MANY REASONS FOR THE ANDERSONS TO BE angry with Robert and Pamela Bily. Robert had done his utmost to destroy PB, Nick, and the church. Pamela, in particular, had been dismissive of Annette's grief after Dawn died. Yet there were also reasons to love them too. Robert had taught both of the Andersons more about Christ's teachings than anyone else had—they were sometimes seen as the Gospel According to Robert, but that didn't discount the power they held. Pamela had been extremely close to Annette, having been there for the birth of the Andersons' two youngest. So when Robert called a second time and asked to meet, Annette reluctantly agreed. Besides, she had a few things of her own she wanted to say. Nick, Nicole, and Annette had spent the day shopping on partial insurance proceeds at Bellevue Square. Robert's war with Nick had been a part of their conversation.

It was after 8:30 P.M. when the Bilys arrived. Robert sat in the rocker next to Craig. Pamela found a place on the couch next to Annette.

After some stilted pleasantries, Annette couldn't hold back: "You know, Robert, I can't believe you'd just come over here and act like this—after all you've done."

"I don't know what you mean," he said.

Annette lost it. "What I mean? I mean, how you sabotaged Nick. He's a widower! How you've pitted everyone against him and PB. Even Ron McClung! One of Nick's oldest and most trusted friends! You've turned everyone against each other."

Robert remained stone-faced. "You don't know all the facts," he said.

Annette turned to Craig, but he was silent, slow to anger. She took up the gauntlet and resumed her attack.

"I know the atmosphere of distrust you've created at the church since Dawn's death." She glanced over at Pamela, who looked as if she was going to say something but thought better of it. "You," she said to Pamela, "used to say we were like sisters. When my heart was broken over Dawn's death, you weren't there for me. You told all of us to get it together and move on."

Pamela started to push back. "How well did you really know Nick and Dawn? Did you know what their lifestyle was really like?" She started to rant about the filthy conditions of the house on Jensen, the lack of smoke detectors, the mess of their finances.

Annette became unhinged with her anger. "What in the world are you trying to insinuate, Pamela? That God punished them for something? For being late on their bills? Dawn died in a horrible fire and you're trying to blame her for something here?"

Pamela tried to defuse Annette's anger with a pat of her hand. "I'm just saying, have you ever wondered if her death might not have been a complete accident?"

Annette jumped to her feet. "Not an accident? Are you here in my home trying to say that Nick's negligence caused his wife's death?"

Pamela ignored that. "And do you know what he's been doing with Nicole?"

Robert saw that his wife, whose genteel manner usually won over the thickest-skinned antagonists, was losing the battle for the Andersons. He turned to Craig.

"You and Annette don't know what's been going on," he said.

"We do. Please leave," Annette cut back in. "Get out and never come back."

The Bilys didn't know what had hit them. Robert felt that Annette had tried to "take him on" and that Satan was calling the shots around the Anderson place. Robert had been convinced that Annette would acquiesce to him. He was the apostle, the senior leader of the church. He figured now that Annette had completely bought into Nick's "cheap grace" preachings—that being in sin was acceptable and that forming inappropriate emotional attachments was fine.

"She has a cloud over her eyes," he said to Pamela after the meeting. "I tried to remove the cloud. She's leading her husband. He's supposed to be in charge. She's answering. This is unscriptural."

Robert had no doubt about God's role for women and he didn't need a Bible in his hands to pull up a quote. He knew the key passages in Ephesians, Timothy, Corinthians, and Peter: Women were to be silent, supportive, and not combative.

What had Nick done to make Annette Anderson behave that way? What was he doing?

IT HAD BEEN A VERY LONG DAY, AND PART-TIME CHURCH secretary Julia DeLashmutt, twenty-two, had been up to her neck in paperwork. From her vantage point, she had seen the number of meetings and discussions between various board members rise to a greater frequency and a larger sense of urgency that spring. She could feel that something was up, but she wasn't sure just what it was. That, she knew, was the trouble with being at the bottom of the totem pole. She watched a downtrodden Nick come and go throughout the afternoon of March 19, 1998, as he prepped for a youth group meeting. When she caught his eye, she asked how Hope's puppies were doing.

He brightened. "You want to see them?"

"Sure," she said, thinking that she hadn't seen Nick smile like that in a long time.

"How about tonight?"

The invitation caught Julia off guard, but rather than face an empty house, with her husband Michael away at a night class, she agreed.

A little after five, she locked the church offices and followed Nick over to Bob and Adele Smith's place on Northwind Court. After they petted each of Hope's pups, Nick invited her inside the empty house. They sat on the couch and talked about the youth group, the puppies, and how focused Julia's husband was on his studies.

Then Nick dropped a bomb, the mother of all non sequiturs.

"You look sexy today," he said.

Julia tensed. It was as if she hadn't heard him right. It embarrassed her, but in a way, the compliment felt good. She was wearing a pretty green waffle-textured vest that she knew looked nice on her.

"Thanks," she said.

Somehow small talk resumed, and the awkwardness of the moment passed. When Nick suggested that they go upstairs to see how he'd set up Lindsey's room as his own, Julia consented.

A picture of Dawn caught her immediate attention, and Julia started to tear up. Nick looked like he was about to cry too. They sat down on Lindsey's old daybed.

"I'm so lonely without her," he said. "Sometimes I just want to drive off the bridge and end it all."

"I miss Dawn too," Julia said, tears streaking her cheeks. "We all do."

Nick's eyes glistened. He reached over and gave her a hug.

"I'd really like to kiss you," he said.

Julia wriggled away. Whatever Nick wanted to happen was absolutely out of the question. For a second she thought she misread his intentions. Julia was not the most experienced and worldly woman. Michael DeLashmutt had been her one and only.

You look sexy today.

I'm so lonely.

I'd really like to kiss you.

Julia knew Nick had made a pass at her. She claimed she needed to get home. Fast.

Rebuffed by Julia, Nick's e-mail to Lindsey later that night was direct and explicit.

> . . . I love you and I am dying to slide into you and make you crazy with passion.

35

THE BILYS, THE SMITHS, AND THE CONNERS MET AT the North Kitsap home of Ron and Carol McClung with one item on the agenda: Nick Hacheney. PB hated the idea of the gathering because he'd already pursued the truth and Nick had told him nothing improper was going on—that Robert was simply pursuing a vendetta. Carol was concerned about the state of Nick's finances, as was Adele. Robert was certain that whatever shenanigans were transpiring—particularly those involving Nicole Matheson, on whom most of the latest rumors were centered—had come from an evil source. It had passed through his mind on more than one occasion that Nick had been possessed by demons.

Robert sized up the room and stared down PB.

"We're looking for the truth here," he said.

The lame-duck pastor doubted that the apostle wanted anything close to the truth. Robert was out to get Nick for reasons known only to him. He was out to destroy a young man who'd suffered a terrible loss. PB, who withheld his concerns about what was transpiring between Nick and Lindsey, was decidedly defensive and bitter.

"I've talked to Nick. Nothing's happening," he said.

Robert didn't back down. "Nick's not being truthful."

"He wouldn't lie to me," PB said, although he knew that Nick had deceived him about his feelings for Lindsey.

"You're being blindsided here."

The rest of the meeting went nowhere. The sides were

chosen. The Bilys, Conners, and McClungs sat across from the Smiths, who were alone in their defense of Nick.

Pastor Bob ultimately and reluctantly agreed to talk to both Nick and Nicole. It felt invasive and out of line, but Nick was a pastor and Nicole was a single woman, and whatever was going on between them—real or imagined—looked bad.

After the meeting, PB caught up with Nick and laid it out squarely.

"Nick," he said, "you can't put yourself in these situations. You have to step back, step away. If you don't, we'll have to discipline you. No more, okay?"

Nick's brown eyes grew wet. "I understand."

The edict had come down: Nick was to have no contact with *any* of the women of the church. It was a dictate impossible for him to follow.

"They need me," he said.

If there was talk that the church leaders were at an impasse, it seemed to embolden Nick even more. Robert Bily was the enemy and God would protect Nick and those who believed in him.

"God is watching over me now," he said as he flip-flopped from viewing himself as a tragic widower to believing he was the anointed one.

Ocean Shores was supposed to become Washington State's version of Atlantic City, with high-rise hotels and gambling casinos along a windswept Pacific coastline. That never happened. Zoning laws and a shortfall of capital made it a land of modest motels, saltwater-taffy purveyors, and noisy mopeds grinding ruts into a broad dune-edged beach. There was one good thing about the location, however, as far as some of the women of the divided church were concerned: It was far away from Bainbridge Island. PB, Robert, Ron, and Nick were meeting that weekend in the church basement, ostensibly to work out their differences and heal the suffering church body.

At least, that was the hope.

Meanwhile, Annette, Adele, Sandy, Holly, and Julie drove

out to Ocean Shores where they'd booked double rooms at the Shilo Inn, the newest and nicest place on the beach. Even though it was ladies-only, Nick asked Holly if he could come, rules be damned. She said no. Everyone could feel the split of the church coming. It was like a speeding train with a congregation pinned on the tracks. Waiting. Hoping. Praying.

Adele ensconced herself at the little telephone table in the room and made several calls to PB to see what was happening back home. The news wasn't good.

"Things are really getting bad," she said to the others. "Bob is talking about submitting his resignation to Robert and just walking away."

As Adele explained it, Robert, Ron, and other board members had presented a united front against PB and Nick.

"Bob's not going to take this abuse anymore," Adele said. "He thinks the church will split."

At dinner in the hotel restaurant, Holly and Adele engaged in a side conversation about a pastor who'd had an affair with a congregant years prior and how it had completely undone the church. Their tone was slightly gossipy, though veiled in concern.

Annette's silence and the expression on her face betrayed her emotions, and she felt Sandy grab her knee from under the table. She looked up. Sandy didn't speak, but her eyes seemed to carry a message.

Don't worry, honey, that's not what's happening with you and Nick.

Although Annette hadn't told Sandy a thing about what had been going on with Nick, she felt that Sandy might have some kind of knowledge about it. Sandy was wise. She seemed to be able to connect the dots on so many things.

NICK MIGHT HAVE BEEN FEELING THE PRESSURE AND BURDEN of splitting the church in two. He practically stomped into Michael and Julia DeLashmutt's house off Clear Creek Road in Poulsbo. His face was red with anger and his eyes nearly popped from his head. His rage was over the content of a sermon about gossip that Michael had given the previous Sunday. Nick hadn't been in church, but he had just listened to the audiotape.

Julia led him to the living room. She and Michael sat on the couch and Nick positioned himself on top of their coffee table. He leaned forward, almost in their faces.

"This was not what this church needed to hear right now. They don't need to hear shame! They need love and grace and forgiveness. You were totally off base, Michael."

Michael said his sermon had come from his heart; he had a need, a Word, to give that message.

Nick wasn't having any of it. He was practically unhinged: It was almost scary.

"That was the worst sermon I've ever heard," he said.

"I'm sorry you feel that way," the younger man said. "That wasn't my intent."

Nick fumed. "And you know what? You know what you've done? Because of your sermon, people think I killed Dawn!"

The statement took Michael's breath away. "I didn't say that! I'm so sorry that anyone felt that way."

"Well, Robert's starting rumors about me. I think you've just added to it."

"I'm sorry" was all Michael could say.

A little while later, Julia dialed Ron McClung's number and told him about their heated encounter with Nick.

"Ron," she said, "was there anything said in any meetings about accusing Nick of killing Dawn?"

"I don't think so," he said. "Robert did tell Nick that he was killing the church. Maybe that's what this is all about."

THE SIDES WERE DRAWN. BOTH PB AND ROBERT HAD MADE their plays for the hearts and minds of the church members. PB's approach was more subtle: He just opened his doors with the offer to talk. Robert, who had all but gained control of the building and all its assets, needed members to keep the place going and to pay the bills. His approach was more insistent. He was on the phone, knocking on doors and asking others to help him make sure that congregants knew that they'd be better off with him than with PB.

Annette, who'd gotten more than her fair share of phone lobbying, couldn't understand.

"Why does everyone want to crucify Nick?" she wondered. "How much more can he take?"

36

I T WAS A CLOUDY, COOL SPRING DAY, AND ANNETTE HAD spent most of it running errands with Nick. She wanted to discuss what she was going through, but Nick was too busy, too self-absorbed to engage. The pair went to Port Orchard, the Kitsap County seat, to retrieve a copy of Dawn's death certificate, and then drove back up to Silverdale to the credit union. While Nick went inside, Annette waited in the Jeep, where she could think about her imploding world and her confusion over what role she was to play in whatever plan God had in store for Nick.

"I'm starting to freak out," she said when Nick returned. "I have no one to talk to about what's going on." She hated being distressed and no longer in control. She wanted a resolution. She needed someone to tell her that she'd be all right, that she'd survive. "Nick, I can't always reach you. I need someone to talk to. I'm dying here."

Nick didn't miss a beat. "I have someone for you," he said as they drove off.

"Who? Who are you talking about?"

"Sandy Glass." He turned his attention from the road for a second and studied Annette's response. The idea that Nick would entrust their secret to a third party surprised Annette, shocking her into silence.

Annette was desperate to talk with someone. Obviously, Craig was out of the question. In the months since she and Nick had consummated their physical relationship, Annette could see that Nick was becoming more and more distant.

His time was being chewed up by the hostilities between Pastor Bob and the apostle Robert. It wasn't that he didn't care for her, but that other, more important things were stealing his time.

"But why Sandy?" she asked. "What makes you think she'd want to be involved in this?"

Nick took a breath. His expression was a mask of smug confidence.

"Because she will do this for me. I'll give you Sandy."

The statement was disconcerting. Annette knew that Sandy held deep feelings for Nick. She'd seen it firsthand when Sandy lingered after services. She also knew it because back in Portland, Sandy's name had been at the top of his list when Nick was complaining of the burden of being wanted by so many women. Even so, it was strange that Nick could be so sure that Jimmy Glass's estranged wife would want anything to do with her big secret. Nick wasn't just suggesting Sandy. He was *offering* her to Annette.

I'll give you Sandy.

Annette wondered if Sandy and Nick had already discussed their encounters from the tanning room to the Ramada Inn and beyond, but she put that out of her mind.

Nick would never betray me by confiding what we've done to someone else, she thought.

ANNETTE AND SANDY WEREN'T CLOSE. ANNETTE KNEW Sandy to be a spiritual woman, one of impeccable judgment—despite what many thought about Sandy's abrupt separation from Jimmy. Her eyes filled with tears as she dialed Sandy's number.

"Hello?" It was Sandy's voice, soft and sweet.

"This is Annette," she said. "Nick told me to call you."

"Yes."

"Do you know why I'm calling?" Annette asked.

"Yes, I do."

And so it began. Over the next few hours, days, and weeks, over the phone and in person, Annette and Sandy huddled in a show of solidarity that seemed sudden and inexplicable.

Annette confided all of the details—the kiss in the tanning room, the rendezvous in Portland, the encounters she'd had that betrayed her marriage and confused her love for God.

Sandy just took it all in, cradling Annette in her arms and promising that God would reveal that all of this had a righteous purpose. By then Annette had begun a kind of transformation that surprised those who hadn't seen her in a while. She wore makeup and colored her hair. She was no longer the earth mother. She stopped eating. She was smoking.

"Nick is the chosen one," Sandy said, urging Annette to stay strong. "He's been anointed by God."

WHETHER IT WAS THOUGHT OF AS CHRIST COMMUNITY OR Life Staff, the church was broken and there was no way to keep it from falling apart further. Those in the inner circles of both camps—the Bily and Smith blocs—had seen it coming for months. Robert had courted people very directly, insisting that PB had lost his way and had given Nick a free hand to wreak havoc on the unsuspecting and undiscerning. PB felt that Robert had twisted the Word to suit his grandiose ambitions.

A defiant PB and Adele Smith stood before the congregation on April 26, 1998.

"We're leaving this church," PB said. "Our door is open today for any who want to talk to us about this. We don't know what we'll do next, but Adele and I love you all."

The church he'd started was his no more. A lifetime of leading a small flock on Bainbridge Island had ended in a bitter and rancorous conflict over who would run it and, just as divisive, how to deal with Nick Hacheney. Countless tears had been shed. Friends who had loved each other no longer spoke. But if PB thought for one second that his life could never take a shadier turn, he could not have been more wrong.

The notes taken during deliverance sessions in the basement offices of Christ Community were a graveyard of skeletons from closets all across Kitsap County. A chilly fear blew across Bainbridge Island. The deliverance counseling files. The secrets. The stuff no one wanted anyone to know. Almost from the moment the Smiths stepped away from the church, their phone started ringing.

"Where is my file?" The question was asked over and over. PB reassured each caller: He'd gone to his office the week before the split and packed up all the files.

"Don't worry," he said, "everything was shredded."

All of this was said with a heavy heart, full of remorse for having been party to this bastardization of the faith that had called him since his boyhood. Only after the secrets of his flock had been committed to paper did he see the ugliness of such recordkeeping. Keeping these records wasn't about helping anyone; it was about *controlling* them.

Adele watched as the shredder consumed page after page.

NICK COULD BARELY WAIT TO GET TO HIS COMPUTER TO tell Lindsey the news that the church had split and that he and her father were going to create a new one, in the gym at Christ Memorial in Poulsbo. They'd call it New Covenant Fellowship. On April 27, he indicated that the state of affairs was joyless, although it had "rightness and a purpose to it." Nick had stood steadfast with her father, which, he was sure, was part of God's plan.

> On one hand, everything feels so orchestrated by God and on the other hand I question myself and whether the things they say about me are true. I am either a David or an Absalom in this battle.

Lindsey sent a note to her father after the split:

> I am glad you got a new e-mail address, especially with that funny business going on. . . . Satan can be really tricky sometimes. Did Nick get a new e-mail address, too?

Two days later, Nick laid it all out for Pastor Bob's daughter:

I keep asking the question—what else do they want to take from me? I guess they feel I'm the weak link in the chain and maybe they can break me.

MANY YEARS LATER, IN A DENNY'S RESTAURANT NOT TOO far from their home in Philomath, Oregon, Gary and Julie Conner sipped ice water and tried to come to terms with the church split. Gary was a bridge engineer, a broad-shouldered fellow with jet black hair and a guarded manner. He saw Nick as an opportunist. "Robert was throwing his weight around for so long, when PB kind of put his foot down on some things. That's why it split. It happened to be about Nick. Because Robert and PB were at odds, Robert couldn't get to Nick's bad stuff because PB was protecting him. Because Robert was attacking Nick so much, PB couldn't see Nick's bad side. It left Nick free to slide under the fence."

Julie, a mother of seven, her streaked blond hair tied neatly back, said they had remained with the apostle's church for four months, a very painful time. "Ron [McClung] stayed and Gary stayed until God just came and lifted us. We feel we were saved out of that. A job opportunity came up and we were out."

37

NICK HACHENEY WAS, QUITE POSSIBLY, ONE OF THE world's worst patients. At the end of May 1998, he was practically down for the count with a case of strep throat. Not so much a complainer as an incessant demander, Nick needed mountains of attention and was able to get it most of the time.

Annette dropped her kids off with her appointed confidante, Sandy, and came by the Smiths' to see Nick. He was holed up on the couch in the basement, wrapped in an afghan like a caterpillar in a cocoon. His skin was tissue white, with dark circles around his dark brown eyes.

Of course he's sick, she thought. *His spirit's broken, which weakened his immune system.*

Nick was upset and worried.

"I need you to get a message to Sandy," he said as Annette hovered with whatever he needed—tissues, cold meds, antibiotics. "I need to speak with her right away."

Annette didn't know what he was talking about, but she didn't question it. By then she'd learned not to question anything. Questioning meant giving up on faith. She left the Smiths' and drove directly over to see Sandy. The two women went to a back room where Sandy had set up her computer along with the odds and ends of her homeschooling efforts with the boys, a stack of unpaid bills, and the kind of assorted clutter that comes with being a busy mother.

The prospect of getting a message from Nick seemed to lift Sandy.

"We haven't e-mailed in a while," she said, indicating that the accusations that had come from Robert and Jimmy had put a stop to that—despite the fact that she had created a secret e-mail account expressly for that purpose. "We've had to be very careful," she said.

Annette averted her eyes as Sandy went to her alternate e-mail account. Annette didn't ask and Sandy didn't volunteer what it was that she wrote.

A day or so later, Annette returned to the Glass compound. She smoked a cigarette on the front porch, while Sandy's emotions ran amok. Sandy had met Nick over at the Smiths' place at a time Nick assured her everyone would be gone. It sounded so mysterious. As Sandy sputtered about the encounter, her words touched not on the subject of their meeting but on how "difficult" and "emotional" things had been and how "happy" she was that she'd been able "to be there" for him.

"But what did he want?" Annette asked, wondering why Sandy and Nick had to continually exclude her from so many things. Hadn't she proved herself?

Sandy was silent, words eluding her once more. By then, her communication was almost always nonverbal. The look in her eyes. The clasping of her hands. The wrapping of her arms around her torso. All these meant something that those closest to Sandy seemed able to decipher. Annette figured she wasn't in their league, spiritually speaking.

Sandy held Annette's hand and squeezed, a gesture that said more than words ever could.

"This is a God thing, honey," she finally said. "This is personal. You can't even begin to grasp what it is that Nick and I are dealing with."

ALWAYS JUST A LITTLE UNCLEAR ABOUT WHAT GOD HAD IN store, Annette patiently waited for the future to reveal itself, for Nick to tell her the Big Plan. It was obvious from the way Nick and Sandy huddled in church and had constantly paged each other that their connection was greater than Annette's bond with Nick could ever be. If Annette had been pressed into service to fulfill whatever physical desires or needs Nick had, Sandy had his soul.

"Sandy's my priest," Nick told Annette during one of their conversations.

"What do you mean by that?"

Nick looked heavenward as if he were reading some important document, a message from the Lord coming in real time.

"She is the one who loves me selflessly," he went on. "She waits for me without any pressure. I wish more people loved me that way. But they don't. They all want something from me and I just don't know how much more I have to give."

It was a slam to Annette and she knew it. Whenever he could, Nick seemed to remind her that whatever she asked of him was more than he wanted to give. It was as if her genuine sacrifices were nothing.

Nothing compared to his loss.

Nick studied Annette's reaction. He always seemed to know just what to say, whether he was before the altar or sitting at his desk at a counseling session.

"And you," he said, his eyes now aimed coolly at hers. "I don't know why God's made me love you. But sometimes I wonder if it's just so I'd get caught."

MONTHS AFTER HER DEATH, THERE WAS STILL NO HEADstone on Dawn's grave. Diana Tienhaara had given up the idea that it would magically appear or that Nick would somehow pull himself together and take care of it. She knew nothing about the real troubles behind the church rift or that Nick had become involved with Nicole, Lindsey, Annette, and Sandy.

Diana's contact with her son-in-law had dwindled. Nick seldom called or answered her e-mails. Yet she thought of him often. Only two people in the world knew the real pain, the depths of agony, that came with the loss of Dawn. Diana was sure that while Dawn's brothers and father grieved, they couldn't know what the loss meant to her. She was Dawn's mother, and the death was out of sync with the natural order of things. Diana was convinced that Nick, so sensitive and loving, was the only person who could comprehend the enormity of the loss.

"Sometimes I go out to the cemetery at night and just cry," he told her.

"Sometimes I don't want to live anymore," she answered.

As always, Nick's big eyes drew her closer. "I know. I feel the same way."

Nick confided that he'd been drinking a great deal.

"It doesn't make me forget," he said, "but it is the only thing that's working, that's helping."

One evening, they parked at the Tracyton boat launch on Dyes Inlet, not far from the first house that Nick and Dawn had renovated right after they got married. Nick turned off the ignition and put his arm around her. They found each other's lips and kissed.

I'm helping him, Diana thought. *I'm helping ease his hurt for losing Dawn.*

38

THE WILD RHODODENDRONS WERE STILL LADEN WITH their pink trumpet blooms in the wooded property along the Duckabush River that Nick purchased with twenty-seven thousand dollars of his insurance money. He and Nicole spent the day there a few days before his twenty-eighth birthday in May 1998. They spread out a blanket, stared at the sky, ate, and talked. Nicole's children were being babysat by Sandy, and for the first time in a while, it was just the two of them. At one point they walked along the river and just enjoyed the noise of the water and the sounds of the birds.

Nicole told Nick how much he meant to her, how she'd come to rely on him. How she'd fallen in love with him.

"You know," Nick said, "in high school I was never seen by girls as the boyfriend type. I was always just the friend. I guess it was my personality." He paused and glanced at her. "And other things."

Nicole knew he was referring to his looks. She had grown to believe that a man's outward appearance wasn't all that important. What she sought was beneath the skin. She'd *had* handsome before. She'd considered her own vanity, realizing what her choice in a man said about her. In the past, it might have been fueled by drugs or lust, but her choice now was being made by her heart and her brain. What kind of man did she want to be with? A man who adored her children. A man who put his family first. A man who understood her past, her personality quirks, her evolving character.

Whatever intimate moments she and Nick had shared up to that point had been mostly about comfort and aiding a man in a dire situation—his needs more than hers. Until then, it was more duty than romance. After the day along the Duckabush River, things were different.

She could no longer deny to anyone she was falling for Nick.

THE VISIONS FROM GOD, FROM GABRIEL, FROM SATAN OR *somebody* kept coming to Sandy. In the late spring of 1998, Sandy disclosed an additional prophecy about Jimmy's impending death. This time, she told Nick, God seemed to want her to take control. This time *her* hands were no longer tied. In her vision, she, Jimmy, and one of their sons were in the Suburban, driving across the Agate Pass Bridge. She reached over, undid Jimmy's seat belt, and grabbed the steering wheel.

"God showed me how I would crash the car by veering into a telephone pole and killing him."

ANNETTE'S EYES FILLED WITH TEARS AS SHE AND NICK SAT in Nick's newly purchased used pickup truck. She understood he had a special purpose, one ordained by God. At the same time, she knew that their intimate relations were wrong, a violation of her vows to Craig. Even in her progressively downward spiral—a woman becoming completely undone by circumstances that brought her an enormous measure of guilt and shame—Annette knew that Nick would sort things out. Pushing her away toward Sandy was only temporary. He'd come back to her as he found his footing in God's plan. That could only happen if he was safe.

And only if he was alive.

The way he was talking now literally put the fear of God in her. It also made her cry.

Nick was agitated, but this time more depressed than angry. He didn't rant about the apostle Robert or Pastor Bob or whine about the unseen forces that stole Dawn from his life or split the church. He was straightforward now. Because his burden was so great, there was only one way out.

"I have a Plan B if things don't go as God promised," he said.

Annette knew he was hinting at suicide.

"You're not serious, Nick. Don't talk like that."

He reached over and produced a firearm from the glove compartment. His movement was slow and dramatic.

"I don't know," he said, holding the gun like a baby. "The only thing that stops me from doing it is how devastated everyone will be. I don't want to hurt anyone. I just don't want to go on anymore. The pain is killing me."

Annette was paralyzed. *What do I do? How do I help him?*

SANDY AND ANNETTE WERE OFTEN SEEN TOGETHER BY the members of the fledgling New Covenant Fellowship throughout the spring and summer months of 1998. Sometimes Nick would join them, but they met less frequently as the year progressed. Apart from Jimmy Glass—who suspected something bizarre and tawdry was going on between the three—most people thought Nick and the two women were still grieving over Dawn's absence.

Those observers, of course, missed the mark by a mile.

Annette was distraught over the turn of events that led her to betray Craig for the love of God and the promises of Nick Hacheney. Sandy was anxious and upset about the holding pattern that her life had taken since the fire.

"I'm waiting," she told Annette, "for my life to begin, for God to do what he's going to do around here."

The words echoed what Nick had told her in the weeks surrounding Dawn's death.

God's going to do something amazing!

Whatever God *was* doing, He was taking His time about it. Somehow Sandy never lost her resolve. However, it was obvious that her patience was being tested.

"I am in the desert now," she told Annette, "but I will soon be in the Promised Land. God has told me to be still."

When Annette probed for something more specific, Sandy seemed incapable of pinning down what it was that she was really waiting for. Her words were strung together more with hope than conviction. That kind of vagueness only exacerbated Annette's eroding self-worth.

God, Sandy, and Nick have one incredible plan in the works. I guess I'm not strong enough, not blessed enough, to be at their level, she thought.

Sandy sprinkled references to Nick into most of their conversations, though it was apparent that the contact between the pair was in a state of decline. But that didn't seem to deter her, nor did the increasing attention Nick was paying to Nicole and her children.

"I got a Word," she said. Her voice was hushed. "God told me I should not doubt Him."

NICK SEEMED TO FIXATE ON ORAL SEX. WHETHER IT WAS IN his relationship with Nicole, Sandy, or Annette or in his sexually charged dialogue with Lindsey, he considered his talent for performing cunnilingus to be one of his greatest gifts.

"I liked to leave Dawn with a big smile on her face every night," he told Annette. "It was my gift to her."

He saw himself and President Clinton, who'd been embroiled in the Monica Lewinsky scandal since the beginning of the year, as kindred spirits.

"I understand what Bill is going through. Believe me. I understand his weakness—his thing for women. How he can't stay away from them."

In another time and place, Annette might have rolled her eyes at the pasty-faced, overweight pastor thinking that he was God's gift to women. It might even have been laughable. There she was, sneaking around with him and hating herself for it. There was Nicole, saying she was in love with him. And there was Sandy, hanging around like the girl in love with the high school stud who doesn't know she's alive.

She pondered it. Nick had something going for him, all right. Maybe it was attitude? Or his own unflinching belief in his sexual prowess?

One time Nick was sitting on the Andersons' couch, contemplating ways to help a Hacheney family foster sister who had bounced from one addiction problem to the next.

"Maybe I should have sex with her," he said. "Maybe that could help."

Annette practically choked at the statement.

"Um, I'm pretty sure that won't help her."

"I don't know," Nick said. "I'll see what God says."

THE PROCESS HAD BEGUN LONG BEFORE DAWN DIED. IT wasn't that Nicole would have had anything to do with Nick romantically if Dawn had still been around. It was more of a personal and emotional connection that she'd forged with Nick as her marriage to Ed crashed and burned. She wanted to tell the world that she and Nick should be together. Her son and daughter adored him.

We're like a happy little family, she thought. *Why shouldn't we be together?*

Nicole couldn't rein in her joy. Sandy saw it. So did Annette. There was some discussion between the two about just how far the relationship had gone. The idea that Nick was romancing Nicole would mean that whatever was going on between Nick and Annette was not sacred but sick. Sandy dismissed Annette's worry, saying, "Honey, you couldn't be more wrong."

When Annette directly asked Nick about it, he stood firm.

"I'm *not* having sex with Nicole," he said flatly. His words nearly echoed his kindred spirit's infamous denial: *I did not have sexual relations with that woman, Miss Lewinsky.*

Nevertheless, they were the words Annette needed to hear.

"But you're always with her. Always with Sandy too. You're attentive. You love them. I've seen it."

"Yes, I love them," he said. "But not in the same way that God has blessed you and me."

"I don't get it. I don't understand how you could be so loving, so important to so many women."

"God made me this way," he said. "I am capable of eros

and agape at the same time. Annette, I can be anything I want to be. I can go anywhere and do or be anything I choose. I've always known this about myself. But I'm here. God's put me here with all of you."

WHEN CHURCH MEMBERS TRAVIS AND SUSANNA PINE LET it be known that they were going to vacate their Bainbridge Island apartment for much of the summer due to work obligations Travis had in Klamath Falls, Oregon, Nick approached them about using their place.

"People are coming over here to the Smiths all the time to console me, and I just wish I had a place I could go to now and then to get away and think, be alone," he said.

The Pines were glad to help. They gave him keys to their second-floor apartment and a car they were leaving behind. Nick seemed very grateful. He indicated he'd only be using the apartment a few hours at a time.

An elated Nick wrote an e-mail to Lindsey that same day. He was excited about his new retreat from everything.

"It has a pool and a hot tub!"

39

THE NIGHT AIR WAS HOT AND THICK. IT WAS ALMOST August, the Pacific Northwest's one good month of summer weather, and Annette Anderson was feeling it. Despite its proximity to Puget Sound, there was little breeze blowing through Suquamish. Just heavy, thick, and oppressive air. It filled the Andersons' bedroom as Annette slumped in her computer chair with thoughts of Nick, Sandy, and Nicole circling her brain like vultures. The kids were asleep and Craig was watching TV, the muffled sounds coming into the bedroom. More than ever, the Andersons were at odds. Craig's anger and concern for Annette's eroding mental and physical health only pushed her farther away. Despite a houseful of children and her husband, Annette felt alone and completely unsettled.

She'd thought of IM'ing Nick, sending e-mails, but she just couldn't right then. Craig, she was convinced, would *never* understand. Sandy was impossible to pry an answer from. Nicole was in a kind of oblivious state that kept her on the fringe of whatever it was that was really happening. But that night, something else came to her. It was another name: Dawn.

What is going on?

Annette wrapped her arms tightly around her withering frame. And almost like a physical touch, she felt the hand of God. It was as if He were grabbing her by the shoulders and shaking her. With the touch came words.

My anger burns against Nick. He has taken what is not his to take. He will answer for it.

The Word sent a shock of sadness through her heart. Images came to her mind: pictures of Dawn looking down at Nick. Her eyes were filled with despair. She seemed sorry, sad, and maybe even heartbroken over the mess her husband had made of his life.

What does this mean? Why is Dawn looking at Nick like that? What is it that Nick must atone for?

Annette walked around her house, went to the store, and changed her youngest's diapers. All of it was done in a nearly rote fashion. There was nothing left of her anymore. She was tired and sick to her stomach. Something had kicked in. *Nick was to blame.* She booted up the computer, but he wasn't online. She sent an e-mail indicating they needed to meet. She was very direct, almost curt. There was no wavering, no second-guessing. God had led her to that moment.

"There's something I need to tell you," she wrote.

A little while later, a response came to her e-mail inbox.

"Okay," Nick wrote back. He didn't bother to ask what she wanted to talk about. He just told her to come over.

IT WAS A THURSDAY EVENING—AFTER A MEETING WITH Adele and Holly to plan for the African mission trip they'd scheduled for that fall—when Annette drove over to the Pines' apartment on Wyatt Way. Nick was on the sofa, quiet and still. She wondered why he was sitting alone in the dark, the blinds drawn. The living room had been hit by the Hacheney cyclone. Clothes were heaped where they fell. Food-caked dishes and utensils were piled everywhere. The disarray was a perfect metaphor for the state of his life just then: a dirty mess.

"Nick," she began, "God said something to me and I need to tell you what it is. God says that His anger burns against you, that you have taken what was not yours to take." She stopped and sucked in some air. "Dawn looks down on you with sorrow."

Nick started to cry. At first it was a slow, soft sob. Within seconds it escalated to a raging bawl. He was crying so hard, the couch rumbled. Annette said nothing.

Finally, Nick spoke. "I know, Annette," he said.

"What?" Annette could scarcely believe her ears. His words and attitude astounded her.

For the first time in more than a year, Annette had a flash of clarity. *This is seriously wrong.* It was only a flash, not a full epiphany that would tell her to stay away from him forever. The idea that God had spoken to her had been no surprise to Nick. But his admission that he'd messed up sent a chill through her. If he'd screwed up, she knew something she didn't want to face: that she'd screwed up too.

In the darkness of the room, Annette could easily make out a smile on Nick's tear-streaked face.

"You want to go to the bedroom?" He looked toward the open doorway.

Annette felt sick. Was this his answer, his admission? A leering look? A lump in her throat nearly made it impossible to swallow. She had only two words, but they came with a force and a finality that surprised her.

"Good-bye, Nick," she said, getting up from the sofa and hurrying for the door. She was abrupt and quick. She never looked back. She *couldn't.* And as good as it felt to walk out that door, it would be a long time before Annette Anderson would really say good-bye.

LINDSEY MIGHT NOT HAVE KNOWN IT, BUT LONG BEFORE the midpoint of 1998, Nick had completely lost interest. Their e-mails had trickled to a scant four in a one-month period; in previous months they'd exchange four or more in a single day. Something was up.

One of Nick's notes suggested the possibility of a little introspection.

> I have been looking hard at my eyes in the mirror for years—sometimes I see things in there that I can't explain.

40

I T WAS NICOLE AGAIN. SHE WAS BUOYANT, BUT NOT WITH-
out a slight hint of hesitation in her voice. She was on the
phone with Annette, talking about Nick and the kids and
their weekend trip together. They'd been to the beach. They
ate out at a wonderful restaurant. Everything was perfect.

"I feel so blessed," she said. "We're having the best time."

Annette could feel her heart sink, her emotions in turmoil. "Sounds like it."

Nicole remained oblivious. It could have been because the
conversation was over the phone. In person, Annette wouldn't
have been able to hide her distress. Annette stood frozen in
her kitchen, her ear pressed against the cordless phone. She
barely glanced at her children as she felt her spirit begin to
slip farther and farther into the dark.

"The kids love Nick so much," Nicole went on.

We all do, Annette thought. "Well, I better go," she finally
said. "Talk to you later."

There really wasn't more Annette felt she *could* say. Nicole hadn't a clue about what had been going on between her
and Nick. Sandy knew. Nicole, who was now having the time
of her life, seemed to be operating in another sphere, separate from the imploding spiritual world that held Annette and
Sandy captive. It wasn't just Nicole's estrangement from what
was really going on that disturbed Annette. There were also
signs that Nick was not the same person with Nicole that he
was around her and Sandy.

Annette had caught glimpses of Nick with Nicole. With

Nicole, he wasn't the doom-and-gloom man. He didn't seem to be one step away from ending it all. In fact, he seemed downright happy.

Annette packed her little ones into the van, drove to the Glass compound, and parked behind Sandy's Suburban. Sandy's boys were jumping on the trampoline, and their laughter filled the air with the kind of joy that was missing from Annette's world.

Sandy let her inside and poured some coffee.

"I don't get it," Annette said. "I don't know what's going on with Nick and Nicole. Any of it."

Dawn Hacheney's chocolate Lab, Faith, ambled through the house.

"You need to pull out of this," Sandy said, her eyes fixed on Annette's. It was an instance of clarity that was meant to propel Annette to a solution. It was as if Sandy, who'd been patiently waiting for something to transpire with God and Nick, now had something definitive. "Break away."

Annette looked so small. Her denim overalls hung on her as if she were made of wire. She started to shake. "I would if I could. I would if I had anything left to pull myself out of this. I would if I had any will left to muster."

Sandy continued to hold Annette's gaze. Her eyes were pleading. What was Sandy telegraphing? Tears fell. Sandy, who had never appeared to be physically strong, now looked especially weak. The months of waiting and hoping had taken their toll on her petite frame too. At that moment, huddled together on Sandy's sofa, neither woman was the person she had been before Dawn's death—before Nick had anointed them in a cause and shown each a future that was full of wonderful but shrouded promises.

Sandy appeared to think, seeming to absorb Annette's pain and her inability to separate from Nick.

"I don't know what to do or how to do it," Annette repeated.

Sandy finally nodded. "I don't know the answer to that." Neither one did.

*　*　*

ANNETTE COULD FEEL HER PULSE QUICKEN AND HER breath draw tight and short whenever Nick summoned her for one of their guilt-inducing clandestine meetings, as he did on a sunny fall day in 1998. Despite her doubts and desire to "break away," he still had a hold on her. Annette drove over from Suquamish, picked up Sandy as he'd requested, and found Nick where he said he'd be, at a secluded park near Bremerton.

Sandy and Nick walked to the edge of the parking lot. From her car, Annette couldn't hear what they were saying, but the conversation appeared to be somewhat animated.

What's going on here? she asked herself.

When Sandy returned, it was apparent she'd been crying. Her eyes were red and she looked shaky. She said that Nick had given her one thousand dollars of Dawn's life insurance money.

"Are you all right?" Annette finally asked.

Sandy stayed frustratingly quiet. "I guess I'm upset," she said, digging deep for the words. "You know, things just don't feel the same."

Annette had an idea what Sandy meant. She could plainly see that Nick was keeping his closest confidante at arm's length. *What happened between the two of them to break their bond?*

41

T HE GLASSES, INCLUDING JIMMY, WERE LIVING ON
the family compound, albeit in separate dwellings:
Jimmy in the trailer, Sandy in the house with the
boys. In August 1998, Sandy called Jimmy's uncle Kenny
Goans for support. She said that she and the boys wanted to
come down to the twin towns of Milton–Freewater for a
visit. Kenny was elated. When they arrived, Sandy seemed
in good spirits and the group went out for pizza.

Later, when the boys were asleep, Sandy confided that
she'd been terrorized by Jimmy. He'd become so fixated on
Nick that it bordered on paranoia. Nick, she said, had been
able to help her in ways that Jimmy, as her husband, should
have but seemed incapable of doing.

She told Kenny about how Jimmy had threatened to put a
gun in his mouth or "run me and the boys off the road."
Jimmy was caught up in the misguided belief that Nick and
she had become too close.

After Sandy left town, Kenny wrote a ten-page letter to
his nephew. Some of the words came from his heart and his
own experience, but in reality the voice was Sandy's. Jimmy
was lazy. He was arrogant. Selfish. The list went on:

Your temper—I've seen where you've gotten so angry it's
almost like a demon possession, Jim.

Sandy, on the other hand, was a paragon of virtue:

Your wife is one of the best Christians I've ever known, the best friend I've ever had, and the finest woman I ever saw. You have used the situation with Nick as an excuse to reach a stage of incomparable criticality in your life. Divorcing Sandy will be the biggest mistake of your life! Nick was helping her though a difficult period of her life.

Kenny made photocopies and sent a set to Jimmy, Sandy, and his sister, Mary Glass. He knew there was some risk in alienating his family, but Sandy needed a soldier.

AUGUST BROUGHT A RETURN TO CAMP GHORMLEY FOR A handful of New Covenant Fellowship members. Annette, who had missed the fireworks of the camp the previous summer, thought that attending this time might help get her out of her deep depression and spiritual funk. She had expected to make the drive with Sandy. Sandy wanted to have her own vehicle there so she'd be free to "minister" as she had the year before.

"I'm waiting on what God has in mind for me. I need to be there for Nick too," she said the night before camp.

When Annette arrived, it became evident that Sandy had given up trying to be a part of the group. She'd set her sole focus on spending time with Nick. Nicole and her kids, Annette and her children, and another church member stayed in a cluster of cabin rooms that shared a central bathroom. Sandy somehow managed a private cabin with the staff, closer to Nick.

As the days went on, Sandy looked more and more unhappy, maybe even a little bitter.

One afternoon Nick asked Annette to watch Nicole's children so he and Nicole could go to a country store for supplies. It was the first time he'd said a word to Annette, and it miffed her to be used as a sitter. She told Sandy about it, but Sandy shut her down.

"I'm not going to do this with you now," she said. Her dismissal was cold, abrupt.

Annette felt about two feet tall. It was as if Sandy had slapped her in the face. Why didn't she understand? What was going on with her that she had to be such a big bitch right then? Annette felt more alone than ever.

Sandy had never treated her like that before.

THE CONCERN—REAL OR IMAGINED—FOLLOWED ANNETTE home from camp. Her dissatisfaction with Nick, Sandy, Nicole, and the rest had been evident to several people there. Even observers outside Nick's spiritual clique had worried about the mother of three. She appeared to be a woman undone. Nick IM'd her the night she returned to Suquamish:

> NHACHENEY: *Everything's ok. You're gonna be ok.*
>
> GRACE23619: *I don't think so.*
>
> NHACHENEY: *This is demonic, and they can't have you. That's what the problem is.*
>
> GRACE23619: *Whatever you say.*
>
> NHACHENEY: *Your rebellion is because of demons. I can help. God has gifted me to fight this battle. I can stop them.*

Annette signed off the instant messenger. She couldn't deny that she no longer felt completely in charge of herself. She didn't feel at all like the woman she'd been prior to Dawn's death. *Maybe demons* are *involved*, she thought. *What else could explain what I've done or how I've doubted Nick and Sandy?*

A few days later, Annette numbly sat through one of New Covenant's Saturday church services in Christ Memorial's gymnasium. After it was over, Nick walked with her to the parking lot. He had something to show her—a van he'd purchased.

"I got this van to help you," he said, opening the door. Annette had no idea what he was talking about. "Sandy and I are going to take you somewhere, park it, and perform deliverance on you."

Annette felt unsure, but offered only vague reservations. "I don't know," she said.

"Satan has a hold on you," Nick said, his arm on her shoulder. "Sandy and I can do this. We love you."

"When?"

"Tonight."

IT WAS DARK. DAWN'S OLD LAB, FAITH, BARKED AS ANnette pulled into the compound. Anxiety cramped her stomach. The plans had shifted. The mobile deliverance van was out. Sandy suggested that her mother's empty house, not far away, would be a better venue. Annette and Sandy drove over to meet Nick there, and the three convened in the living room.

"God will help you, Annette," Nick said. "*I* am going to help you."

Nick's pager went off. "It's Nicole," he said, making a face. He returned his attention to Annette. "I'm ready to do battle," he said.

Sandy looked on from her corner in the room, with a serious but beatific expression on her face. Nick put his hands on Annette's shoulders, and Sandy closed her eyes and started praying and speaking in tongues. Her voice was soft, and it faded into the background as Nick took center stage.

"I'm going to call upon God and cast the demons out of you!" he said.

Sandy stopped praying and called over, "Amen!"

The darkened room seemed to close in around Annette. She felt Nick put his arms around her.

"Satan! I want you to leave!" he yelled. "I *command* you. Get off of her, you vile spirit, spirit of rebellion and death. Get away from her! In the name of Jesus, I command you!"

Annette let out a little cry and Nick slumped over. The

demon had been expunged. Nick had sweated and huffed and puffed through the deliverance as though he had just finished a lap around a high school track. He could barely move. Sandy appeared spent by the session too.

"You know how much I love you, little lamb, and that I'd do anything for you," he said, tilting up Annette's chin so she would look right at him. "I've loved you in every way possible."

Annette felt a rush of sadness for Sandy. It was true that Sandy knew most of everything she and Nick had done together, but his acknowledgment of his love for her felt hurtful toward Sandy just then. Annette never felt the kind of love for Nick that she imagined Sandy might have.

Before they left, Sandy did a once-over of the living room.

"I don't want my mom to know we were here," she said.

MAYBE THE ONLY WAY OUT OF THE NIGHTMARE WAS IF Nick actually left Kitsap County, as he'd threatened every now and then. First, he said he would disappear into the wilderness with his dog, rifle, and yurt—a kind of Jeremiah Johnson or Chris McCandless character on a mission of self-discovery and retreat. Alternately, he threatened suicide. If Nick had deceived others about his feelings for Nicole, Sandy, Lindsey, Dawn, Diana, or herself, Annette had too. Despite the fact that she pleaded with him not to disappear, deep down she saw it as the only true way she could save herself and her family.

When his plan shifted yet again and he no longer seemed desperate enough or ordered by God to leave, Annette felt herself sink deeper into the darkness. She felt used by the very man who'd promised that her sacrifice had genuine value and purpose.

"I'm not doing okay with this, Nick. Look at me. I'm falling apart here."

In fact, Annette's physical deterioration was obvious to many at the church. The deliverance session at Sandy's mother's home had lifted her spirits with hope, but it was short-lived. She was barely hanging on.

Around that time, Travis and Susanna Pine returned home and were stunned to see that the place they had left so tidy was completely trashed. Garbage was everywhere. The carpet had been destroyed. The liquor cabinet had been completely emptied. It was as though Nick had had a big party there, packed up his stuff, and left without a thought to the condition of the apartment. On the nightstand in the master bedroom, Susanna found an array of lotions and creams; on the floor, a pair of panties. It wasn't hard to figure out what had been going on, nor was it difficult to deduce who the woman was. In the bathroom, Susanna found two small life jackets in the tub.

Nicole Matheson, Susanna thought. *This stuff must belong to Nicole.*

AFTER A LONG AND JOYOUS TRIP VISITING EINAR'S RELAtives in Norway, the Kloven family was met by Nick behind the wheel of their dark blue Suburban in the passenger pickup area of Sea-Tac airport. He was his usual effusive self, always ready to help. When Nick moved his backpack to the backseat so Einar could drive home, Holly stumbled upon, of all things, a condom in its wrapper. Nick was the youth pastor of New Covenant Fellowship. He wasn't married; why would he have a condom? She had been worried about Sandy and Nick in the past; lately, she had been increasingly concerned about Nick and Nicole.

She told her husband later. The Klovens agreed that it really wasn't any of their business, but since Nick was their children's youth pastor, Einar said he'd ask Nick about it.

That Saturday night he cornered Nick in a quiet place at the church and held out the condom.

"We found this in the car."

Nick locked his eyes on Einar's. "It's not mine. I don't need those."

"Then were did it come from?"

"Maybe you should ask your son."

When Einar got home, he showed the condom to their teenage son, Stewart. The kid looked completely clueless.

"No, it isn't mine, Dad. What is it?"

The next time he saw Nick, Einar mentioned his boy's denial.

Nick shrugged. "Maybe it's my dad's. I borrowed his backpack."

Nick's *father's*? Einar would have laughed out loud if he'd been a more demonstrative man. The idea that Nick would pin the blame first on a boy, then on his own dad, was indefensible.

CONFRONTING NICK WAS NEVER EASY, BUT ANNETTE KNEW that whatever had made her risk her future and family had to stop. She prayed over it. As far as she could see, Nick's maneuvering, justification, and self-absorption had precipitated her mental and physical decline. But she wouldn't allow it any longer.

"You have no idea how sick and tired Sandy and I are of your BS," she finally said.

Nick looked astounded. It wasn't every day that he was challenged.

"You're just like Robert," Nick hissed back, offended. "Yeah, you and Robert." It was the ultimate put-down and he knew it. "All you two care about is words," he said.

Annette refused to let it go. "I care about words that make sense."

"I don't. I care about feelings. I go on how I feel, Annette. I go on what God tells me. Words just aren't that important. It doesn't matter if I said something or not. I go with how I feel."

Annette didn't know why Nick would say something like that, but she didn't think to question it.

THOSE WHO'D STAYED WITH PASTOR BOB SMITH AND NEW Covenant had been without a real home for their church since the split that spring. Many, like Einar Kloven, could barely drive by what had once been Christ Community Church without feeling a heartbreaking sense of loss. Hours of time, gallons of sweat, and an unbridled faith had fueled the construction; now, in late fall, with the cover of maple leaves gone, it was easy to see what they'd all lost. They knew that a church building was just a building and that the spirit of the Lord had no real need for walls, stained-glass windows, or any of the trappings that went along with organized religion. Even so, it still pained them every time they shuffled past the sanctuary to the gym at Christ Memorial. They were refugees. Their pews were metal folding chairs; the altar, a blank wall. PB set up a high school band's black metal sheet-music stand as the pulpit.

It was a far cry from the beautiful carved wooden pulpit that master carpenter James Glass had fashioned as a testament of his own love for Christ. Now the Glasses were gone. They'd stayed with Robert Bily's Life Staff Ministries. So many others had too.

Nick took to the makeshift pulpit in late October and gave a sermon that was far removed from his typical feel-good routines. Usually, churchgoers could count on Nick to mix a few laughs and personal anecdotes as he drove home a meaningful message from the Scripture. Nick's sermons frequently bordered on over-the-top hysterical, but not that evening. Certainly, this sermon was rife with drama, but this time, there was a decided darkness to his words.

He wrote about it to Lindsey the next day:

> I basically said I was expecting God to show Himself to me and show me what is next and give me some sort of anointing for ministry and that if He didn't, I don't want to be around anymore.

Lindsey, who expected Nick's long-awaited visit to Africa in less than two weeks, had no idea what he would be like when he got there: martyr or boyfriend. She counted the days, wondering what Nick's future would be and, by extension, what hers would be as well.

PB's youngest daughter held her breath.

JIMMY GLASS CONTINUED TO FEEL ISOLATED AND EStranged from everyone. That October, when Sandy finally filed for legal separation, he'd felt that his parents had allied with her—possibly out of fear of being shut out of their grandsons' lives. Jimmy knew that the church had sided with Sandy. Jimmy wasn't the kind of guy driven to deep introspection. He was a man who enjoyed working with his hands, having a home-cooked dinner, and singing as loudly as he could from the back of the church. He wondered what it was that had really driven Sandy away. They didn't argue. Certainly, they hadn't before Nick had become his wife's chief spiritual adviser.

What could I have done differently? Jimmy asked himself over and over. *Why wouldn't Sandy give me another chance?*

His entire life, Jimmy had felt dwarfed by other people's achievements: his father's unmatched skills as a wood craftsman and leader in church; his younger brother's success at West Point; Sandy's gift of prophecy . . . Everyone in his life was a star, while he was only a bit player.

Before she bonded with Sandy, Annette liked Jimmy. As the two women grew closer, Sandy began to confide small details of her relationships with God, Jimmy, and Nick. Periodically, Annette would glean information about Sandy through conversations with Holly or Adele. In turn, she'd ask Sandy about them. One time, she pressed Sandy for details on Jimmy's impending doom.

"God told me a long time ago that Jimmy was going to die," Sandy told Annette. "I prepared for it. I bought life insurance so the boys and I could get by, so that I could fulfill my dreams."

Annette prodded. "But he *didn't* die. God was wrong."

"He hasn't died *yet* and I have waited a long time," Sandy

said. "All of this needs to progress by God's plan. I'm sure it will happen. I'm waiting."

Sandy looked so disappointed that Jimmy hadn't given up the ghost that Annette wanted to hug her and say something about how God would take care of Jimmy. All would be okay. But something stopped her. It was almost as if by doing that, she'd be wishing Jimmy was dead too. *What about those four little boys? Even a purportedly lousy father was probably better than no dad at all.*

Jimmy might have been fighting to save his marriage or to prove that Sandy had betrayed him, but Sandy took another approach. At times she almost seemed to pity her estranged husband. She even suggested that Jimmy couldn't really be completely faulted for his endless list of shortcomings.

"God told me that there's something wrong with Jimmy. It was like he was born with a birth defect. A part of him is just missing. There's nothing that can be done for him."

Annette didn't get it.

"Oh, honey," Sandy sighed. "God told me that Jimmy has something like a physical illness or like someone being born without an arm or a leg. He just was born without the ability to be a husband. He just can't have a relationship."

In person, Nick always came across as concerned, deeply interested, and supremely confident. But sometimes, over the phone—where he couldn't employ body language and a gentle touch on a knee, or tears in his eyes—his tone seemed smug.

Annette was struggling with the meaning of some passages she'd been studying in the Bible. The Scripture was at odds with the reading material Nick and Sandy had given her. One morning she was pacing the small space of her bedroom. Craig and the kids had gone somewhere. Annette increasingly stayed home alone. She called Nick.

"I'm trying to follow the Bible," she said. "But what we've been doing doesn't fit. What you've told me doesn't exactly fit."

Nick let out a long laugh. "Annette, you don't get it. I'll tell you something. Listen carefully. I don't read the Bible anymore. To be honest, I never really 'got it' before any of this happened, anyway."

"You're kidding, right?" Annette was so shocked, she wondered if she'd heard him right. Nick not believing in the Bible? That wasn't like him at all. "You're close to blasphemy, Nick. This isn't you."

He laughed again. "It *is* me. I'm sorry if this shocks you. I guess it would be surprising to a lot of people, but it's never been important to me."

42

NICK HAD BEEN TALKING ABOUT HIS TRIP TO AFRICA for months. But each time Diana Tienhaara, then forty-seven, heard him mention Tanzania, she felt a little jab at her heart. Dawn had so wanted to go on the mission trip too. She was frightened about getting the immunizations, but she told her mother that nothing, "not even the shots," would keep her from doing the good work that they'd been called to do.

Nothing but the fire.

When Nick contacted Diana to see if she'd like to get together one last time before his big trip, he suggested the Boat Shed, a steak and seafood restaurant on the shores of Dyes Inlet, just under the Manette Bridge in Bremerton. Diana agreed. After all, she was lonely. Donald never took her anywhere. If he'd been shut off from her before their daughter's death, there was even less connection between them now. Diana was living on the Internet. Donald was stuck on graveyard shift at the shipyard. They barely spoke.

Nick picked her up at her home on Rimrock Avenue, a place he seldom visited anymore. He was upbeat, excited about Africa. They ordered wine with dinner, and although Diana hesitated—she was never one for much drinking—she had a glass or two. Within an hour she had fallen into those sad brown eyes.

"Do you want to go somewhere?" Nick's tone wasn't overtly flirtatious, but Diana knew what he meant even before he uttered the next line. "To be alone?"

"All right," she said. "But where?" It tripped through her mind that she wasn't sure if he was thinking of the Smiths' house or maybe a motel. She remembered the kiss at the boat launch.

Nick reached for his wallet to pay. "We can go back to the house."

"I guess so," she said, a twinge of fear percolating. Diana hadn't been to the house since the fire. She knew Nick and people from church had been working on it over the summer, fixing it, getting it ready for sale. She wanted the place sold and the memories gone.

Nick prattled on about Africa and things he was doing, while Diana kept her mind on what she would see when she got there. When they arrived, he parked on the street and she looked up at the house. A window was still boarded up. Soot framed the bright new wood. They walked up the steps and went past the bedroom window. Nick seemed oblivious to the significance of the moment. For Diana, it was the first time she'd come to the place where her firstborn had died.

She felt confused and a little dizzy.

"We can go up to the yurt," Nick said.

His casualness calmed her as they forced their way through soggy ankle-high grass. *A flashlight would be handy about now*, Diana thought as Nick parted some brambles and they ascended a second set of steps up to the yurt. *But Nick knows what he's doing. He knows the way.*

The contents of the yurt were sparse and scattered. Light from the moon was the sole source of illumination. Diana knew what would happen when she sat next to Nick on the sofa, the only piece of real furniture.

They started to kiss. She knew where they were headed. She felt sorry for Nick; he'd been so lonely too. He told her time and time again how much he missed Dawn, how much he missed the touch of a woman. The closeness of being with someone he loved.

In that moment—with the wine, the moonlight, Nick's pleading eyes—Diana Tienhaara knew what she was being called to do. Nick had led her there.

"I want to be Dawn for you," she said, offering herself.

Nick stared at her. "I don't want you to be Dawn," he said. "I want to be with *you*. You are special on your own."

They kissed again, this time with more passion.

"I feel lucky that I can love both of you," he said.

That was all she needed. Diana was a pleaser and Nick wanted attention that she felt only she could give. It wasn't about sex just then, but about a man in dire need. Diana performed oral sex on him and he returned the favor.

"Tell me how good I am," he instructed. "I want to hear it."

Diana complied and in a few minutes it was all over. She stared off into the night, thinking of her daughter and what she'd done. She wasn't sure why or how it had happened. Nick stood to get dressed. He seemed to know what she was thinking.

"This won't happen again," he said.

THINGS WERE BECOMING CLEARER TO ANNETTE. WHATever Nick felt for her, he seemed to feel much more for Nicole. Sandy appeared to have been shut out altogether. One evening he summoned Annette to come to his father's garage in downtown Winslow. He was working on a car that he'd bought for Nicole.

Again it was about Nicole.

Nick was in a flirty mood, telling Annette how gorgeous she was. He didn't see that the stress of what she was carrying had cost her her health. She'd lost more weight. Her skin was no longer perfect, and her eyes were smudged by dark circles.

None of that mattered. Nick cajoled her into joining him in the back of the garage, where they were intimate once more. The act was devoid of excitement, joy, or even pleasure. Annette felt completely defeated and disgusted. Once more, Nick didn't notice.

Annette stopped by Sandy's on the way back to Suquamish, and the pair sat on the Glasses' front porch. Sandy poured coffee and Annette, her nerves frazzled, smoked a cigarette.

"Well, I saw Nick just now," she said. "We fooled around. I feel like crap. I need to stop doing this."

Sandy set down her mug and narrowed her focus on Annette. There was no "Oh, honey," no smile on her face. "Yes, it is time for you to stop." Her tone was stern and judgmental.

Annette left a little while later, thinking, *Where did that come from? I thought she was here to help me.*

PASTOR BOB AND ADELE PUT NICK ON A PLANE TO LONDON the first Sunday in November with a single suitcase for himself, a carry-on for Lindsey, and two blocks of cheese, a scarce commodity in Tanzania, which Adele insisted he take at the very last minute. Nick had a long layover before continuing on to Kilimanjaro.

Back home, Robert Bily and the church split continued to trouble PB, who wrote in an e-mail to Lindsey while she waited for Nick's arrival:

> [Robert] continues to tell people (from our body) when he sees them on the street that he has the full truth if they want it. How sad, but we move ahead.

43

SANDY GLASS WAS ON THE VERGE OF TEARS WHEN Nicole came to pick up her children, whom Sandy had been babysitting. With Nick out of the country, Nicole was feeling lonely, so she lingered a bit as Sandy began to crumble. Like many of Sandy's conversations, the erratic nature of her speech, bouncing from one subject to another, made it nearly impossible to grasp what she wanted to convey. Nicole, moving the discussion along, said God had showed her that she could be released from her marriage.

"I feel like He wants me to be on my own," she said. "Ed's not coming back and I need to focus on the future. Focus on my babies."

Sandy didn't point out the patently obvious: that Ed *had* moved on. They'd divorced. He was not coming back, no matter how much Nicole still hoped for a divine miracle to save her shattered marriage.

Sandy wrapped her arms around herself in a defensive posture. Her lips trembled. She said she'd received an e-mail from Nick. Then she started to cry.

"What is it?" Nicole prodded, not really wanting to ask. When Sandy didn't respond, she changed the subject slightly. "What are you hoping for, dreaming of?"

Sandy stayed quiet. "I don't know anymore," she said finally. "I don't think what I thought was going to happen is going to. What I *wanted* to happen. I guess I'll be off in the woods somewhere. Alone."

The comment was so bizarre that Nicole struggled to

make sense of it. She put her arms around Sandy to comfort her. It was all she could do.

JIMMY'S TRUCK WAS PARKED IN FRONT OF THE ANDERSONS' place when Annette arrived home with the kids from another afternoon at Sandy's. By then Annette had had her fill of Jimmy and his bleating suspicions about Sandy and Nick, and Sandy and *her*. To her his behavior seemed paranoid and delusional. Sandy had told her that Jimmy had even suggested that their relationship was a lesbian love affair.

"Jimmy's such a fool. He's so off base. He's being a jerk," Sandy said.

Wherever Jimmy went, he left a trail of poison. Annette braced herself, opened the door, and let him have it.

"What are you doing here?" she asked angrily.

Jimmy barely looked at her. Instead, he kept his eyes trained on Craig. "I'm leaving now. See you later, Craig."

Annette barely moved out of his way. She glanced over at her husband, who rolled his eyes.

The children filed in and the door shut. Jimmy's truck revved and he drove away.

"What was going on here?" she asked.

"Oh, Jimmy's flipping out over Nick. He told me that Nick took his wife away from him and that I should watch out . . . that Nick's after you too. He claims that Nick has some harem or something."

"A harem?" Annette laughed. "Jimmy said Nick's got a harem? Jimmy's an asshole."

Craig nodded. "Yeah, he's really off his rocker. I told him that he had to go, that I didn't want to hear it, that Nick's a good guy and Jimmy's wrong to be running around making accusations."

PASTOR BOB SMITH CONTINUED TO TURN A BLIND EYE. Instead of focusing on Nick's role as the alleged puppet master of the women of the former Christ Community Church, he laid most of the trouble at the feet of Annette and Sandy. He wrote to Lindsey about how Annette had elevated Nick to the role of an "emotional spouse." He was concerned for Nick's personal pain.

> It is a dangerous thing because in our attempt to help people we end up being their substitute and they never press into God's true answer.

ANNETTE HAD GIVEN SANDY HER E-MAIL ACCOUNT PASS-word with instructions to call if anything came through from Nick while her family was at her parents' house in Portland for Christmas of 1998. While the holiday passed, it never left Annette's mind that it had been exactly one year since Dawn died. She wondered how Nick was faring in Africa with Kim, Godwin, and, of course, Lindsey. But mostly she ruminated on the disaster her own life had become. Craig was always angry. Sandy was forever in tears. Nick had gone off to sort things out with Lindsey, but in doing so, he took with him the lifeline that he'd tethered to her and Sandy. The church that had given her so much hope and support was gone.

She had written an angst-filled e-mail to Nick, but there had been no reply. Her life had been nothing but waiting for the past year: waiting for God to do something. Waiting for Nick to tell her the meaning of everything.

Sandy phoned Annette in Portland. She'd been crying.

"Oh, honey," Sandy said. "Things aren't good. I'm not doing too well. Nick sent us some e-mail," she went on, her voice flagging. "I'll read yours to you."

In a halting voice, Sandy started reading. Nick acknowledged that Annette might feel abandoned, although he insisted that was not his intent. In fact, he turned around all of her fears and worries, to point out that his was the direst of the situations.

> [I am] a man who has lost more than most people ever have, I did so willingly because it was requested by God. I have been left behind by the one I love, I have been betrayed by my closest friends, accused of every manner of evil imagin-able, followed and spied upon, lied about and constantly

> questioned, I am pursued by a madman who wishes me
> dead and will stop short at nothing to either prove I am who
> they say I am or try to make me become that. . . . Even in my
> place of refuge I am constantly being monitored.

As Sandy continued, Annette felt uneasy. She didn't see
what he was saying as a play for sympathy or a statement of
martyrdom. It was simply the truth as God had told him. But
it was a truth that rankled her.

> If you had any idea what I have risked in this damn war you
> would lose sleep more often.

He ended the missive with words of love and support. He
loved her "a ton." She was his "little lamb." When he returned to the States, he'd prove to her that she wasn't being
set aside.

> If you respond with a letter about how unworthy and doubt-
> ful and incapable you are and how much you don't want to
> play anymore I'm going to come home and beat your ass.

The e-mail stoked Annette's anger. Her world was completely shattered, yet Nick—God's man—kept playing the
"poor me" or the widower card as if she'd risked nothing of
her own. She'd gone out on a limb for him and for God, and
it felt as if he was just saying thanks and moving on.

"This isn't right, Sandy. What did he say to you?"

Sandy was crumbling on the other end of the line. "I can't
go there right now," she said. "I just can't."

The message was clipped. Nick and Sandy, *whatever*
they had been to each other, were history.

Over in Suquamish, Nicole Matheson also got an e-mail
from Nick. Hers was a far cry from Sandy's electronic kiss-
off. Instead, it was a vague confession of mistakes that he'd
made—inappropriate things involving Sandy.

Nicole allowed herself to imagine the smallest of all inappropriate transgressions that might have occurred be-

tween Nick and Sandy. She figured that they'd become too close, too emotionally connected through the marital counseling sessions.

That has to be it, she thought.

Nick said he loved Nicole, but he conceded he hadn't done things right: "We have a lot to work through."

Nicole knew he was right. They'd had sex too soon—way too soon—after Dawn's death, and the foundation of their relationship had been compromised. Something else gave her pause. Ed did his own thing, of course, but he was passive in every real measure of a man. Nick was far from passive.

Nicole wasn't sure she could make a go of it with such a strong man.

JUST AS LINDSEY HAD WONDERED ABOUT DAWN WHEN SHE fell deeper and deeper in love with Nick, Annette also thought of her friend. Annette, however, wasn't thinking about whether or not Dawn would condone *her* relationship with Nick; it seemed to her that Dawn would understand how she had offered herself to him to help him survive a terrible loss. Instead, as the relationship became darker—as the venues for Nick's insatiable lust became more and more reckless—Annette considered what Dawn might have told her had the two of them become close enough to share the things that friends sometimes whisper to each other. Had Dawn ever felt as used as she did? Had Nick taken Dawn to places in the woods of Kitsap County where a stranger could have encountered them? Did they have sex at church when PB went about his business in his office? Did Dawn feel as though she had no choice but to satisfy her husband's desires—that her sole purpose as a woman was to submit to her husband's authority? Did she lose herself too?

Had Dawn ever said no to Nick?

44

IT HAD BEEN A TERRIBLE WINTER FOR KENNY GOANS and Mary Glass, who had lost their father just before the Christmas season. When Sandy Glass picked up Kenny at Sea-Tac airport in late December, surprisingly her focus wasn't on Kenny's grief, only her own.

"Things have gotten worse since your last visit," she said. "Things aren't good between Jimmy and me right now."

Kenny had seen himself as a kind of marriage counselor, which amused him a little, as he'd never walked down the aisle. He loved Jimmy and Sandy and thought they'd be able to pull it together for the sake of their sons.

At the same time, he was wrestling with feelings he'd developed for Sandy.

When they arrived at the Glass compound, Kenny stayed with James and Mary, and Sandy went home to her boys. Jimmy was exiled to the guesthouse.

Jimmy sought out Kenny right away.

"I have something to show you," he said, his voice more animated than normal. Sandy had said he'd been drinking and Kenny wondered if he'd had a few.

"Just read them." Jimmy held out a couple slips of paper. "They're from Nick. I got them off the computer. One of my boys told me Sandy's password."

Jimmy had been ignored by everyone. But no more. Now he had proof.

Kenny scanned the letters. As he read, uneasiness came

over him. *Hey, there just might be more to Jimmy's side of the story.*

"She's been lying to me," Jimmy said. He said he'd been rummaging through her things at the house while Sandy was away. "Sandy doesn't realize I know a lot more about computers than she thinks."

"We shouldn't read those," Kenny said. "It isn't right to read someone's mail."

"But this *proves* it. It proves that something's going on with her and Nick."

Later, with Kenny, Jimmy, and her husband, James, standing by, Mary read the letters too. She shook her head slightly without saying a word. She wanted to know just what the truth was. She'd been sitting there day after day, wondering why Nick was coming over or why Annette and Nicole were hanging around when they should be home. And, of course, the teddy bear and Christmas note the year before came to mind.

One letter was written to Annette. The other was addressed to Sandy. Jimmy, providing his own interpretation of what he'd read into the letters, considered Annette's note to be just another of Nick and Sandy's brand of over-the-top, misguided, God's-doing-amazing-things brand of Christianity. Annette was having problems with Craig, and Nick told her in the letter that she could continue to go to Sandy for moral and spiritual support. She needed to pull herself out of her funk and get her head on straight.

If she didn't? "I'm going to come home and beat your ass," he'd written.

Sandy's letter was an unmistakable Dear Jane letter that left little room for doubt that their relationship was an intimate one. Jimmy's big hand trembled as he offered it to his dad.

Finally, someone's going to believe me, he thought.

But neither James nor Mary let their faces betray any disappointment toward Sandy. Neither could they really wrap their arms around their son and tell him that they were sorry for everything he'd been going through. They just didn't want to believe the worst. Nick's note, they read, told Sandy in no uncertain terms that he was finished with her. They would not be moving forward in life together with their ministry or anything else. It was over.

"I don't know what we can do about this," Mary finally told Jimmy, handing back the computer printouts.

IT SEEMED SO STUPID, A LITTLE EMBARRASSING; HOWEVER, it had to be done. Kenny Goans hoped that Sandy would have some plausible explanation. On January 2, 1999, he telephoned Sandy and asked if she'd like to take a drive. She agreed. A half hour later they parked the Suburban in a spot overlooking Puget Sound on the Kitsap Peninsula, halfway between Poulsbo and Bremerton. The water sparkled and the mountain range in the distance had been frosted with a fresh mantle of snow. They walked down to the rocky beach and he reached into his pocket.

"Jimmy found these, Sandy. They seem to indicate a relationship between you and Nick."

Sandy looked at the papers and started to cry.

"What's the situation here?" he asked.

"This is going to hurt a lot of people," she said. "But it isn't what you think. Nothing happened between us. We just got close."

Sandy would never lie to him. She was a godly woman. That was good enough for Kenny.

THE TWO MEN—A KIND OF MUTT AND JEFF PAIR, WITH Jimmy tall and leaner and Kenny shorter and stocky— walked along the perimeter of Battle Point Park, the ninety-acre recreational area that had been the site of a naval radio station before it became a magnet for soccer players, picnickers, and those with deep secrets. Kenny had put up with Jimmy's suspicions for months. He'd heard how Jimmy had tried to bug Sandy's telephone with a listening device from RadioShack.

"I know you think I'm crazy," Jimmy said, "but I really

think Sandy and Nick had something going on. I think they had an affair. The e-mails prove it."

"Never happened," Kenny said. "That's not Sandy and you know it. You need to remain calm about all of this. If you lose it, you'll lose any chance of being with Sandy again."

"I know," Jimmy said. "I'm trying. But I don't trust Nick. He's a wolf in sheep's clothing, that's what he is."

Kenny didn't like Nick much, either. But although he wasn't a very nice guy, he was a pastor. Jimmy, on the other hand, was drinking and hanging out in topless bars. At least that's what Sandy kept saying. Sandy didn't think Jimmy was a good influence on the boys, and Kenny sided with her.

"You have to pull yourself together," Kenny said. "PB will help us figure this out."

The next day Kenny and Jimmy drove over to the Smiths' place on the other side of the island. Jimmy was pumped up because he finally had some "proof." Kenny tried to remind Jimmy of the fact that the truth really wasn't clear and that he shouldn't jump to any conclusions. Kenny thought Sandy's relationship with Nick was nothing deeper than a personal connection through their love for Christ. Sandy would *never* have an illicit affair. She was a hardworking Little League mom who put her children above everything.

PB, Adele, Jimmy, and Kenny gathered around the Smiths' kitchen table and recited the Lord's Prayer. That finished, PB reviewed the e-mails, his mouth a straight line. Whatever he was really thinking inside, he held it close. Adele also stayed mum as she served coffee.

Kenny told PB how Sandy had admitted that while there was no sexual involvement, she and Nick had become spiritually close.

"There was an inappropriate emotional connection," he said. "It came up through the marital counseling."

"All right," PB finally said. "The letters are out there; we don't know what they mean for sure, but we have to deal with them. Even if Nick and Sandy weren't intimately involved—and we don't know they were—this is wrong on Nick's part."

Jimmy couldn't believe his ears. "What more does everyone need to see to know what's going on?"

"Jimmy," Kenny said, agreeing with PB, "we don't know the extent of this."

"Well, I don't care. All I want is my family back."

THE NEXT DAY, WITHOUT TELLING JIMMY, KENNY MET with PB at Captain K's restaurant on Bainbridge Island. Kenny felt things were under control because Sandy had assured him that her perceived relationship with Nick was all a big misunderstanding. PB had also talked to her. Both men agreed that it was Nick who was at fault.

"He needs to repent for what he's done here," PB said.

"But what about Jimmy?" Kenny asked. "What do we tell him?"

PB took a breath. "I think that Jimmy's beating a dead horse when it comes to his marriage. He needs to give her some time, some space."

Kenny nodded. "Pushing her face in it right now will only drive her farther away."

The two men finished their lunch, agreeing that Nick needed to be held accountable for interfering with Sandy and Jimmy. PB promised he'd take care of it. It was a little over a year since the fire; a little over a year since Nick looked into PB's eyes and said he'd stop romancing Lindsey.

ON MONDAY, JANUARY 4, 1999, NICK—STILL OVERSEAS— logged on to a computer and told Lindsey that he'd just sent off a seven-page dispatch to her father. He had some explaining to do. And while he didn't mention the letter that Sandy Glass had received and Jimmy had shown around town, it was clear those things were on his mind.

> My e-mail may not be secure. I think that maybe your dad and possibly others have access to it.

He added:

I am learning a lot about free will and holding a spiritual gun to people's heads. . . . I suppose I deserve this treatment for all I did at Christ Community.

A short time later, Lindsey told her sister, Kim, that her relationship with Nick was not moving forward. In a staggeringly long e-mail, Lindsey also told a friend about her relationship with Nick and their month together in Africa. She wrote of their swimming with wild dolphins off the coast of Zanzibar, a high point of the trip. Despite the fact that she was still in love with him, he broke it off.

Nick was really honest with me as to what he wanted and it didn't include me. I can't really say or describe the time that Nick and I had together. . . . I don't think either one of us will ever speak of it again in this lifetime but it is time that God gave me and him to savor for a lifetime.

IN A COFFEE BAR IN POULSBO, MANY YEARS LATER, LINDsey tried to shake off the naïveté of her youth. Yes, she did receive a Word from God that they'd be married, but it was Nick who ended it. He represented himself as a broken man.

"When he was in Tanzania, he said, 'I'm not going to marry you. I have to marry somebody else.' He didn't say Nicole, but I knew it was. He was a martyr. Poor guy. His wife's taken from him. He's lost everything. His home has burned down. People are turning on him. Robert's on his back. What can I do to make him happy?"

She felt stupid for a long time.

And, of course, she wasn't the only one.

45

I F NICK THOUGHT THE TRIP BACK FROM AFRICA WOULD be a version of the return of the prodigal son, he was misguided. Things had vastly changed during his absence. Despite Kenny's attempts at damage control, the gossip surrounding the e-mails was in full swing. It was true that Annette and Sandy still loved Nick and saw him as their embattled spiritual leader. But that was eroding with the drama of the kiss-off e-mail to Sandy and the one to Annette that told her to get over herself and buck up.

Neither woman went to the airport to welcome him home.

The next day, Annette's forgiving nature rebounded when Nick came to see her. It was hard to stay angry at Nick. What he'd done to Sandy was cold and beyond cruel, but in his e-mails to Annette he'd been kinder. She felt she could absolve him of anything. He arrived with a bag of photographs and some little gifts he'd picked up in Tanzania and Zanzibar. He looked tan and, for Nick, surprisingly fit. Without the convenience of a drive-through window at a fast-food place, he'd lost a few pounds. He was animated and unable to conceal his joy.

At the same time, he was also conspiratorial in his tone.

"Lindsey and I went for a weekend in Zanzibar," he said. "We had an amazing time together. Don't tell PB." He spread out photos of Lindsey on the white sandy beach of the island, charming images of native children with gorgeous smiles, and a beaming Nick surrounded by it all.

He presented a blue sarong for Annette and some exotic

spices for Craig, who Nick knew was doing more and more of the cooking. He also brought a knife with an intricately carved handle.

"Lindsey and I picked out your gift together," he said.

Next came the real agenda. "You know, Annette, I have something really important to tell you," Nick said. "God spoke to me in Africa."

He was working his own damage control over the letters, and Annette knew it.

"He's given me a new direction for my ministry. It is the first time that I've felt God and I'm really excited. He wants me to take on a leadership role in the church and start helping all of you again. Like before."

Nick's enthusiasm, and a specific direction from God, was enough just then. She didn't feel compelled to probe for details on his new ministry.

"I'm going to need your help through this," he added. "I need you to keep me on track when we're together."

He was talking about their sexual intimacy. In a way, Annette was relieved. The note to Sandy had been so unbelievably icy that she had wondered if she'd be shut out of his life too. But Nick still loved and needed her. On some level, that felt good. Good enough, almost, to forgive him for his cruelty to her closest confidante. Not only that, Nick's general mood and tone were so gentle and soothing, it left her completely unprepared for what came out of his mouth next.

"Oh, yeah," he said, as if what he was about to utter was just a postscript to the conversation, "I want you to know that Nicole and I are going to give a relationship a try and start dating. You know, see where that leads us."

It wasn't so much his words that grabbed her by the jugular; it was his off-the-cuff attitude. When Sandy wasn't around, Annette had *seen* the kiss-off e-mail. She knew that Nick wasn't being entirely honest. In the e-mail he made it clear he was going to *marry* Nicole.

Annette told a friend about the content of Nick's note ending his relationship with Sandy.

"Nick's letter to Sandy talked about the promise that they

shared, of being together after their spouses died. And that he was sorry but he was going to break the promise," she said.

Annette tried her best to reconcile the deceptions between Nick, Sandy, PB, Nicole, Craig, Jimmy, and herself. It was like a sixteen-car pileup and she was buried in the middle of it, unable to crawl out. She knew only one thing to be true: Nick needed her. He'd lost everything. God was taking him in a new direction. She was going with him because she could see no alternative.

To stay behind was to die, Annette was certain.

ONE OF NICK'S FIRST STOPS ON HIS WAY HOME FROM THE airport was Nicole's house, where he told her straight out that he'd done some "inappropriate" things and just wanted to start over without having to reveal details. There was something else too.

"I feel like what we've done wasn't right, either," he said. "I want to do this right. I want to start over and date. If things go right, I'd like to see about marriage then."

He told Nicole that he needed to get with Diana and resolve the issue of Dawn's headstone once and for all. It was both a logistical and a monetary issue. He indicated he also had some fences to mend with the Glasses, which was a good step toward healing whatever had happened between him and Sandy.

Finally, he wanted to save up the money to take Nicole on a honeymoon trip. "You and Ed didn't have much of a honeymoon," he said. "And I really want to bless you with one."

This new Nick, this *cautious* Nick, puzzled Nicole somewhat. She wasn't sure she could turn off her feelings and "start over." She wasn't sure how long she could wait, but she knew for sure that she loved him.

Losing Dawn was like losing himself, she thought. *He's going to make things right. He's going to find himself.*

AFTER NICK ANNOUNCED HE'D BE DATING NICOLE, Annette went over to Sandy's, where she found her friend stoic and full of resolve. Annette wanted her to get angry and call Nick a jerk, but Sandy was playing the martyr this time. She said nothing against either Nick or Nicole. She was somehow above it all.

Sandy, Annette knew, still believed in Nick and the great purpose he'd promised for her life.

Whatever it was.

46

IN MANY WAYS, JAMES AND MARY GLASS WERE THE PER-
fect couple—two halves of a whole. He was one of those
men who preferred giving his two cents only when asked
to offer it. He was a thoughtful and calming influence, and
when he spoke, whoever was in earshot knew they'd better
listen. Mary, on the other hand, was the type who would put
two and two together and then double-check her math. She
was a kind woman, but she didn't suffer any fools.

More than that, she didn't like to be made a fool.

The Glasses knew they were embroiled in a sticky situation. Sandy was their daughter-in-law, the key to their grandchildren. If they sided with their son, angering Sandy, those
four little boys could be plucked from their lives forever.

James liked the direct approach. "Calling Robert or PB
won't do any good," James said. It was clear that Robert and
PB were so bitter and biased that talking to them was futile
when it came to discussing Nick. "But I know who we should
talk to."

A little while later, he dialed Nick's number.

"Nick, get on over here." James's voice was stern. "*Now.*"

Nick was like a big puppy with his tail between his legs
when he showed up. He had a good inkling why he'd been
summoned. He scooted up to the front door, and Mary let
him inside. With Jimmy looking on, his father held out the
printed evidence.

"What is the meaning of this?"

Nick sat there, searching for words. The man who'd been

able to debate anyone at any time—who could sell fleas to a dog—now choked.

"I'm sorry," he said. "I'm just sorry."

James pressed him and Nick said that nothing physical had happened between him and Sandy. He admitted, however, that they'd formed a very strong "emotional" and "spiritual" bond.

"It went too far emotionally," he said. "That's all. Forgive me."

"That's *all*?" Jimmy prodded.

"I'm sorry, Jimmy, but I swear to you nothing like what you're thinking happened."

The apology seemed hollow as a drum. There was nothing behind it.

Yet to the older Glasses, the words "forgive me" were the holy grail of contrition.

"All right, Nick," James said. "We forgive you."

Later, when they were alone, James cornered his wife in the kitchen.

"Okay," he said, "he's not repentant."

Mary agreed. "Yes, his voice, his attitude were all wrong."

Mary could almost buy the idea of Sandy and Nick's emotional and spiritual union. She knew how much Sandy had wanted to lead a Christian ministry. After her boys, nothing had been more important to Sandy. Jimmy had made it to Tanzania with one of the first groups from Christ Community. Sandy hadn't been able to go. Nick had been talking about creating a youth ministry, and it would have been hard for Sandy not to have been drawn into the scheme.

Mary felt sorry for Sandy. She was searching for something deep and meaningful. She was absolutely *not* an adulteress.

NICK KNEW THAT HE'D SCREWED UP. PB SMITH HAD backed him to the hilt over questions about his relationships with Sandy and Nicole before he left for Africa. In fact, some people close to the situation would later say that PB's blind defense of Nick was the primary reason he lost control of his church. A few openly suspected that demons might have been behind everything.

"You know why there are so many scandals involving churches? Satan likes to embarrass Christians where it counts the most: at home, in God's house," one congregant said.

Pastor Bob had been the victim of evil, and Nick must have felt he was in the center of it, because when he joined his dad and PB on a duck-hunting trip in the New Year, he tried to use the occasion to lift PB's spirits and, more important, repair their faltering relationship. The e-mails intercepted by Jimmy were the latest evidence to cast aspersions on his character.

Nick wrote Lindsey about how PB broached the subject in the car.

> He started telling me that we had a pretty big mess to clean up and then thought better of it and changed the subject. . . . He seems a little distant, but it may be just my imagination, too.

SERVICES IN THE CHRIST MEMORIAL CHURCH GYMNASIUM had a distinctly different vibe than those held in a traditional place of worship. Certainly, banners adorned with symbols of Christ helped, but such window dressing didn't change the fact that basketball hoops were the real focal points and the smell of sweaty teenagers still lingered. Pastor Bob Smith made the best of the situation, telling himself—and his congregation—that the church they left behind on Bainbridge Island was merely a building.

"The body of Christ is all of us here today," he said.

To lessen the echo in the cavernous space—and to diminish the fact that half the congregation was missing—the gym was partitioned with a folding wall. Folding chairs faced the stage; a mic stand stood there for the preacher. There was still singing and prayer, of course, but for at least a small portion of the congregation, there was something strange and even irritating about the services. Nick and Nicole were openly dating. No one faulted Nicole for starting a new relationship. She'd hung in there so long waiting for Ed, even after divorcing, that the young woman deserved a decent guy.

The only thing people wondered was whether or not Nick *was* a decent guy. Rumors of an improper relationship with Sandy, of the flirting he'd done with Lindsey, and of his involvement with Nicole prior to Dawn's death ran rampant among the congregants.

To Sandy and Annette, the image of Nick playing the bongos while Nicole sang on the worship team seemed completely at odds with the great plan that had been foretold, put on hold, then rekindled, but had yet to materialize. It seemed as though the relationship with Nicole was a distraction, a diversion from what God—according to Nick—had ordained. How in the world did Nicole and her kids fit into any of the "amazing things God is going to do"? It just didn't add up. By then Sandy and Annette had inseparably entwined, like two old vines, impossible to pull apart without breaking one or the other.

Sandy showed up in a purple jacket, her shoulders like wire hangers and her eyes puffy. Every now and then, she wandered the gym with her hands in the air as if they were lightning rods to God. A few times she fell to the floor, sobbing. Sandy lamented how she felt discarded. Nicole had replaced her in every way in Nick's life.

While she knew things were very wrong, Annette still had her connection to Nick. She still saw him almost every day. Sometimes he flirted with her in front of other people, as if to wink at the world without telling anyone what they'd done.

"But what about Nicole?" Annette asked. "What are you doing with her?"

"We're taking it slow," he said, "seeing if God wants us together."

Nick never stopped talking about Nicole and her kids. It was as if none of the other women in his life mattered. Sandy had retreated from almost everything when she was put on hold. Lindsey tried to deal with unresolved feelings after Nick. Annette searched Scripture and psychology books at the Bremerton library to try to figure out what had happened and if God had had a hand in it—or if it was all Nick's doing.

Whenever Annette asked for help for anyone affected by the events surrounding the ravaged church or promises not kept, Nick just pushed her away.

"I've given you Sandy. You two work it out." Then he added: "Look, Annette, Nicole is the only one that I can really help. God wants me to help her and the kids. They *need* me. I can still be a hero to them. . . . You have Sandy and Craig and your own kids. What am *I* supposed to do?"

Every now and then, in moments of stress like this, Nick would recall the story of his parents rushing him to the hospital as a baby and how he'd been handed off to God to raise.

"Sometimes I wish I just could have been a normal kid," he told a friend in an instance of introspection. He wished his own father had been more involved, his mother less absorbed by the tragedies that befell the family. "None of this has been easy for me. A lot of responsibility comes with being God's son."

SANDY GLASS HAD NEVER BEEN THE BEST HOUSEKEEPER. She cleaned the homes of fellow islanders for a living, but her own home was often in utter disarray. The great thing God and Nick had promised after Dawn's death had still not come to pass, and Sandy's world spiraled out of control. Her flower garden—usually ready for early sowing by that time of year—was a weedy patch of rotting debris. Dirty dishes were heaped in the kitchen sink. If Einar Kloven hadn't fed and cared for her horses, they'd have been in a sorry state too.

Annette noticed the clutter and discreetly picked up Sandy's mess. Sandy didn't seem to notice how far she'd let things go. She'd change one of her son's diapers and just leave it in a ball on the floor. Her mind was never on the task at hand.

Sandy was still waiting for something to happen. *It.* Annette was a shell of what she'd been before Dawn's death.

Yet she and Sandy clung together. They answered Nick's infrequent e-mails on the computer. Sandy had an old upright piano in the living room and Annette brought her guitar, but they never quite found the inspiration to play or sing.

As Sandy's dog and kids ran rampant, Annette wondered why Nick allowed the fragile mother of four to drift toward self-destruction.

"Why don't you help her?" she asked him more than once.

"She needs to get herself together," he said. "This is *her* fault. I can't do everything for everyone. I have to think about me."

Since the church split, Nick's needs seemed to override everything. Annette thought of how he had told her that God had granted him special privileges so they could have sex.

"Did you ever consider you might be a sex addict, Nick?" she asked.

He bristled. "No. And I'm not."

"I've been doing some reading. It seems like you might fit the profile."

Nick blew up. "You must be reading the wrong things. I'm not in those books you read."

Annette stood her ground. "I think you are."

A few days later, Nick called to see if she wanted to go to the Bremerton public library.

"I want to prove to you that you're wrong about me. You've been reading the wrong books."

Annette agreed to go. She was disgusted with how Nick had treated everyone, but she still loved him. She hoped she was wrong. She also saw other words in the books she was reading that seemed to describe Nick's self-centered personality: "Narcissist." "Sociopath." Somehow she held her tongue.

"Sandy's falling apart and it's killing me," she said as they pored through psychology books that day. "I can't take it anymore."

Nick flipped through books and shrugged. "Sandy's problems are rubbing off on you. She's the cause of your doubts. If it weren't for her, none of us would be feeling like we do. Sandy's to blame."

The remarks were pitiless, his tone decisive. Annette was crushed.

Why would he say those things? All she ever did was love him, she thought.

And the summer rolled on.

ON AUGUST 4, 1999, NICK WROTE TO LINDSEY. THEIR CORrespondence had tapered off to almost nothing by then. There were no "I love you's" or promises of wild nights together. He focused his concern on Lindsey's dad.

"Pray for your dad," he wrote. "He has been in a major funk lately. Really doesn't do much with the church."

He didn't mention any role he might have had in PB's despondency.

INVESTIGATORS USUALLY PAY CAREFUL ATTENTION TO A husband whose wife has suddenly died in any kind of accident. Nick was questioned, to be sure, but he wasn't challenged. He told the police, the coroner, the fire department, and insurance investigators varying stories of what might have happened on December 26, 1997. He'd even suggested that the fire was caused by the heater in the master bedroom. He also said that he'd left the house at 5:00 A.M., half an hour earlier than what he first told the coroner's assistant. None of those points were challenged.

Years would pass before Lindsey Smith would be asked what time she and Phil Martini met with Nick on the bridge the day after Christmas. The passage of time clouded her memory somewhat, but she was sure it was at least an hour later than Nick had suggested.

No one had asked her that question when the memories of that fateful day were still fresh in her mind.

47

S ANDY GLASS KEPT LATER AND LATER HOURS. SHE
seemed to care even less about herself and the condition of her home. She'd be up all night, but the laundry
would remain undone, and pots and pans stayed in the sink
on permanent-soak mode. She'd put the littlest one to bed,
but the other three boys had to fend for themselves. She sat
up in bed waiting for the phone to ring.

When it did, it would be Annette. The conversations
would almost always be the same. Annette had been on the
computer talking with Nick. Sandy would interrogate her in
her sweet, supportive, and nonjudgmental way.

"What did he say? How is he doing?"

Sandy would no longer remark on what Nick had said to
her or how she felt about something she'd seen him do. She
was on the outs. She would concentrate instead on Annette's
fragile state.

"I'm here for you," she repeated. "I just love you, because
you're you."

Annette wanted to draw Sandy out. "But what about you?
Are you doing okay tonight?"

"Just waiting on God. I feel so alone sometimes, honey."

WHERE IS HE? ANNETTE THOUGHT AS SHE LOOKED OUT AT
the driveway. *Nick's never late.*

Craig was gone on a road trip, the kids were fed and
watching TV, and Annette was getting ready to leave for a
healing group meeting at Nick's mother's house. Nick, who'd

usually been so helpful, was nowhere to be seen. Then it crossed her mind where he might be. She dialed Nicole's number. Nick got on the line.

"Hey," she said, "what's up? I thought you were coming over."

"You know, darn it, I can't," he said.

"You promised. You know how much your mom's group means to me. Your mom will flip if I call her at the last minute and tell her I'm not coming."

"Shoot, I'm sorry about that. But I promised Nicole I'd take her and her kids up to the school for the open house."

Annette steamed. "That's it. I'm done with you and all this crap that comes with being your friend." She hung up; her face was red. The trap of being involved with Nick had finally come unhinged. She wanted out. She wanted someone else to talk to, someone to confide in. Someone who wasn't part of the utter craziness of Nick, Sandy, Nicole, and herself.

Nick speed-dialed her back.

"I'm sorry, little lamb," he said softly.

"Fuck off, Nick. I'm not going to your mom's. I don't know what I'm going to do."

And she hung up a second time. She poured herself a glass of wine. Nick called again and again, but she didn't answer.

Maybe Robert Bily was right after all, she thought. *Maybe Nick wasn't what he seemed to be.*

A few moments later, Nick appeared on the Andersons' doorstep.

"We need to get you some help. I don't know what to do. We need to call Sandy. I'll call her right now."

Within minutes Sandy was over, watching the kids, while Nick had Annette alone in the master bedroom. Annette had been double-teamed by Nick and Sandy before; the purported exorcism at Sandy's mother's house was certainly the most dramatic example.

"I'm thinking about going to PB and telling him about this," Nick said.

It was clear that he was referring to their sexual relationship.

"Really?" Annette wasn't buying it, but the idea that some honest and decent person like PB could be brought into the toxic mix—and maybe fix it—gave her a glimmer of hope.

"Yeah, I should just get it all out in the open so that you can get the help you need."

A couple hours later, after he and Sandy had left, Nick called Annette. He and Sandy had had another discussion and they both agreed it would *not* be a good idea for PB to be dragged into the mire.

"We need to fix this—fix *you*—on our own. It would devastate too many to let this out."

Sandy telephoned next with the same message, almost word for word.

"There is no need to devastate so many undeserving, innocent people."

There was a time Annette would have accepted the statement at face value. A lot had changed as the lies grew and the subterfuge escalated since Dawn perished in the fire. Nick's credibility had eroded as his words failed to match any genuinely godly outcome. Finally, she understood: *Nick* was the reason she was so sick.

He was the reason Sandy was so sick too.

Annette looked at herself in the bathroom mirror. Her skin was pale, which was to be expected, given the Northwest's seasonal gloom. But it was deeper than that. She was no longer the picture of young womanhood. She was thirty-two, and the stress of the last two years had stolen her beauty. Her skin was marred by blemishes. Cigarettes had replaced meals. A glass of wine had turned into two or three. Annette was not the kind of woman who paraded herself around like some prize in a short skirt and pumps that made her tiptoe. But neither was she a woman without vanity. The sallow face in the mirror belonged to a stranger.

As she began to understand the true cost of what had happened and how she'd been duped into an illicit relationship with her pastor, she grew angrier. Her rage was directed at Nick.

How could you do this to me? How could you do this to Sandy? To Nicole? To Lindsey? To anyone?

She wanted to tell him off, but she knew he'd say she was wrong or crazy. It would be one lie after another, designed to obscure reality and keep her in perpetual need. Annette sat on her bed and started to write out a list of things that she knew to be true: situations that Nick had caused.

1. You took away my ability to have honest relationships with people.
2. You coerced me to follow you and have sex with you without giving me enough information to make an informed choice.
3. You exploited my faith in God and my belief in you.
4. You stole the innocence from my marriage and my family.
5. You lied to me—you didn't need me for love and comfort after Dawn died; you had other people available for you.
6. You took away my ability to walk into church and feel like it's a safe place.
7. You ruined my friendship with Nicole.

She called Nick and told him to come over. It was his day of reckoning.

It was almost 11:00 P.M. when he arrived. He refused to take off his coat—a sure sign that he didn't want to be there and didn't want to stay. As she read her list aloud, her voice quavered. She worked hard to keep the paper steady as she ticked off each item. Nick looked at her with defiance and irritation.

Then the tears started. Annette couldn't count the times she'd seen Nick cry. He was an emotional guy. Tears were a part of who he was. But this wasn't the usual cryfest. It was a deluge.

"I'm sorry. I'm so sorry. I don't know what more I can do."

"I don't think you can do anything," she said.

Nick threw himself on the floor, facedown. He continued

to sob in the exaggerated manner of an attention-seeking two-year-old. Annette just sat there stone-faced. She wanted him to feel every bit of what he'd done.

He needs to own up to this, she thought. *So much of this is his doing. Feel every bit of it, Nick.*

Annette knew what she had to do. She had to tell someone.

As the two-year anniversary of his wife's death neared, Nick was oblivious to what Annette was thinking. He was getting his life in order. His *new* life. He cashed the last of the insurance checks, which brought the total paid out for damage and property loss to $52,219.97. That, added to Dawn's death benefits (excluding her life insurance policy that didn't go into effect) of $58,066.98, made for a grand total of $110,286.95. Most of the money was gone, spent on fixing the house, gifts for his female friends, the purchase of the Jefferson County property, and other debts. He'd also bought a boat, a motorcycle, and a pickup truck.

If Nick thought his problems were finally behind him, he was mistaken.

48

T HE SEDATE ATMOSPHERE OF THE POULSBO OFFICES OF Alpha Counseling Services had been designed to offer comfort and familiarity to the troubled souls who filed in there, hour after hour. The walls in the Christian counseling offices were papered in blue with a border design of antique maps. A framed print of Mount Rainier and the town of Gig Harbor dominated one wall. When Annette Anderson made her first appointment, she sounded shaky and frightened. Counselor Richard Maxwell, fifty-one, knew Annette was barely holding herself together and wasn't sure if she was strong enough to come in.

It was late December 1999 when Annette arrived there, a woman who'd been buried under a bone-crushing burden for almost two years. Richard had seen the look on her face many, many times on other clients. She was afraid and ashamed.

"No one can find out about this," she said.

Of course, when she said "no one," she was thinking mostly of Craig. She'd found herself spiritually adrift, living a lie and not knowing how to reach out to the one person who could help: her husband.

"I was involved with my pastor," she finally said, unable to look the counselor in the eye. She didn't say it was an affair, because she knew it hadn't been that. She wasn't sure what it was. Abuse? Rape? She pondered the possibility that demonic possession was somehow involved. She pulled tissues like a stream of magician's handkerchiefs from a Kleenex box. Richard let her cry. Every now and then, Annette would regain her composure and sputter what had brought her there. It wasn't the first time that he'd heard of a church leader becoming involved with a church member. In his tenure at Alpha he'd counted nine instances in which a man in a leadership position—a pastor, a choir director, or an administrator—had forsaken his commitment to God and engaged in sexual relations with a vulnerable woman.

"Which pastor?"

"His name is Nick Hacheney," she said.

It was a name that Richard Maxwell had already heard. In fact, he'd seen half a dozen former members of Christ Community Church already.

Although adept at treating the victims of trauma— Richard had been a medic in Vietnam—he worried about Annette. Her depression and shame had overridden her ability to think clearly. The fight to become whole again was going to take time.

She's come just in time, he thought. *If she hadn't come, she might have killed herself.*

They agreed to meet again, but a few days later Richard got a message that Annette was canceling. She just wasn't ready. He prayed that she'd be back and shortly thereafter, she returned to his office.

"Nick told me that God wanted us to be together," she said.

"God didn't want that, Annette. Nick did."

Annette knew it was true on one level, but she couldn't openly admit that she'd been duped by someone she truly cared about.

"I should have known better," she said. "This really is my fault."

"No," Richard told her repeatedly as she cried, "you were manipulated by people you trusted."

He quoted Scripture and read other passages from the Bible. One from 2 Corinthians seemed to fit perfectly with what had happened on Bainbridge Island:

> For such are false apostles, deceitful workers, trans-
> forming themselves into the apostles of Christ. And

no marvel; for Satan himself is transformed into an angel of light.

RICHARD MAXWELL WAS IN THE UNENVIABLE POSITION OF having all of the pieces to the puzzle, but because of confidentiality commitments, he had to keep his mouth shut. No matter what former members of Christ Community Church confided, no dots would be connected. He had the only big-picture view. He could see the similarities in the people who'd found their way to that particular church. Some had come from Christ Memorial, the Poulsbo church that defined spirituality for much of the region. While not a mega-church in the truest sense, the church was big enough that congregants desiring a more intimate experience were sometimes left wanting. Those spiritual refugees had been called across the Agate Pass Bridge by pied pipers Bob Smith, Ron McClung, and Nick Hacheney. The congregants had answered the call because they'd wanted to be in on the cutting edge of a movement, a church in which people actually got their hands dirty by doing the really hard work God needed done.

Come over here. Come across the bridge. God's working here. We're a family.

As the counselor sat in his office after a session or drove to or from his Silverdale home, he thought about how the people who'd come to worship Jesus Christ with pastors Nick and Bob and apostle Robert Bily had only wanted to do the right thing. They were waiting for a payoff that never came.

This is like Amway, he thought. *Hang on, any minute . . . you'll bust in at a hundred thousand dollars a year and get a new car.*

WHEN SHE RELUCTANTLY RETURNED TO SEE RICHARD Maxwell for another session, Annette disclosed how it happened: how she and Sandy had been called into Nick's service. How something "big" was about to happen and how Dawn's death was foretold in one of Sandy's prophecies.

"I didn't want it from the beginning," she said of Nick's insistence that God had ordained their physical involvement. "I still don't want it."

"You can say no."

"But God says—"

"Bullshit." Richard cut her off with an epithet he seldom used. "God doesn't want this, Annette."

"What do I say when Nick calls?"

"You say *no*. If he says he's coming over, you call the police. You have him written up for unwanted attention or harassment."

Richard started each session with a prayer of forgiveness for those who'd harmed Annette—forgiveness for herself too. Sometimes he diagrammed the human experience as he saw it, mapping out how the soul, mind, and body worked together in a healthy existence only when God was in charge.

Annette saw the diagrams as a literal roadmap to physical, spiritual, and mental health.

Sandy, by then taking counseling sessions of her own with Richard, didn't see it that way. Whereas Annette began to feel that genuine healing was a possibility and that her life might not really be over, Sandy came out of each session angry.

"I'm so mad at Richard," Sandy said one afternoon over ice tea at the Glass compound.

"Why are you mad at him?"

"I just am."

As Annette continued to employ Sandy as her sounding board for what was going on with her counseling, Sandy just spoke of vague concepts. Annette wondered if Sandy could even be direct with Richard. She had a feeling that "Oh, honey" would only go so far with a trained professional.

"What did you talk about today?"

Sandy looked away. "Things. I don't know. I'm just so terrified of all of this, where this will lead. I'm not sure if he can help me. I left there in tears again."

Annette's confidence grew with each session. But Sandy

resisted and fell deeper into depression. Annette tried to probe to see what it was that was making her confidante come up short.

"Is it about your separation with Jimmy? Is he coming down hard on you for that?"

"No, he thinks that I need to stop the limbo of separation and move into a divorce if that's what I'm going to do, but I'm still waiting on God for that."

Annette understood Sandy to mean that she was still hoping, *praying*, for Jimmy to keel over, making it unnecessary to go through the humiliation of a failed marriage.

"He thinks I might need some medication—you know, see a doctor."

It was a sound idea. Sandy was getting weaker and weaker. Recovery through talk therapy wasn't making any inroads.

"That's good," she said. "That might help."

DURING A SESSION IN MID-SPRING OF 2000, COUNSELOR Richard Maxwell lobbed a bomb at Annette from his side of the library table in his office.

"Have you ever considered Nick might have done it?"

"Done what?"

He paused, searching her face. "Killed his wife?"

Annette flashed to the night when the Bilys came over to win her back by saying Nick was a killer: *Have you ever wondered if her death might not have been a complete accident?*

Originally posited by Pamela Bily, the idea was inconceivable then and it was inconceivable now.

"No," she said, emphatically. "He *didn't*, and I won't have a conversation like this."

And that was that. No more discussion. End of subject.

Annette couldn't wait to get home to call Sandy. She liked Richard, but his suggestion that Nick might have killed Dawn was way out of line.

"How could he even say such a thing? We know that Nick's far from perfect. He's bad enough; why make him into something even worse than he is?"

Sandy didn't respond. She just waited for Annette to wind down.

"Richard had no reason to even *say* that," she finally said. "I'm sorry you had such a bad session, honey."

49

JASON VERTEFEUILLE, A TWENTY-SIX-YEAR-OLD BREMERton police officer, found his way to Robert Bily's Life Staff Ministries when a childhood friend joined the former Christ Community Church as a minister. Like a good buddy, Jason showed up to lend his support. However, all the claims of prophetic Words from God made him uncomfortable from the outset. At first he assumed it was because he wasn't as experienced as the other church members. That was true. He hadn't seen prophetic gifting at any other church he'd attended.

These seem no better than horoscopes, he thought.

The prophecies reported were vague. They could be about anyone or anything. Yet Robert and Pamela Bily and their dwindling flock seemed to revel in each one. People would fall over from the force of the Holy Spirit at the services. That seemed bizarre and appealing to Jason at the same time.

I want to feel what they are feeling, he told himself.

The deliverance sessions that the church promoted also disturbed the young man. He had a roommate who he knew was deeply troubled, but church members insisted a deliverance would cure her of all of her demons. Two straight nights of yelling, praying, and pounding fists on the wall did nothing. The last Jason heard, the woman was living in a rest stop off I-5 near Portland.

One morning in the early months of 2000, Robert approached Jason at the entrance to the church. The apostle was as intense as ever.

"You're a police officer," Robert said. "I've just come from a prayer meeting. The word 'murder' came to us. I think it is in connection with Nick and Dawn Hacheney."

Jason barely knew the names, but as Robert filled him in, he remembered the fire. Indeed, almost everyone serving on the Bremerton Police Department remembered the case of the preacher's wife killed the day after Christmas in 1997.

"Yeah," Jason said, "some of us have always been suspicious about that fire. Guy goes out hunting with his favorite dog, gone an hour, comes back and his wife is dead. Looked pretty suspicious to me."

Robert neither smiled nor frowned. He had the solemn countenance of a man who had been living with a truth that no one could seem to grasp. That no one wanted to believe. He'd told Pastor Bob. He'd tried to warn Annette and Craig.

"I've always thought so too," Robert finally said.

Later, when he got back to work, Jason wrote a note to his supervisor about the apostle's suspicion.

Robert expected he'd get a call from the police about Nick, but none came.

He didn't know that Jason's note had slipped between the cracks and wouldn't be seen by anyone for months.

It was as if someone or something was protecting Nick.

NICK FINALLY FOUND A WAY TO REINVENT HIMSELF, SERVE God, and potentially make some decent money. He and Godwin Selembo, who had moved to the area from Tanzania with his wife, Kim, and their baby, joined forces to start up a Christian video production company they called First Light Media. Bob Smith's son-in-law was the brain behind the enterprise; Nick, the sales manager. For the creative side, they enlisted Jon McClung, the artistic and tech-savvy son of former Christ Community pastor Ron McClung.

The demands of the day job forced Nick to adopt a new approach with the women in his life. There was simply not enough time during the day to ping-pong between Sandy, Nicole, Annette, and Lindsey as he had when he was a pastor. He also e-mailed, instant-messaged, and telephoned Dawn's mother, Diana, mostly during the evenings.

"I can't sleep," he said to Annette during one of his rambling phone calls.

"Why not?"

"I'm afraid of the dark," he said.

"What are you talking about?"

"The demons, Annette; I'm terrified of the demons. I see terrible things in the dark."

Annette was sure he was talking about the nightmare of losing Dawn. She could think of no other reason for his inner turmoil. He needed to release it.

"You've never really grieved for Dawn," she said.

"Maybe that's it."

For all that Nick had put her through, Annette still offered him the kind of love and support that she once thought would be his salvation—that she once believed would be her own salvation. She saw the irony in these exchanges between the two of them. She was helping him, even though he'd undermined her marriage, usurped her ability to go to church, and damaged her friendships with those who loved her.

Nick had no idea that Annette was spilling her guts to Richard Maxwell about their intimate relationship. He didn't know that Sandy was disclosing her secrets about God's plan for her and Nick to the same counselor. Nick was solely focused on Nicole, who was still irritated by his close relationship with the other women of the former Christ Community Church.

On school mornings Nicole, Nick, and the kids would pile into his car and drive down to the school. It was on some of these drives that they would occasionally run into Annette and her children making the same trek from her house on the other side of town. Nicole waved the first few times during these drive-by encounters, but she stopped doing so after she saw the look on Annette's face.

"Wow," Nicole said, leaning closer to Nick, who was driving. "Annette sure looks upset about something. She must be having a really hard time."

Nicole felt that Annette, because of her sometimes-tumultuous marriage with Craig, was jealous. *That has to be it*, she thought. *Annette is jealous of what I found with Nick.*

"Why can't she be happy for me?" she asked Nick. "I know she probably wishes she could have somebody like you."

During their off-and-on courtship, Nicole tired of sharing Nick with Sandy and Annette. It seemed that no matter how much *she* needed him, all those two had to do was telephone and he'd be gone.

I don't know how Dawn could put up with this, she seethed. *I just don't want to share Nick.* Nicole thought guilt was driving Nick: that on some level Nick felt responsible. He was their pastor. He'd counseled them in their marriages. Their bonds were deep. Nicole knew that both women had troubled marriages; Sandy's was over and Annette's had been teetering on the brink for a couple years. Nick was their counselor, but he could not fix relationships that were so badly broken.

"Can't you just let that part of you be over?"

Nick said he wanted to do the right thing. But for now he insisted the women still needed him.

Nicole would sit on her sofa and fume before settling back and realizing that her anger should be replaced by understanding and compassion. She understood she was suffering from some kind of survivor's guilt when it came to having a decent and loving relationship with a man.

I have Nick, she thought. *I have the real deal going and they don't.*

Despite their connection, the couple's ups and downs continued into the third week of May 2000. Nicole wrote in her journal:

We had a major brawl, we practically ended it. It was that we are both doing the best job we can and we're still not making it for each other. So we prayed. . . . I feel bad, what's new?

BY THEN ANNETTE KNEW THAT THE ONLY SOLUTION TO her problem—the only way she could save herself—was to leave Kitsap County. Leave, or die. She fully expected that the weight of the burden of what she'd done with Nick was ultimately going to kill her. When Craig suggested that they move, she agreed.

50

WORD HAD GOTTEN OUT THAT THE ANDERSONS would be relocating to a town an hour or so south of Portland. The chain of communication that Debbie Gelbach had so effectively worked the morning of Dawn's death had lost some vital links, but by the end of May, most of the original members of Christ Community Church knew the Andersons would be leaving.

Although she held great resentment, Annette still loved Nick. One day around that time, she and Nick drove out to Port Gamble to see the new First Light Media office space above the old post office.

"I know you're doing this," he said, "but I can't figure out what this move means for us. What will it be like when I come down to see you?"

Annette chose her words carefully. "It won't be like anything because I won't be seeing you," she said.

He looked as if he was going to cry.

"I need to do what I can to get better, to start over," she went on. "I'm sorry, but I can't seem to get better when you're in my life. Just let me get better. Let me take some time and then, when I'm better, I'll be in touch with you."

Nick looked at her with dark, hurt-filled eyes.

"This idea of me not talking to you won't work," he said.

Annette steadied herself. "But that's how it will be."

"But *why?*"

She wanted to say, *Because you've fucked up my life*

beyond belief and if I don't get out of here—and away from you—I'll die.

"I don't have a choice," she finally offered. "Not seeing you or talking to you is the only way I can do it."

WITH THE MOVE ONLY A FEW WEEKS AWAY—PLANNED FOR the first weekend in July—Annette saw no reason to cut Nick out of her life while they still lived near each other, had friends in common, and shared a history that had made them confidants. He came over one Thursday evening in June to watch the kids while Annette went to his mother's healing group.

When she returned home, the pair sat on the couch and he hugged her. It was the kind of hug that had no end: part bear hug, part leg trap. He wouldn't let go. She hugged him back, then tried to release him, but he held her close.

"I can't help myself," he said, his voice low. "I just wish we could have just one more time."

Annette got up and went to the front door. She was crying then, feeling the pain of rejecting a man she cared deeply about. But she knew that loving Nick was like drinking poison with a straw.

There would be no "one more time."

HER LAST DAY IN SUQUAMISH, ANNETTE KNEW THAT FOcusing on the task of moving would be the only thing that kept her from breaking down. There were so many unknowns associated with uprooting her family, but it had to be done. Annette had unspooled the garden hose and was rinsing off the drawers of the refrigerator out on the lawn when she saw Nick's truck come into view. She barely glanced in his direction.

Gotta keep my focus, she thought. *No matter what he's done, leaving him hurts like hell.*

Nick chatted with Craig for a while, but Annette stayed resolute in avoiding him. She wanted to cry. As Nick went to leave, their eyes locked for a second.

"See ya," he said.

She nodded. "Bye."

And that, she hoped, was it.

Craig loaded a big U-Haul truck and Annette looked around the yard. The lilacs, the tangle of strawberry plants, the rhododendrons: All had been planted in the years that the place had been their home. A white park bench sat on the front porch. It had been a cool spot on summer days like this, a place to rock the children, drink ice tea. Memories came flooding back, so many of them good. But there were the others too—memories that a weaker person would have purged from her mind rather than battle with, as Annette had done in Richard Maxwell's office.

It was dusk when she got in her car and made her way over to Sandy's place, where her children had been spending the day. The next morning they'd all leave for Oregon.

They had no choice.

THE OREGON CONTINGENT OF THE FORMER CHRIST COMmunity Church had remained in touch, mostly because Gary and Julie Conner were so concerned about the Andersons. The Conners had left Washington for a new life in Philomath, Oregon, and the Andersons moved a short drive away in Dallas. Dallas, a part of the orchard and vineyard region of western Oregon, was the perfect place to heal. In the summer, that meant hot days and cooler nights as the marine air tiptoed in from the Pacific. Annette appeared to be getting stronger every day, away from Nick and what had occurred in Kitsap County.

She could go shopping in Dallas without the worry that she'd run into someone from the old church or, worse, a judgmental member from Life Staff Ministries. Julie witnessed her friend's slow climb out of the darkness, but was wary. If she and her husband didn't keep tabs on Annette, not only would her marriage disintegrate, her health might deteriorate even further.

In mid-July 2000, Annette and Julie were on the phone talking about what to take for a day at the beach with the kids—blankets, picnic food, and sunblock—but then the conversation took an unexpected turn.

"I'm still bothered by Nick and how he victimized Nicole and Sandy," Julie said. "He was completely out of line having relationships with those two. It could not have been more wrong."

Annette muttered something in agreement, then let the comment fall flat. But Julie persisted, this time a little harder.

"How was it," she said, "that something like that never happened between you and Nick? You two were together all the time."

Annette's silence confirmed what Julie already suspected.

"Okay," Julie said. "Now it makes sense. I get it."

For the first time in a couple of years, Annette exhaled. She could feel her body relax a little, now that her secret was exposed, now that it was clear that Julie understood.

"I love you," Julie said. "Will you tell me more tomorrow?"

Annette decided at that very moment that she'd release herself from her nightmare. She hadn't planned on it before that phone call, but it just came to her: *Now is the time.*

"I'll try," she said.

Her pulse racing, Annette hung up and dialed Sandy's number. She wanted Sandy to know that soon she would no longer be the only one holding her secret. Annette filled Sandy in on the conversation she'd had with Julie.

Sandy seemed confused. "Why are you telling her?"

Annette wondered if there was some fear in her voice too.

"I need to get better, Sandy. I can't hold this inside forever. I can't carry this anymore. Telling the truth is what sets you free."

"This is a little scary," Sandy said. "What if Julie doesn't understand?"

"I trust her," she said. "Like I trust you."

THE NEXT MORNING ANNETTE PACKED UP THE KIDS FOR the trip to Fogarty Creek Beach, an idyllic spot on Oregon's coast. The park was an equal hour's drive from Philomath, where the Conners lived, and the Andersons' new home in Dallas. As she started to head for the coast, she reaffirmed what she was about to do: *I'm going to get well. I'm going to tell Julie.*

As the kids played in the creek, which sent a silvery braid of water to the ocean, the two women started to talk.

"I really don't understand Sandy and what she had going on with Nick," Julie said as they walked along the beach. She mentioned the letters, the e-mails that Jimmy had threatened to share with the world, one person at a time. Julie knew the gist of the content but had never read them.

"It isn't about Sandy," Annette said, suddenly feeling a little defensive. "Nick wasn't all that innocent, you know. He isn't what he seems to be." Annette took a breath. She looked at her youngest children playing in the creek. The ocean loomed in front of her. She knew her words invited Julie to take that next step, to broach the subject in a direct way.

"Did you and Nick ever do anything—" Julie paused, "physical?"

Even though she expected the question, it nearly took Annette's breath away. It was the first time anyone had actually asked her that. There had been speculation about Nicole and Sandy, but no one ever hinted to Annette that they thought she might have been intimate with the chubby youth pastor.

"Yes," she said. "We did."

They continued walking along the shore, away from the kids. Julie held Annette's hand and then hugged her. "I guess I already knew in some way," she said.

Both women cried.

"You must think I'm a terrible person."

Julie took Annette's hand in hers. "No, no. I forgive you, Annette. It wasn't your fault. God will forgive you too."

More tears flowed and the wind blew against their damp faces. The surf roared and Annette felt very small, but her problems had also become smaller. Just saying it out loud made it better.

"Nick and I had sex," she said.

Julie didn't really react, at least not in the way that Annette figured she might.

Instead, Julie slowly nodded. "That makes sense," she said, indicating the downward spiral that Annette had taken since the split of the church. Maybe even before that.

"He said God wanted it."

Julie stared hard into Annette's eyes. "That's a lie."

"I know."

"You need to tell Craig," she said.

Annette dug in. "I can't."

"Your marriage can't survive without telling him."

Annette knew that Julie was right. The web of deception had become a wall between her and Craig. She felt embarrassed and ashamed and humiliated. She was unsure if Craig would forgive her.

"You're underestimating your husband."

Annette stared out at the ocean, watching the older kids playing in the ocean's surf.

"I'm not ready."

On the drive back home to Dallas, Annette felt a genuine sense of relief from having told someone her terrible secret. No stones had been thrown. No one had said she was foolish or a bad person. She'd made a mistake. She thought of one more person who needed to know that she was getting better: Sandy Glass.

She remembered how a bald eagle had soared into the twisted conifers above the cliff at the beach and how she and Julie had watched it land.

"See that, my friend," Julie had said, motioning to the eagle. "I'm taking that as a sign that this was exactly the right thing to do and that you're where God wants you to be."

Annette smiled—her first heartfelt smile in a long time. She couldn't wait to share with Sandy how unburdened she felt. Telling Julie had been difficult, but it was also a great gift.

51

ANNETTE HAD BEEN CAJOLING SANDY TO PACK UP the kids and head down to Oregon before the summer was over. She'd been telling her how much better she'd been feeling since sharing with Julie what had happened between her and Nick. She was also in the mood for a connection with the past. She didn't think that she had to run away from that part of her life anymore. Sandy's enduring support was the one aspect of her past in Kitsap County that had been affirming, not damaging.

Sandy finally agreed, and she and her boys drove down to the Andersons' at the end of August 2000. After spending a day in Dallas, they planned on a beach holiday at Fogarty Creek Beach with Julie and her children. But almost from the moment Annette embraced Sandy on her arrival, it was plain that something was awry. Sandy seemed out of sorts. As the children blended into a blur of activity—video games, TV, basketball—Sandy tugged at Annette.

"Let's go out back," Sandy said. "I have something I need to tell you."

Annette poured some ice tea and the two women went outside. The air was still and hot, with the sounds of the children playing in the background. They found some lawn chairs in a patch of shade.

Something big was coming. Annette could feel it the way a cat senses an earthquake.

Sandy started to cry and Annette reflexively put her arms around her friend's shoulders, as Sandy had done for her again and again. Annette had told Sandy before her arrival that her confession to Julie had set her free. Nick had been an abuser. The entire setup of the church as Robert Bily had organized it had been a pathway to her ruin. She'd been foolish, yes. She'd been victimized too. Whatever Sandy was about to tell her—about Jimmy, about the church, about whatever was causing her tears—they'd get through it together, as they always had.

"What is it?" Annette asked.

Sandy opened her mouth, but nothing came out. The words were stuck in her constricted throat. She tried to speak, but spasms of grief prevented it.

"It can't be that bad," Annette said softly. She looked over her shoulder. The kids were occupied. They weren't noticing Sandy, who was rapidly dissolving into tears.

"It is," Sandy finally said.

"Tell me," Annette prodded.

"I had sex with Nick too," she said.

The words were direct and clear, but to Annette, they seemed incomprehensible. She replayed them in her head slowly so that she could be sure she understood them. *Sandy had had sex with Nick.* Annette stood up and hovered over Sandy, her anger building as she began to really absorb what she'd just heard. *Sandy had had sex with Nick too?*

"What? *When?*"

Sandy's eyes were full of tears. "Before *you.* Before Dawn died."

Annette felt her heart stop and her stomach turn a full rotation, then thud like a jet landing hard on the tarmac. It hurt.

"Are you telling me that the entire time I've been talking to you about the things that happened between Nick and me, you'd already done the same things?"

Sandy melted into her lawn chair.

Annette pulled back and then moved closer. She thought of all the times she'd poured her heart out to Sandy. All the times when she'd unveiled the most intimate moments of her personal life. And all this time, Sandy had kept her mouth shut about Nick. A feeling of disgust welled up inside. The lie seemed like an extraordinary betrayal. Annette wanted to know *everything*, just as a betrayed husband would want to know all the sordid details, to wallow in the hurt and to make the cheater pay.

"When? Where? How often?"

Sandy sputtered her story. She and Nick had sex at the trailer on the Glass property. At the church. At a motel. In his car.

"Not at the dump on Bainbridge?" Annette asked, feeling a sickening mix of betrayal and shame.

Sandy nodded.

By then Annette knew she was going in for the kill, but she felt she had a right to. Sandy Glass, the holy prophet of Christ Community Church, had been the biggest liar and conniver she'd ever known. Maybe worse than Nick, whom she'd come to loathe for all he'd done to her.

She asked her where Sandy's baby had been during the trysts.

"We brought him with us," Sandy answered, unable to meet Annette's gaze. "He slept in his car seat."

Annette wondered if Sandy had been told to use Benadryl too.

She got up and circled Sandy's lawn chair. Her fists were tight with anger and she fought to keep her voice from echoing across the backyard fence. "How could you have kept this from me?"

Sandy didn't answer. She just sobbed.

Annette pushed harder. "It would have changed everything!"

Sandy found her voice, but it was feeble. "I'm sorry. I'm so sorry."

"You did all of this before Dawn died?" Annette didn't have to ask, but she couldn't help jabbing at this woman who'd just admitted a secret that she'd had no business holding for so long.

"Yes, and sometimes after."

"Were you having sex with him when I was confiding in you?"

"Yes."

Annette wanted to heave onto the lawn. Everything that Nick had told her about God's plan had been tested on Sandy Glass. All of Annette's tears had been cried on the shoulder of a conspirator, a woman who'd betrayed not only their friendship but Dawn's as well. Annette hated Sandy, but she felt sorry for her too. She remembered the e-mail in which Nick dumped Sandy for Nicole. Annette had had no designs on marrying Nick. Sandy, on the other hand, had been in love with him.

At that moment Annette found herself in a very dark place. One question remained.

"Did Nick have anything to do with Dawn's death?"

Sandy was hunched in a pathetic ball in the lawn chair. She looked up at Annette. Her eyes were sunken and red.

"No," she said, shaking her head. "No."

THE NEXT DAY, ANNETTE LOADED UP HER VAN, HER KIDS, her beach blankets, a cooler. She was numb. She could barely face, let alone speak to, her houseguest. Sandy said she'd take her own car for the drive to the beach, and Annette was grateful for the separation.

At the beach, the conversation was brief.

"I'm sorry. Please forgive me," Sandy said.

That seemed impossible, but Annette forced a sympathetic smile. She knew that Sandy's secret had been enormous and that getting it out must have been agonizing. She couldn't even fathom how Sandy really felt inside, because she wasn't sure that she had ever known her at all.

Annette glanced away, refusing to look into the eyes of the woman who'd betrayed her. "I forgive you, Sandy. Give me some time, okay?"

AS IF IN ANSWER TO A PRAYER AND A MOM'S NEED FOR RE-demption, Annette's mental malaise lessened in September

2000. Craig was away on a business trip and her period was late. She took a drugstore pregnancy test.

For the first time in years, a little joy came into Annette's heart. If she'd missed a moment of her three other children's lives because of her depression, because of what had happened between her and Nick and Sandy, this was her second chance. She could do this right. She knew it.

Despite her anger at Sandy, Annette called her with the happy news. She despised Sandy for her duplicity, but they'd been so close, it was impossible not to still think of her as her dearest friend, her closest confidante.

"Oh, honey, that's great news," Sandy said.

When Annette visited a midwife in nearby Salem, a due date was set that sent a wave of nausea through her body: May 20.

Please, God, don't let my baby be born on Nick's birthday. Please, she thought.

YEARS LATER—LONG AFTER EVERYONE HAD HAD HIS OR her say with investigators and lawyers—Nick Hacheney, his skin pale and face fuller, folded his hands on the Formica tabletop and disagreed with Sandy Glass's assessment of their relationship as she'd laid it out to Annette Anderson. He insisted they'd had sex only one time. He recalled how she told him to come over to the Glass compound early one morning in the summer of 1997, when her boys were asleep.

"It was out of bounds. I shouldn't be going there. I knew that nobody would approve of it. I walked over to the house and she watched and said, 'I knew the path you were going to take. God showed me the exact path you were going to take to get here.' I went to the camper and she said that she made the bed with sheets that God told her to buy. At the time, we both said, whatever that was supposed to be . . . that was it. Her attitude was 'Now we've spiritually tied the knot.' She said, 'Well, I wanted to experience true love one time in my life and I realize this is it.'"

52

S HE WASN'T GOING TO CALL HIM. SHE COULDN'T WRITE a letter. She certainly couldn't go and have it out with him face-to-face. Annette didn't have a plan for confronting Nick once Sandy disclosed her ongoing betrayal. It wasn't that she didn't want to confront him; the problem was where—and how. She didn't want Craig to know, so that ruled out most direct forms of communication.

Her chance came one November afternoon when she saw Nick was online. On impulse, she activated instant messenger. It was that sudden. In one click, she was able to pop into his world and throw ice water on his face. He tried to brush her off. It was nice hearing from her, he said, but it wasn't a good time to chat.

> NHacheney: *Nicole and I are working on the computer now.*

Annette wasn't going to let him scoot her aside in cyberspace. He'd lied to her. Sandy had lied to her. *They* had lied to her together.

> Grace23619: *I really want to talk with you now.*

The screen remained empty as he typed. Annette's heart thumped. An introvert by nature, it took a lot of guts for her to push Nick just then. *He will answer me*, she thought. *He owes me.* She imagined that he must have made up some excuse to get Nicole away from the computer. His response was brief, just two letters.

NHACHENEY: *OK.*

Annette pounced and typed and hit the Send button.

GRACE23619: *Sandy told me the truth.*

Another pause came from Nick's computer. The IM window remained a white void. Finally, it flashed that Nick was typing.

NHACHENEY: *What did Sandy tell you?*

Typical Nick, Annette thought, *always fishing before taking action. He always needs to know exactly what someone was calling him on before he'll cop to anything.*

GRACE23619: *She told me she had sex with you before Dawn died.*

Another pause.

NHACHENEY: *Yeah, I'm really sorry about that.*

That was it. He said nothing more about it. Annette found herself just leaving the subject alone.

A second later he wrote that he'd heard she was pregnant.

NHACHENEY: *That's great!*

Annette didn't have time for a response before he came back.

NHacheney: *Gotta go.*

NICOLE MATHESON WAS A DOODLER. HER JOURNALS WERE decorated with wavy scribbles, circles, X's, whatever shape soothed her mind as she tried to come up with words to fill the blank pages that mocked her. The past few days had been rough. She and Nick had been arguing. Nicole could feel her anger pushing him away. She wanted to stop, wanted to change, but it was so hard. She wasn't sure exactly where she stood because she didn't know what had really happened between Nick and Sandy. She didn't see what had been on the computer screen when Nick shuttled her out of the room so he could IM with Annette. On the morning of November 13, 2000, there was no lag time between forming words in her mind and putting them on paper.

The IM exchange between Nick and Annette had brought a journal entry that just poured from her pen:

> I haven't written for awhile. I had a blow out with Nick regarding Annette's instant message. Hard to work through that. I feel a lot of old garbage and old fears regarding Sandy and that there's something more that I don't know. But I have to trust him. And it helps me to remember that Dawn was alive then and I know that he wouldn't do anything more than the kiss, because he loved Dawn. Nick is not that person anymore that is everything to women. He is everything to me.

IN THE WAYS THAT REALLY COUNTED, LINDSEY SMITH WAS over Nick. She no longer saw him as the man in her life. Even so, she still loved him. She could scarcely help herself. They had known each other since she was a girl. Their lives and histories were entwined. It hurt when she felt he avoided her.

Several weeks before the holidays, Lindsey wrote in an e-mail to a friend:

> I just don't know what is going on with Nick and I, but I do know that it's not just his busy-ness. I don't know

how he's feeling about me and that scares me! He
doesn't "have time" to talk about it, so pretty much I
have no idea what is going on in his head.

Adele Smith laid it all out. She'd heard enough about
Nick and no longer wanted her daughter to be caught in his
web: "Just break it off and be done with it."

It was the best advice any mother could give.

DIANA TIENHAARA WRESTLED WITH THE GUILT OVER HER
encounters with her son-in-law. She'd meant to comfort him,
to show her love for him by "giving him" Dawn. She was
now separated from Donald, the grief of losing their daughter having exacerbated a bad marriage. Why had God taken
Dawn away? Why had Nick turned his back on all of them?
Why hadn't Nick honored Dawn's memory with a headstone?

53

THE SIGN HAD BEEN BECKONING ANNETTE. IT WAS almost cruel in a way, the big black letters conveying a message that she wanted and resisted at the same time. Every time she passed by, she'd catch a glimpse of the reader board that dominated the winter-brown front lawn of Dallas's Grace Community Church:

WOMEN'S BIBLE STUDY
OPEN TO THE COMMUNITY

Annette was in the second trimester of her pregnancy when the sign was put up. Every day she drove by, a small voice in her ear told her that she had to stop and go inside. Despite her need for answers to the questions that haunted her, Annette resisted. Back and forth, she passed by. The sign was always there, telling her in big black letters: COME INSIDE.

Yvonne Basso, petite and pretty, was the consummate pastor's wife. She loved God. She loved her husband, Guy. She adored their three daughters and their bounty of five grandchildren. She never had a harsh word for anyone. And she was self-effacing, doing most of her work behind the scenes. Some members of the congregation didn't even know that Yvonne was the pastor's wife.

In January 2001, Yvonne was leading half of the women's Bible study group that met on Thursday mornings. She took the younger women, those with children in school. Not yet fifty, in an aging congregation, she was one of the younger ones herself. She was talking about God and being a mother when she noticed that the new woman who'd joined the circle that morning had started to weep.

"It's so important," she said, "to apply the love of God in your home, especially with your children. Children can be difficult. They need an awful lot of love and acceptance to grow up and be whole."

Annette, her head bent low, was sobbing audibly, but Yvonne went on. She toyed with the idea of stopping the class, but thought better of it. She didn't want to embarrass Annette by calling attention to her.

Lord, there's someone there who really needs help.

When the class finished, a handful of women rushed up to Yvonne as they always did. By the time she took care of them and turned to talk to the troubled woman, Annette was gone.

Yvonne told her husband about the woman and how she worried that she'd missed an opportunity to help someone who undoubtedly needed it. She didn't know her name. She didn't know anything about her.

So she prayed.

Scott Nickell, age forty, could no longer ignore his guarded emotions. With his marriage headed for divorce, he knew there was only one woman who could fill his heart. He'd known her since high school, although they hadn't been in the same class. She was the island girl who had stayed true to her roots, never jumping off Bainbridge for Seattle success but content raising her boys on a little acreage overlooking Battle Point Park. Scott, a barrel-chested Navy commander who split his time between Bainbridge and the naval air base on Washington's Whidbey Island, was away on Navy business in Virginia when he worked up the nerve to call Sandy Glass.

"I love you," he said not long after the first call, when they met face-to-face on Bainbridge Island. "I know it probably can't go anywhere. I'm still married."

He didn't even know what she'd say, but the answer that came was not one he could have imagined.

"Why?" she asked.

Why love me? Why would anyone ever love me? She didn't say those words, but her eyes, then in tears, conveyed her feelings as if she'd written them in indelible black ink.

I'm garbage. I'm no good. Why love me?

Scott didn't know what to do. He hugged her and patted her shoulders. Nothing he said or did could ease her torment. He told her that she was worthy in every way, but Sandy just cried.

SOME COUPLES FIND THE ROAD TO ENGAGEMENT A LITTLE rocky. For Nick Hacheney and Nicole Matheson, it was more like a hundred miles on a washed-out unpaved winding highway in the dark. They'd gone back and forth so many times that casual observers doubted they'd ever end up tying the knot. Being together shouldn't be so hard, but all who knew Nicole knew that her loyalty to a man could never die.

But Nicole was also controlling. It was her method of coping with the chaos of a life without brakes. When it came to setting a date, Nicole wanted to ensure that this time she'd have a ceremony closer to the wedding of her dreams. She'd been pregnant when she wed Ed, and their wedding was more a means to a necessary end. Not this time.

While Nick worked on establishing First Light Media, Nicole let her attention shift to the wedding. When she shared her ideas with Nick, it invariably led to a fight. She wanted Van Morrison's "Someone Like You" played at the wedding. She loved the message of finding the right person, the long search and the sacrifice that brought them together. It moved her.

"Absolutely not," Nick told her.

"But the words mean so much; it's as if they've almost been written for us."

Nick held his ground. "No secular music. Period."

She pushed harder. She wanted *that* song.

This time Nick shut her down in a way that was impossible to counter.

"It reminds me of Dawn and the times we had together," he said. "Every day, I see Dawn."

Nicole wrote about that glimpse into Nick's hidden, vulnerable self in her diary on the morning of February 21, 2001:

> It makes me a little fearful because he always acts different than that. He looks, acts, big and tough.

She was unsure if he was ready to get married, or if they even *should* get married. He hadn't grieved for Dawn. That bothered Nicole, but she loved him. Regardless, a week later, on her birthday, she accepted his engagement ring.

A date was set too. They'd wed on Nick's thirty-first birthday in May 2001. They told friends and family. Within a few days, everyone who'd ever known them knew that this time they were getting married for real.

Only one thing would stop them. And it was coming from Oregon.

BOOK THREE

Judgment Day

*God told me that I'm not to
defend myself.*

—NICK HACHENEY

54

PASTOR'S WIFE YVONNE BASSO WAS SURE SHE'D SEEN the last of the teary-eyed pregnant woman who'd exited her Bible study so hastily, but to her surprise, Annette Anderson returned to Dallas' Grace Community Church. Once more, as Yvonne talked, Annette began to cry. Yvonne could barely look in her direction, because when she did, Annette would cry even more.

I'm not going to let this woman go this time, Yvonne thought.

As soon as she finished the morning's lesson, Yvonne went to Annette.

"Please," she said, "I'd like to talk with you. Stay."

Annette said that she would. A few minutes later Yvonne finished with the other women and found Annette standing in the hall. Yvonne took her by the arm and they started down the stairs.

"You have something that you're hiding that you just need to get out. I want you to know that what you say to me is confidential. I won't say anything to my husband."

Annette looked at the floor. "I've done something that I need to tell my husband about, but I don't know how."

Yvonne had heard other women share the same thing. Annette must have had an affair.

"I don't know a lot of things, but I know if you don't have honesty in a marriage . . . no matter how hard it would be for you to tell your husband what you've done, you've got to tell him."

Annette nodded.

"Don't put it off. The longer you put something off that's eating you alive like this, the harder it is going to be to tell him. We all do things that are wrong. There isn't any unpardonable sin in a marriage. You stand before God and you commit to for better or worse. We all want to take the better."

Annette said she was looking for the right time to tell Craig.

BUT BY THE SPRING, WELL INTO HER PREGNANCY'S THIRD trimester, Annette knew that there would *never* be a good time to tell Craig. She knew that her husband loved her and she owed him the truth, but she was afraid. By telling on herself, she'd probably have to reveal Sandy's role in things. That made her even more reluctant.

Nick held part of her too. She could still hear him whispering in her ear that Craig wouldn't love her, wouldn't understand. That the only forgiveness she ever needed was from God.

"Look, Annette, you tell Craig and you hurt everyone," Nick had said on several occasions. "What's the point of that?"

As Annette picked up the living room of their Dallas home, the moment came. It was unexpected. Craig was flipping through the pages of the Salem newspaper when he brought up the subject they'd avoided for almost a year— Nick Hacheney.

"Heard anything from Nick lately?"

Annette stopped what she was doing and looked at her husband. "No, and I don't want to hear from him ever again."

"Give him a break. He's a good guy."

"Nick's *not* such a great guy," she said. She just floated the words out, but they were angry and they hung in the air, provoking Craig.

Craig looked over his paper. "You know, Annette, you really need to let go of your anger here."

She said nothing. Her silence pushed at Craig a little.

"What's wrong with you that you're still upset?" he asked.

They'd moved hundreds of miles away. They'd severed most ties. Yes, Craig understood that she had had a falling-out with Nick, but he wasn't really clear about why.

In a flash, the urge to tell the truth began to rise in Annette. She was finally going to tell Craig. In doing so, she knew she was risking everything. Would he leave her? Would he kick her out? Would he understand and forgive?

"What is this about? Nick and Sandy?"

Craig thought back to the e-mails Jimmy Glass had found and the rumors that swirled around Nick and Sandy's "emotional" affair.

"Did Nick and Sandy have sex?"

Annette found her voice. "Yes, but that's not all."

He stared at her. She was crying then, shaking. Something in her face, her eyes, prompted him to ask a question that no man ever wants to ask.

"But you didn't have sex with Nick. Did you?"

Annette didn't answer.

"You had sex with Nick too?"

Finally: the truth.

"Yes," she said.

Annette saw the shock on her husband's face and felt like dying. Craig was devastated. Through her tears, Annette told him that her liaison with Nick hadn't been an affair but a bizarre mix of Nick's twisted desires and God. When she could see he wasn't grasping it, she took the next step: She told him that Sandy had been caught up in the same thing.

"He said God wanted this," she said.

By then Craig was headed out the door. His world had been shattered, but within his anger he carried a measure of resolve too.

Nick Hacheney is not going to get away with this, he smoldered.

Later, Annette called Sandy to say she had told Craig.

"You didn't tell him about me?"

"I'm sorry. I had to," Annette said.

"Well, I don't appreciate that, Annette. You can do whatever you feel you need to do with your part in this, but you had no right to drag me into it."

It was a different Sandy speaking. Her words carried a kind of desperation, not her usual love and understanding.

"I had to tell the truth," Annette said.

Sandy seethed on the other end of the line. "You don't have any idea what you've done. I'm going to have to figure out what I'm going to do now."

Before Annette could say anything more, Sandy abruptly ended the call.

It was the last time they'd talk as friends.

55

I
T WAS ALL COMING OUT. NO ONE KNOWS FOR SURE HOW
Sandy Glass felt when Annette dropped the bomb that
she'd told Craig and that he was within hours of telling
PB and the other church members that Sandy had been lying
to everyone, making her husband Jimmy look like a paranoid, delusional creep for years. Up until that point, few who
knew her would have considered Sandy anything other than
a paragon of virtue. Truthful. Trustworthy.

After the phone call from Annette, Sandy's hand was
forced. The affair with Nick was going to be broadcast across
the island. No one would ever look at her in the same way.

No one who had looked into her eyes and believed her
facile lies would ever trust her again.

She was backed into a corner and she had a decision to
make. Sandy had to save herself.

SCOTT NICKELL WAS BACK ON WHIDBEY ISLAND, LIVING IN
an old Holiday Rambler motor home with Levi, one of the
puppies whelped by Faith, Dawn Hacheney's old dog, at
his feet. He'd bought the dog from Sandy the season before.
He wondered what it was that would make Sandy say that she
was unworthy of love.

I don't get it, he thought. *Don't you see what's loveable
about you? I see so many things. You're a dedicated mother.
Nothing is more important to you than your family. I see the
great lengths you go to to provide for them.*

He was thinking about the grueling cleaning jobs she

added to a full roster, just so the boys would have the base-ball uniforms and equipment they needed. Sandy always put her sons first, not so much as a sacrifice, but because it was the only right choice she could make.

Sandy could appear to be all sorts of things. For many she was the consummate mother and hard worker—a housecleaner with more elbow grease than a mechanic. A deeply spiritual woman.

Scott saw something else. Sandy was a woman beginning to unravel. He drove down from Whidbey and they met for a walk with their dogs at Battle Point Park, where he applied all the listening skills he'd acquired in Navy personnel training. *Let her get it out.*

"I'm not worthy of happiness," Sandy told him. The air was chilly and they picked up the pace. Finally, Sandy stopped in order to force out what she'd been holding inside.

"I had an affair," she said.

Scott didn't flinch. He'd expected as much.

"That doesn't surprise me. I figured you had the affair, not Jimmy. Just your demeanor. You know, you're not the first woman who has had an affair, and you won't be the last. People make mistakes."

Sandy wanted to say more, but she stood silent.

Finally, she spoke again. "I had an affair with the pastor of my church."

Scott didn't know what to say, but in his head a single word came to mind: *Wow.*

They walked back up to the house after Sandy regained her composure. Scott knew there was more to the story.

SCOTT MIGHT AS WELL HAVE BEEN IN TIMBUKTU, SO RE-mote did Whidbey Island feel from where he really wanted to be: with Sandy. Her affair with her pastor had been such a stunning revelation, he wanted nothing more than to rev up the RV and plant it on her property. With Jimmy out of the picture, Scott wanted to help Sandy sort out her life. He'd also like to give the no-good preacher a word or two, but

Sandy hadn't disclosed who it had been. At his first opportunity, Scott drove down once more to see Sandy.

Back on Bainbridge and in the park with their dogs a few days later, Scott gently prodded Sandy for additional details. It was distasteful and he knew it, but he realized that what had happened to Sandy couldn't really be over until after she talked it out. It passed through his mind that perhaps the affair was still going on and that was why she'd been so cryptic. He didn't pussyfoot around.

"Is it over?" he asked.

She nodded. "Yes. For a long time."

"Does anyone else know about it?"

"No."

While their dogs tugged at their leads, it was clear that Sandy's mental state was fragile. Scott felt there was something more about the affair, something even darker than the fact that the man had been a pastor.

"I'm worried about losing my boys," she said.

"Losing your boys? Sandy, lots of women have affairs."

She was silent.

"There's more, isn't there? What's the problem?"

Once more she was unresponsive.

Scott sensed that she'd been alone with her secret for far too long. Letting it out would free her. But she wasn't forthcoming. She seemed to want to tell him, but it just wasn't within her ability.

"What is it? Was it an abortion?" he asked, thinking of the worst secret she could hide.

Sandy shook her head forcefully. She'd never kill a baby. "No, I've never had an abortion."

The answer surprised him and he said so.

"Is it worse?" he asked gently. "It can't be worse."

He caught a look in her now crying eyes.

"The only thing worse is murder," he said.

There was a long pause. Sandy looked around the park, mostly empty save for another dog walker or two. Seagulls picked at garbage from overflowing cans, and the chilly wind coming off Puget Sound had never felt so harsh. She looked directly into Scott's eyes.

"Yes, it is," she finally said, tears falling like a rainstorm. A stream. An anguished cry. "It is murder."

"Did you murder someone?"

"I didn't. Nick did!"

Scott couldn't believe it. "Fuck. Shit! You're kidding."

His eyes popped. He was a man who could take a lot. Yet at that moment he needed a little space. While Sandy sat weeping, he left her and took a short drive, his mind working on what she'd just disclosed. *A murder. Sandy knows of a murder!* He gathered that she'd been unhappy in her marriage to Jimmy. And Nick Hacheney had come along and prayed his way into her pants. Promised things. *Loved her.*

This is too much. But I need to know more.

Scott drove back over.

"Okay, Sandy," he said, "you gotta tell me all of this. Every bit. Okay?"

Sandy seemed unburdened then, maybe a little hopeful that just talking about what had happened would save her from the torture she'd been enduring since the fire.

With the dam of silence broken, a deluge of information spilled forth. She talked about the prophecy of Dawn's death. She talked about how Nick phoned her the morning of December 26. He was in his car on the way somewhere. His only words were "I did it," but call waiting interrupted the conversation before Sandy could respond. Debbie Gelbach was on the line, leading the prayer chain with the news that Dawn had died in the fire. Sandy thanked her for the information and went back to Nick and asked what he meant. He said, "It's done."

Scott was completely astonished. Sandy was shell-shocked, but she took a breath and went on. Nick had confessed to her how he had killed his wife. A few weeks after Dawn died, she said, Nick told her that he'd held a plastic bag over Dawn's face after overdosing her with Benadryl. He said that Dawn could see him through the plastic and knew what he was doing.

Sandy was sobbing, barely able to get out her words. "Nick told me that God spoke to him to 'take the land.'"

The phrase was a biblical reference from Joshua 1:11, when God spoke to the prophet and told him to take the land that had been promised to the children of Israel.

"What about the fire?"

"Nick said he'd set it up to look like a space heater accident."

"Wow" was all Scott could think to say. "Did you tell the police?"

"No. I was afraid I'd lose my boys."

Although much of the story didn't make sense, that small disclosure did. If Sandy was anything, she was a devoted mother. No one could take that away from her.

It was too late to drive back to the RV on Whidbey. Scott, adrenaline rushing like a torrent through his sturdy frame, rented a room at the Poulsbo Inn. He could barely sleep. The thought that Sandy could hold such a devastating secret had stunned him. She'd been cryptic in her disclosure and he didn't push too hard. In a way, Scott saw Sandy as a trapped animal. She needed to be released from whatever it was that held her captive.

Scott called in sick to the Navy base the next day. Later, when he was sure his estranged wife was away at work, he let himself in the house they shared and sat down in front of the computer. In a few attempts at searching for keywords— "fire," "pastor," "Christmas," "death"—on the Bremerton newspaper Web site, he found several stories.

With each line from the paper, Scott felt there had to be something real behind Sandy's story. His concern escalated. He wanted to protect her, to find out more. He called her right away.

"I read the articles about the case," he said. "I need to see you. We need to talk some more."

She agreed, and over the course of the next few hours, Sandy heaved up details like poison from the bottom of her stomach. So black. So toxic. That she had survived all those years was a testament to her unbelievable strength.

At least, that was how Scott saw it. He knew others wouldn't see it that way at all. They'd see it as hiding something. Maybe collusion. Maybe even direct involvement. He would wonder about that too, but he had known Sandy since high school.

She is not a murderer, he thought.

She told him how it had started, how she had a Word from God that first led her to believe that she had a connection with Nick. She didn't know what it meant, but the message she received was that God wanted them to be together.

"He was the aggressor," she said. "He kissed me first. He told me one time . . ." She stopped herself as embarrassment overcame her.

"What?" Scott pressed.

" 'My penis will show you what love is.' " The horror and confusion on Sandy's face twisted her features in agony and shame.

Scott nearly blew a gasket. He was a sailor, and when necessary he used the vernacular of the men with whom he'd served for two decades.

"He's a fucking scumbag and he used you."

Sandy fell quiet, but Scott kept it coming. He wanted to build a wall around her to protect her from all that she'd been through. He felt she needed to hear the tough truth about the man who had used her love for God to get into her pants.

"He's a predator. You are the victim of a predatory sexual attack."

She told him that she had a hand in the relationship too. "I thought he loved me. I thought I loved him."

Scott's face was red, so angry was he about the pastor who had manipulated this woman to the point of convincing her to accept culpability for an affair that had nothing to do with romance.

"This isn't about being in love, Sandy. This is about a man abusing power. Rape isn't about sex, it's about power. He acted out of the power he had as a pastor of his church and he fucking abused it."

Sandy appeared to understand, but she said she was deeply

ashamed of how she let herself be manipulated by something so obviously false to any outsider. It was the mix of religion that had clouded everything.

"Do you still think the Word came from God?"

She looked away. "No, it came from Satan."

Scott nodded. Progress, finally. There was one more step she had to make.

"You have a moral obligation to go to the authorities with the truth. I don't know what your legal obligations are, but you have a moral obligation."

Sandy thought for a moment. She had likely known that answer since the day Nick told her what he'd done. "I know," she said. "But what about my boys? I didn't report it right away. Can I go to jail?"

He didn't think so, but he couldn't be sure.

"You need a lawyer," he said.

NICK WAITED A LONG TIME BEFORE HE EVER TOLD ANYONE else what had transpired in the Smiths' basement, where Sandy claimed he told her how he'd killed Dawn. He flatly denied the bit about the plastic bag and "Take the land." He conceded it was a very emotional visit: Both of them were crying.

"I told her that God didn't kill Dawn; it's my fault. It was because I wasn't the husband that should have been there for her. I committed adultery. *That's* why. I should have been home. I should have taken care of the house. Instead, I was out having an affair. This is the conversation she's talking about."

But why had Dawn just stayed put that morning? Why hadn't she found her way from the bed? Had she been too groggy from the Benadryl she'd taken the night before? Or had she struggled and fought when Nick slipped a plastic bag over her nose and mouth?

"He looked into her eyes," Sandy told Scott. "He sat up all night with her after he killed her."

SANDY'S RECOLLECTION OF NICK'S CONFESSION WAS DIFFIcult to follow: Details morphed; specifics became obscure.

She pinpointed the date as being in the summer of 1998 and the location as the Smiths' residence, where he helped with New Covenant Fellowship business. She said she had sought to "share the burden" by getting Nick to offer the details of what happened the night his wife died. She recalled how he mentioned that Robert Bily might have bugged the room before he made the "Take the land" disclosure.

Sandy said she had kept Nick's secret out of fear. Neither did she want to drag others through the mud. But there was something far darker at play too.

"I was afraid," she said. "I didn't know if I had a part in this."

That was as close as Sandy Glass would come to an admission of culpability. If not for her prophecies, her need to be a part of Nick's great plan, would Dawn Hacheney have died?

Your hands are no longer tied.

WHEN SANDY GLASS FIRST POINTED AN ACCUSING FINGER at her former lover, her pastor, the man for whom she lived and waited for so many years, it didn't take long for others to piece together what might have happened. They presumed Nick had been looking for the opportunity to kill Dawn for months, in order to be with Sandy, Lindsey, Nicole, or any number of other women. The chance to rechart his life came Christmas night at the Smiths' when he, Lindsey, and Phil Martini spontaneously planned to go hunting the next morning. Was his plan to incapacitate Dawn with Benadryl, set the fire, and leave? The trip was the ideal alibi to cover his absence during the fire.

There was one thing Nick likely couldn't wriggle out of: Dawn's autopsy would likely show she was dead *before* the fire burned the master bedroom. There was no carbon monoxide in her blood, no soot in her lungs, and nothing in her medical history that could point to anything that caused her death. There was nothing that indicated she was alive before the fire ignited.

But wriggle he did.

56

IF THE WORLD HAD TURNED UPSIDE DOWN IN DALLAS, Oregon, it didn't take long for the shock waves to reach Bob Smith, now living in a 1920s farmhouse on Sawdust Hill Road in Poulsbo. PB was doing the bane of his existence, church paperwork, when the phone rang midday on Friday. It was Craig Anderson on the line.

At first PB was delighted that Craig had phoned. It had been a long time since they'd talked. He knew that Craig and Annette were expecting their fourth baby soon and wondered if he was calling about that. But immediately he detected something awkward or unsettling in Craig's tone: He seemed a little off, a little upset. The call was clearly *not* about catching up with old friends.

"I'm going to be up there on Monday," Craig said. "Gary and I want to meet with you."

"Oh, great!" PB said, happy that they'd be getting together. He'd missed Gary Conner too.

"We want to meet at Richard Maxwell's office in Poulsbo, with him there for support."

Like a mosquito bite in a place he couldn't reach, the thought that something serious was brewing bothered PB after they hung up. It was only Friday. He wasn't sure if he could last the whole weekend worrying and wondering what the matter was. He immediately thought of the one person who might know what Craig and Gary were upset about: Nick Hacheney.

He reached Nick and told him to come over.

* * *

A LITTLE WHILE LATER, NICK SHOWED UP AND PB MET HIM at the door. PB's face was stone. Nick's smile faded.

"Gary and Craig are coming up from Oregon. I want to know if there's something I don't know about."

Nick looked surprised and shrugged his soft shoulders. "I don't know anything."

PB felt a familiar pang of anxiety. Nick had lied to his face about Lindsey at least twice. He'd seen the evidence that something inappropriate had gone on with Sandy Glass. But at every turn Nick had professed innocence, and PB wanted to believe him.

Nick phoned PB Sunday and said that he and Nicole wanted to come over. Nick had something important to tell him. They gathered in a travel trailer parked on the Smiths' property.

"I wasn't exactly honest with you," Nick said as Nicole looked on with hurt and contempt. "I made a mistake."

As PB listened, Nick poured out his heart, confessing that he'd had a relationship with Annette and Nicole after Dawn's death. He knew he had been wrong, and he was very sorry.

PB felt foolish and bewildered. He'd loved Nick like a son. He'd defended him at every turn. Whenever Robert Bily had said something nasty about Nick, it had been PB who shut him down. Nick asked now for forgiveness, and his childhood mentor led a prayer.

"Nick, it's not going to end with this, obviously. We're talking about members of our church, and I have to respond to that."

THE NEXT DAY, CRAIG ANDERSON, GARY CONNER, BOB SMITH, trusted friend and church deacon Eric Kruse, and Richard Maxwell gathered in the conference room at Alpha Counseling. Craig was emotional but somehow held himself together. The other men let him say his piece, mostly directed at PB.

"My wife has confessed to me that she had an affair with

Pastor Nick. You have to do something about this. Sandy was involved with Nick too."

Sandy Glass? Nick hadn't mentioned Sandy's name when he and Nicole came over. He'd specifically said he was only involved with Nicole and Annette.

PB was confused and humiliated.

"The church will discipline him," he said. "I've talked to Nick. He understands that. He's sorry."

FINALLY, IT HAPPENED. BAINBRIDGE ISLAND WAS HIT BY AN earthquake of sorts, just as so many of the church prophets had predicted. But it was not one of tectonic plates shifting and scraping, as Pamela Bily had foretold in a Word from God. It was about a deception revealed.

Sandy looked pale, thinner than usual. She hadn't had a decent night's rest in quite some time. Those that knew her had a theory that was far from sinister: She had had a late night with one of the boys, which would explain her haggard appearance. She was a good mother. Mary and James Glass were among those who could easily have adopted this theory.

But not this time.

James and Sandy were pounding nails on a chicken coop next to her place on Arrow Point Drive one spring afternoon. New grass was everywhere, and the canopy of trees behind the property had exploded into a lovely green shield. Sandy had become quite a carpenter under her father-in-law's tutelage. The connection they shared was natural and close. Sandy had lost her own father, and James Glass had stepped in to fill those big shoes.

"I have something to tell you," she said. Her words were tentative, like falling raindrops off the end of a reed. She was slightly shaky, but not overly emotional.

"What is it, Sandy?"

"I have to tell you that Nick and I had an affair."

James set down his tools. He thought of all of the comings and goings; the denials; the hurt that his son, Jimmy, had surely endured after being made the fool.

"I'm asking for forgiveness," she said.

James stared into her eyes. "Okay, Sandy. I forgive you. You have acknowledged what you've done is wrong."

Little more was said about it. Sandy didn't have the nerve to tell Jimmy in person that she'd repeatedly lied to him too. Finally, she gathered the courage to call him. She cried as she admitted the affair.

"I'm sorry. I wanted you to know before the word got out."

Jimmy didn't know what to say. He did not feel vindicated or elated. He'd known all along that Sandy had deceived him. He was hurt by the revelation, but not out for blood. He felt sorry for Sandy.

In a way, he still loved her.

SCOTT NICKELL WAS LIVID. NICK HACHENEY DOMINATED his thoughts. There could be no defending a pastor who had done what Sandy had tearfully said he had: murdered his wife and carried on with other women in the church. Anyone who'd use his position as a marital counselor to molest a vulnerable woman was completely amoral and depraved.

Although Scott trusted Sandy and would stand by her, it crossed his mind that she was withholding something. A moment before, he couldn't have fathomed a secret bigger than a murder confession.

Sandy, he thought, *you don't even get it. You were mind-raped.*

It was too explosive for Scott to keep to himself. Shortly after Sandy disclosed that Nick had murdered Dawn, Scott had told his commanding officer at Whidbey, his parents, and his estranged wife. The reaction of each was nearly identical.

"You need to drop that friendship. It will ruin your career."

"You can't be involved with any of this."

"How do you know Sandy wasn't involved in the plot?"

Scott carefully considered the first two comments, but he knew that in the end he couldn't just drop Sandy. He had deepening feelings for her. He trusted her, partly because he wanted to. So much of his own life had been in disarray as his marriage crumbled and his relationship with his youngest daughter became more and more strained.

How do you abandon someone who has opened up to you and told you something she is so ashamed of, so tortured by? Do you just say, "Hey, you're a fucking nut job and I'm not going to have anything to do with you"? *Not me*, he thought.

The last comment provoked a little more uneasiness. What if Sandy *had* been involved? What if Nick had killed his wife so they could be together?

He asked her directly a little later.

"Did you have a part in Dawn's murder?"

Sandy was emphatic. "No. I was at home with the boys." There was no murder pact. Why would there be? She went on to say that she'd already "felt that God had released" her from being with Nick. The "appointed time" of the prophecy for Dawn's death had come and gone.

By then Scott had fallen in love with Sandy. It was more than just the two-decade-long connection they had shared since high school. That had been so long ago, and there had been other relationships in between. In a very real way, he'd seen himself as her protector from the moment she'd confided her darkest secret. Their relationship had intensified and become physical. He was in love with her in a way that he hadn't been with his wife. Sandy *needed* him.

At the naval base on Whidbey Island, he packed up the RV for the ferry ride and drive to Bainbridge Island, where he planned to park it on the Glass property. He wasn't moving there. He'd rented a basement apartment on Whidbey that would be better for him and his dog, Levi.

It was very late when his phone rang. The number on the display belonged to Sandy.

"He knows," she said.

"Who?" Scott wasn't sure what she meant at first.

"Nick *knows*. He called me."

"What did he say?"

"He said, 'Do you know what you've done? Do you know how many people this is going to hurt? Do you think God would want you to do this?'"

She hesitated. "I told him, 'It is the truth.' "

It was obvious by the timbre of Sandy's voice, slight and hesitant, that she was very frightened. She felt threatened by Nick. She wasn't sure what he would do, now that he knew she'd broken her silence. She didn't tell him that she had sought legal representation. She told Scott that she was scared that Nick might harm her, that he might seek revenge.

She didn't have to say "he's already murdered once" to lend credence to her panic.

Scott wanted to solve the problem and protect her. He asked for Nick's phone number and dialed right away.

"Hello?" Nick sounded as if he'd been asleep.

Scott jumped on him. He didn't identify himself. He didn't say hello back. "I know what you did. Sandy told me. She's told the authorities. Stay away from her!"

"Huh?"

"You heard me."

Then he hung up.

HE SURE LOOKS SERIOUS, JON MCCLUNG THOUGHT AS HE glanced over at Nick talking on his cell phone. Nick was in his van, parked next to the Dumpster that served the apartment complex where he and Nick shared a place while working together at First Light Media. Jon pushed open the Dumpster and threw the bag of trash inside. He looked back over at Nick and jokingly made a face at him through the driver's-side window. Nick was focused on whatever the other person was saying to him.

It must be about a client. An unhappy client, Jon thought.

Jon went back inside, thinking he'd hear about whatever it was at the office.

Nick's pretty good at handling those things, he thought.

NICOLE HUDDLED IN HER SAGE GREEN BEDROOM AND sobbed until she could shed no more tears. In some ways the feelings that took hold of her seemed unnervingly familiar. She'd been betrayed by Ed, of course. She'd been lied to by other men in her life. But never *Nick*. She wondered what

had made her the type of woman who was repeatedly victimized by men. She wanted to sort out the fiction from the
truth, but Nick wasn't completely forthcoming. He was vague
in his admission to her.

"It was inappropriate," he said of his relationships with
Sandy and Annette. "What I did was wrong."

Nicole bought a new journal because she knew there were
not enough pages in the one she'd been writing in to contain
everything she had to say. She wrote to God on April 3,
2001:

> I don't know who to trust, I'm having a hard time believing
> Nick about much. . . . Help me to walk away for a season to
> heal and help me not to destroy Nick.

THE PICTURE OF NICK AND HIS DOG HOPE SEEMED TO MOCK
Pastor Bob from the Smith family's Wall of Fame as he sat
down with the telephone and a photocopy of the church di-
rectory. Each name was that of an old friend, a supporter
who'd followed him from the split with Life Staff Ministries
and Robert Bily. There was no other way but to start at the
top of the alphabet and work his way down—Nick Hacheney's
sins from nearly A to Z.

He moved through the rolls like a telemarketer who really didn't want the answers to a survey.

"At any time since Dawn's death"—he stopped himself,
and amended his script—"or before Dawn's death did Pastor
Nick do anything that you felt was inappropriate or made
you feel extremely uncomfortable?"

All the voices on the other end of the line were female, of
course. All, with only a sole exception, answered in the af-
firmative.

"When my husband wasn't around, he came over crying
about how he lost Dawn . . ."

"He put his head on my breast."

"He mentioned things about me, about my appearance."

PB was completely caught off guard. He felt foolish that
he could have been so blind, when it turned out so many

people felt that Nick had been out of line. He could feel the resistance and skepticism of some of the women and their husbands. It was as if they were saying: *How do we know we can really trust you? You carried Nick for so long; you didn't even want to listen.*

PB asked God how he could have been so oblivious to Nick's deception. The answer came to him that a spirit was involved in the scenario, a specter of evil. A spirit from the dark side.

The next day, Monday, PB dragged himself before the New Covenant Fellowship board, whose membership now included Dan Hacheney, Nick's father. Looking into Dan's worried eyes was probably the most difficult thing PB had been called to do. Dan sat there glumly, knowing that something bad about his precious son was about to be revealed.

"We've got a serious problem," PB said. "Here's what I found out. . . ."

57

DAN HACHENEY FELT LET DOWN BY BOB SMITH AND the church board. *Some new covenant.* He knew his son could use help—he'd lost his wife, for God's sake—but he was not a man without a path to redemption. The board convened amid the service bays and engine smells at Dan's garage. Nick's father's eyes betrayed what he thought was a poker face. He was angry and deeply hurt.

"The Scripture calls for public discipline," PB said. The other board members concurred. "If Nick asks for forgiveness, then we're going to forgive him."

Nick had agreed to go before the church and get counseling, so that wasn't the issue that Dan was upset about. The board, however, didn't want to stop there.

"He will need to leave the church and go under another pastor, besides me," PB said. "He'd have to fully confess his past to the new pastor, at a new church."

Dan flinched. "You're kicking him out?"

"It isn't right that he stay, considering the women who feel victimized are members of this body too."

PB left Lindsey out of the conversation.

Dan started pacing. "That's not forgiveness."

"That's what's best for Nick."

With that, the small group departed, leaving Dan to face the consequences of his son's actions alone.

Later that day, Dan called PB with the request to meet him in the bank parking lot on High School Road on

Bainbridge. Dan stood next to his truck. PB got out of his car and walked over.

"I'm going to have to resign the board, the church," Dan said.

"You don't need to do that," PB said, though he wasn't trying hard to be persuasive.

"I just can't be in a church that would treat my son the way you are."

PB was moved but he wouldn't give in. "He's done nothing to make us trust him."

Dan's desperation was gut-wrenching. He had lost one boy already. Nick had been the apple of his eye since the day he held him as a dying infant on the way to the hospital. He had pleaded with God to take his son and raise him right there. And He had. The Almighty came through.

But PB refused to budge.

ON APRIL 10, 2001, SANDY GLASS AND HER LAWYER MET with Kitsap County prosecutors in their offices in Port Orchard. On the table was an agreement that assured her immunity from prosecution in any matters concerning Dawn Hacheney's death. Later, observers close to the church would consider it a "deal with the devil."

Sandy signed the document.

NICOLE MATHESON HAD NOT HAD IT EASY SINCE SHE WAS fourteen. She'd made more mistakes and put herself at more personal risk than she cared to remember. All of that was behind her. All she wanted was to be a good mother and a good wife to a righteous man. She had serious doubts that Nick was that man. And yet, possibly because she hated being told "I told you so," she sucked in the bad news and kept her mouth shut. With the exception of Nick, she really had no one to talk to, or blast. Nicole hated being judged or questioned by anyone. To talk it out with a girlfriend or a family member at that point was to risk being told that she'd been duped by a fat little preacher. So Nick got it with both barrels.

Nick was beside himself. Nicole *had* to believe him. None of what had transpired between him and Sandy had been by design. It wasn't his doing at all. He wasn't driven by lust. It just happened. When he finally admitted to what had occurred, he told Nicole how it all started in his office in the summer of 1998.

Sandy had been crying, inconsolable, almost unreachable.

"You look like you've never in your life been loved," Nick had said.

Tears streaming, Sandy finally looked up. "You're right. I haven't."

That was the invitation. He leaned in to her and kissed her on the lips. Just once.

Sandy had said that they were going to be married. Maybe this was part of a spiritual marriage.

"I knew it was wrong," he said years later, "but somehow I figured that God would okay it because it was part of the prophecy."

In the days following Nick's mea culpa, Nicole wanted to extract every single detail she could get. She fired questions at him in person and over the phone and didn't let up. This was the Nicole who could wage war and who no one wanted to go up against. She was petite and pretty—and absolutely relentless.

"Did you have intercourse?"

"Where did you have sex?"

"How many times did you have sex?"

"Did you have sex with Sandy or Annette on the same days that you were intimate with me?"

"Did you tell them they were special?"

And so on. There was no open Bible or pad and pencil to write down all that was said, but in every other way it was like one of the church's basement deliverance counseling sessions. Nicole wanted to know every damn detail, and she wanted Nick to be man enough to tell her the truth. Nick remained vague in his denial and apology. The specifics weren't important, he said. He said he was sorry.

For Nicole, at least at that moment, being seemingly repentant wasn't nearly enough.

She wrote in her diary the morning of April 16, 2001:

When the thoughts come that show me all the different times he lied to me in the present, about the past, it makes me either angry and want to know now every detail of every situation of it. I just feel the sickness come up inside me and the tightness inside my body. When I badgered Nick at this time, it felt good to hurt him.

NEW COVENANT'S CONGREGATION WAS STILL MEETING IN the gym of Christ Memorial Church when Nick stood to confess that he'd sinned. He was vague about what he'd done, the line he had crossed, the sins he had committed. Only two of the women he might have been addressing were in attendance: Nicole and Lindsey. Nicole stood by him but without exhibiting the starry-eyed love she'd once felt. She'd been betrayed. Lindsey, a young woman with a new man in her life, was hurt by the humiliation of knowing that Nick had played with her innocence. It had not been God at all.

Nick's apology seemed flat, any authentic contrition overwhelmed by the emotions of everyone around him.

"He's only sorry he was caught," one observer said.

Later, when the Smiths were home alone, it crept into their conversation that perhaps they never really knew Nick at all. Maybe Dawn never did, either.

When it occurred to PB that maybe Nick had killed Dawn, he swiftly suppressed the thought.

No. It can't be. Nick loved her.

ONE PERSON CLOSE TO THE CASE WHO WEIGHED WHAT HAD happened the night Dawn died and Sandy's story of murder put it this way several years later: "I wonder if he'd [Nick] needed to alter his plans. Surely he was smart enough to know that an autopsy was in the offing and that it would be discovered that Dawn hadn't breathed in any CO_2 or smoke.

Maybe the Benadryl plan didn't go off as smoothly as he'd hoped and planned? Maybe he had to suffocate Dawn? Too bad none of the cops thought to examine his body to see if he'd been involved in a struggle. I wonder if Dawn might have fought for her life."

58

AFTER HEARING FROM MARY GLASS THAT SANDY had confessed to a sexual affair with Nick, Kenny Goans thought he was going to burst a blood vessel. Being made a fool of didn't sit well at all. He'd listened to Sandy bad-mouth Jimmy for more than two years. She'd cried on his shoulder. She'd acted as if his counsel had meant something—as if *he* had meant something to her. He was so ashamed of how he'd sided with Sandy, he could have kicked himself and not felt his own steel-toed boot.

"I feel so deceived by her," he told his brother, Bill. "How could she just look at me and lie about her and Nick and make Jimmy out to be some kind of a nut?"

"The kind of lying Sandy has done, Ken, you just don't develop in one day."

Mary's words dangled in the air. Kenny thought of Dawn Hacheney's death and his sister's immediate reaction that something fishy had gone on with it.

"There was no smoke in her lungs," she had told him not long after the fire.

"No smoke in her lungs means Dawn was dead before the fire," Kenny said now.

"But the police investigated."

"They didn't know what we know now, because if they did, they'd have worked the case a lot harder."

Kenny took a seat behind his computer on the afternoon of June 10, 2001, and wrote a three-page letter touching on the primary events that had turned his world upside down.

He felt as if his role in Sandy's deception had betrayed Jesus Christ.

> Concerning Pastor Bily, I can't remember how many times I heard from Bob Smith and Hacheney the phrase: I have seen how that man operates, and I just don't trust him. Given the confessions of you [Sandy] and Annette, I now ask what was the man supposed to do? Poor Jimmy . . . I cringe to think how often I was your agent against him.

He saved the best for last. On the subject of Dawn's demise, he wrote:

> The Teddy bear note proves that your relations with Nick were prior to Dawn's death, which up to fore has been known as a tragic accident. I personally now believe that he killed his wife.

What he didn't say was that he was carbon-copying the Bremerton Police Department. "No more secrets, Sandy. No more lies," he wrote.

He sent the letter the next morning, registered mail. When he returned to Milton–Freewater, he found it in his mailbox. Sandy had refused delivery.

"I just couldn't go there," she told a friend at the time. "I didn't want to read any of it."

ON JUNE 12, TWO DAYS AFTER KENNY GOANS WROTE HIS letter, Sandy and her lawyer met with Kitsap County prosecutors to tell them a story that would have made *Elmer Gantry*'s saga of sex, greed, and God look like a road map to sainthood. Alternately guarded and excessively emotional, the thirty-nine-year-old mother of four told the prosecutors a tale of a lonely church secretary seduced by a charismatic young preacher. Nick was strong, decisive, and deeply spiritual. She told the prosecutors how Nick had wished Jimmy were dead so that she'd be free to marry. Nick told her that it was God's will that Dawn was going to die, and Sandy had bought into it. They purchased custom wedding rings. She'd even had prophetic dreams that it was all going to come true.

Sandy tried to convince everyone in the room that Nick had plotted the murder on his own. She had been an unwitting bystander in the tragedy. Sure, she felt guilty, but it wasn't because she'd taken any particular action. She felt shame for sharing God's Word of Dawn's impending death.

She had managed to make a deal with the Kitsap County Prosecutor's Office that she wouldn't be charged for anything relating to Dawn's murder. Considering how central she was with her persuasive prophecies urging Nick along, for her the document she signed was truly a gift from God.

APART FROM SOME LESS THAN CANDID CONVERSATIONS with her parents, Lindsey Smith hadn't really discussed how profoundly she'd been hurt by Nick's betrayal with Annette, Sandy, and Nicole. It seemed too deep a wound, too fresh, to even talk about with her older sister, Kim. She was also embarrassed by her gullibility, the consequence of her need to trust and love a man who portrayed himself as broken by the loss of his wife.

Kim could understand how her sister and the other women of the church might fall victim to a man's charm—not his appearance. Nick didn't exactly have movie-star looks; he was more like the Pillsbury Doughboy. She pondered how he could seduce so many attractive, seemingly intelligent women. She discussed it with her husband, Godwin. It was a mystery to him as well, but when Kim finally came to a conclusion, Godwin couldn't help but agree.

"Nick had such a way of making people—especially those going through difficult times—feel great about themselves. He'd shower them with attention," he said many years later.

Both had seen it time and again. Needy women readily

congregated around Nick Hacheney to scoop up whatever he was selling, whether it was affection, concern, or compliments. Some were married; some were single.

All were emotionally ripe for a charmer, a schemer.

59

A CROSS KITSAP COUNTY, THE BREMERTON POLICE DE-
partment swarmed over those who knew Nick, had
access to his financial records, or had originally investigated the case. Embarrassment energized their every move.
They had let a potential killer walk free in December 1997.
There were so many reasons for that: He was a pastor; he had
a good marriage; although they were deep in debt, he and his
wife had perfect credit; her life insurance policies were not
enormous; and the coroner ruled a flash fire as the explanation
for Dawn's empty toxicity screens for carbon monoxide.

No one from the church had told them what they suspected. No one had given them a single reason to dig deeper
into the case.

IN THE KLOVENS' LIVING ROOM, WITH ITS PRETTY COUNTRY-
style furniture and river-rock fireplace, Einar and Holly sat
quietly and wondered about Sandy, Nick, and the prophecy
that Jimmy was going to die. Einar wondered aloud where
Sandy had been the night of Dawn's murder.

"She was at home with the boys. She told me that," Holly
said.

By then, what Sandy told them didn't carry much weight.

They considered what, if any, connection could be made
to the prophecy and the affair. Holly mused that Sandy might
have had an idea about what God wanted her to have in life.

Jimmy Glass just wasn't that person. Nick was.

"Maybe she couldn't wait for God to give her what she

thought He wanted for her," Einar said. "She had an affair to try to attain that."

Holly nodded. In a strange way, it made a little sense.

"She felt like God would give her somebody better than Jimmy," she said.

What the Klovens didn't know was that Jimmy Glass had begun dialysis treatment for kidney failure earlier that spring of 2001. Investigators on the Hacheney case spoke to doctors about the possibility that a deliberate or accidental poisoning might be the reason. Despite a battery of tests, no determination could be made that Jimmy had been poisoned.

NICK'S TIMELINE FOR DECEMBER 26 WAS THE SUBJECT OF much interest among those working in the offices of the Bremerton Police Department and the Kitsap County Prosecutor's Office. Certainly they had Sandy's story of the confession, Nick's blatant womanizing, the insurance money, and his mounting debt. But what about the fire? Had it burned as long as Nick had initially maintained? Some fire investigators had questioned that from the beginning, indicating a burn time of under one hour—certainly not more than two hours. Nick had told investigators on the scene that morning that he'd kissed Dawn good-bye and left the house around 5:30 A.M.

Working backwards from the only time for which there was physical corroboration—the 9:27 A.M. credit card transaction at Mitzel's restaurant—put that in some doubt.

9 A.M.	Nick, Lindsey, and Phil arrive at Mitzel's in Poulsbo.
8:25 A.M.	They leave the hunting grounds at Indian Island.
7:50 A.M.	They wait in the duck blinds.
7:40 A.M.	They arrive at Indian Island.
7:15 A.M.	They depart the Hood Canal Bridge.
7:13 A.M.	Nick arrives at the Hood Canal Bridge.
6:45 A.M.	Nick leaves the house on Jensen Avenue.

According to that time sequence, the fire started almost immediately after Nick left his home on Jensen Avenue. It burned quickly until neighbors spotted the smoke at 7:13 and called 911.

CRAIG AND ANNETTE ANDERSON WERE NOT HAVING AN easy time. In the weeks after she confessed her infidelity, Annette couldn't feel more ashamed if she'd had a capital *A* tattooed across her forehead. She cried. She begged. She told Craig that she was sorrier than he could ever know. But he continued to hammer at her.

"Look," she finally said, "I can't be any more sorry than I have been, so get over it or leave me."

There was no way Craig could do that, of course. They had three children and Annette was due with their fourth.

On May 19, Annette's water broke. She did the math and the horror set in. God was going to give her a new baby on Nick's birthday. It was a cruel irony that she just couldn't handle.

This baby can't be born after midnight, she told herself. *This can't happen to me.*

That afternoon, the midwife came into the hospital room.

"What would happen if I asked for a C-section?" Annette asked.

"Your baby will be here in an hour."

Annette didn't hesitate. "I want a C-section."

And so her baby came as promised, not on Nick's birthday, but on the birthday of a friend who'd helped her through the roughest time—Gary Conner.

It was a miracle.

60

NICK LOOKED LIKE A RUMPLED MESS WHENEVER HE arrived in the office at First Light Media, but on that particular day he looked worse than ever. Jon Mc-Clung and Godwin Selembo had seen Nick in dark times, in the weeks following Dawn's death, but that was before Nicole. Supposedly, his life was now on track.

Godwin put his hand on Nick's shoulder. "What is it?" he asked.

"They're out to get me," he said. "They are going to take me to jail."

"Who? Who's out to get you? What are you talking about?"

Nick told them that a man he didn't know but whom he suspected was Sandy Glass's boyfriend, Scott Nickell, had phoned with a threat that he'd be arrested for Dawn's murder.

"What?" Godwin asked. "Who is going to take you to jail?"

"They are. The police. Scott told me that Sandy had told him something. He said, 'I know what you did.'"

"But did you do anything, Nick?" Godwin could feel First Light slipping away just then. Practical man that he was, Godwin immediately processed the latest Nick misstep in terms of how it would harm the business. When someone points an accusing finger, there are grave consequences.

"I didn't do anything," he said. "Sandy's been pressured

by Scott to make this up. Sandy would never hurt me like this. This isn't her doing. I'm going to jail."

"You need to talk to a lawyer," Godwin said.

NICK'S FACE WAS WHITE AS PARCHMENT. HE HADN'T SLEPT in a couple of days. His dark eyes had sunk deep into their sockets. Yet he tried to keep a positive attitude. The day after he dropped the bomb about Sandy Glass's charges of murder, he and Jon McClung caught the ferry to Seattle to see a lawyer at a downtown law firm. Nick was worried that Sandy's accusations could take on a life of their own. Being a minister on the make was one thing. Saying that he killed his wife was a colossal leap.

Jon took a seat in the waiting room while Nick disappeared inside the lawyer's private office.

"Well, what happened?" Jon asked as they walked to their van afterward. "What did the lawyer say?"

Nick's mood had lifted. "He said for me not to worry about it. Sandy's probably after money. He said she'll probably try to sue me or the church, if it goes that far."

Over the next few weeks there was only more silence.

NICK INSISTED HE NEVER HEARD SANDY'S PROPHESIES OF Dawn's impending demise. He'd heard that Jimmy was going to die and even mentally prepared for it. But there was one prophecy for which there could be no preparation. He told Nicole and his lawyers about it but didn't mention it to other people. During the early part of 1998, Sandy had told him that she'd had yet another message from God.

"Jimmy and [one of our boys] are going to die," Sandy had said. "God showed me how I was to reach over and unbuckle Jimmy's seat belt and grab the wheel and ram the car into a tree or off the Agate Pass Bridge. [The boy] would already have his seat belt unbuckled."

This was different. Her boys had never come up in any messages from God.

"Sandy," Nick had said, "this is not what God wants. Gabriel doesn't want this. No one wants this. This is not right."

Sandy refused to back down.

It was significant that she'd mention that particular son and not the other boys. He looked the most like his father and, among the boys, seemed to be the one who sought the closest relationship with Jimmy. Sandy complained about that to Annette and others. It was pathetic and heartbreaking at the same time. It was as if she hadn't bonded with the boy as she had the others. Her way of handling his education was proof. Despite his special needs—slight cerebral palsy from a premature birth—he was the only one of the three oldest Glass boys to be sent off to public school. In keeping with the tenets of the church, she homeschooled the boys.

Some wondered if having him around reminded her of the husband she'd so badly wanted to be rid of so she could be with Nick Hacheney.

Later, Sandy would tell the prophecy about the fatal crash without mentioning her son's involvement. Nick's reply would be different too.

"I could tell you what to do, but don't expect any help," he claimed he said, responding to her Word.

"Help"? Had there been help with Dawn's death?

THROUGH THE SECOND HALF OF 2001, NICK AND NICOLE lived under the specter of a Bremerton Police homicide investigation, the whispers of former friends, and the shame that he'd brought to their relationship. Nick went in for counseling after his vague confession of his sins, but even that seemed too little, too late.

He wrote in his journal:

I just got off the phone with Nicole who is very angry and asked me about counseling and then started asking questions about the counselor—how she looks and if I'm attracted to her. . . . I am torn between hope for future reconciliation and fear that something will be taken away again. I feel somewhat concerned about Nicole's fears because I cannot undo what I've done and the level of craziness that I have been involved in is pretty deep.

ACROSS THE AGATE PASS BRIDGE ON BAINBRIDGE ISLAND, Sandy spoke to few people apart from Scott, her lawyer, and the county prosecution team. All of the women who'd been so closely connected were now cut off from each other. Sandy was the crucial witness in the mounting case against Nick. Lindsey was back in the States at her parents' house, Annette was down in Oregon, and Nicole continued to go about her daily life and plan her wedding. The date had moved to October 20, the May date having been ruined by the public disclosure that Nick had been unfaithful with several women in the church. It was hard, but Nicole had forgiven him. He was, she was sure, a changed man.

Nick, Nicole, and her two children spent September 7 picnicking at the Jefferson County property—the place that had been Dawn's dream, then Sandy's. It was as if all of the nasty things that Sandy had said really had blown over, as Nick's lawyer had said they would. The next day they went to Ocean Shores and had another great day.

Nothing was going to happen to them. God was watching them.

She wrote:

> I just prayed for the kids that they'd sleep well because we got home late and God would give me the wisdom and strength to get everything done.

WHEN ANNETTE CONTINUED TO REVISIT THE EVENTS FOLlowing Dawn's death, one memory that stood out was of Dawn's purse. It was not like Dawn to leave her purse in the car. It wasn't like *any* woman that Annette knew. She remembered how Nick had been so lucky to have it after the fire, and yet he had cavalierly wanted to toss it in the trash. Annette kept the purse in a bedroom closet in her house in Dallas. Something told her to get it one day. She remembered something, but she didn't know what it was.

In the purse, she found two little Benadryl pills inside the zippered pocket. Nothing more. It was strange. Why those two pills? Of all the things that could have been left behind . . .

Could it be a message from Dawn?

THE DAY AFTER THE ATTACK ON THE WORLD TRADE CENTER and the Pentagon, Nicole Matheson took her two children to school, feeling the fear that was consuming the nation. She prayed for God to intervene and provide wisdom and comfort. It was so needed. She planned on meeting Nick at the Poulsbo library before their counseling appointment to discuss diet, health, and the need for submission in their relationship. She was working on it. He was too. It was a terrible day and she needed him.

She didn't know it, but that was the last time she'd see him outside of a correctional facility.

61

NICHOLAS DANIEL HACHENEY, THIRTY-ONE, WAS picked up by Bremerton Police detectives Sue Schultz and Dan Trudeau in the parking lot of the Silverdale Kinko's copy and mailing center just after lunch on September 12, 2001. He immediately insisted that he didn't have anything to do with Dawn's murder and, in fact, said that members of his old church led by the apostle Robert Bily had waged an evil campaign against him.

"You have no idea what these people are capable of," he said. "I did not kill my wife."

A half hour later, he was in an austere interrogation room, emotional, belching, and gasping for air. His heart pulsed through his shirt. Sweat beaded on his brow and glistened in the sparse goatee he'd grown.

"We know what you did. We know about 'take the land,' the plastic bag over Dawn's head, the affairs," Dan Trudeau said. "We know about the Benadryl. We know you drugged her. Dawn was dead before the fire and you were the last one to see her alive."

"You're deceiving me," Nick shot back, trying to pull himself together.

"You are under arrest for first-degree murder," the detective said.

"You're making a mistake," Nick said, crying.

The detective filled out the booking sheet with bail set at $750,000. It was 2:30 P.M.

Nick's belongings were logged: his clothes, wallet, a Mead composition notebook, and some loose papers.

Among his possessions was a to-do list. One item seemed to indicate that he was still in contact with Sandy Glass, who'd specifically told investigators that she hadn't talked to him in years. He'd detailed the songs of a mix tape he was making for her. The lead song was "Who Is This" from *Winds of Worship 12*.

Nick had also carried a typed "character bio" for a possible video he was going to produce for First Light Media.

He believes deeply in the existence of God and has known Him on a personal level since childhood. He has experiences that he knows are real and yet is suspicious of anything that men would call a "word from God" or a supernatural event. A deep involvement in a cult like environment have [*sic*] created huge holes in his confidence to really know that something is God and is not a psychological trick.

ANNETTE ANDERSON BROKE DOWN WHEN SHE GOT THE call from the prosecutor's office that Nick was in custody. She wanted to talk to Sandy, but her e-mails and calls went unanswered. Now divorced from Donald, Diana Tienhaara cried too. She just couldn't accept that her fun-loving and playful son-in-law could have killed her beautiful daughter. Lindsey Smith sought comfort in the arms of her boyfriend, Chris. Bob Smith felt sickness in his stomach that reminded him that he'd been made a fool of by a young man he'd loved as a son.

Only Robert Bily felt satisfied. Vindicated. Nick had been possessed by evil long before Dawn's body burned in that fire. The apostle's congregation had shrunk by then to a handful, and his marriage to Pamela was in trouble. Still, he was undeterred. Justice, he was sure, would come not from the courts but from God.

* * *

"I JUST HAVE TO SEE WHAT THIS DON JUAN OF THE HOLY Roller set looks like," an employee in the Kitsap County Clerk's Office declared as the courthouse buzzed like overloaded power lines with news of the pastor's arraignment for murder and arson. She wasn't alone in her curiosity. About half a dozen of those who spent their days patiently waiting on the county's troubled and confused public put their phones on hold and trundled over to the courtroom. They'd heard Nick Hacheney had bedded half the women in the congregations of *two* churches. Bainbridge Island women, no less. These were females of supposed class and intellect: privileged women who should have known better than to fall for a good-looking guy with a line. To be duped by the likes of Nick Hacheney, observers were certain, meant he had to be something special.

Nick ambled in, looking like a flabby, sweating average Joe instead of a cool, suave lothario who could charm the underpants off any woman he wanted.

"Jesus," one clerk sniffed in disappointment as her eyes lit on the defendant. "Either he's really let himself go, or he's got something going for him that doesn't meet the eye."

Her colleague rolled her eyes. "Yeah, that has to be it."

Of course, she was right.

AS THE TRIAL SPUTTERED OVER MONTHS OF DELAY, THOSE close to the case continued to wonder about Sandy Glass—what she knew and when she knew it. An internal memorandum distributed among the Kitsap County prosecution team put it quite bluntly: They might have struck an immunity deal with Sandy, but that didn't mean they believed all of her story. The memo writer wanted the prosecution's investigator to see if Sandy had been in contact with Nick—by phone or in person—since his incarceration pending the trial.

> My apologies if this is labor intensive. However, if we interviewed her without the benefit of knowing about communications between them, we'd take a significant risk. One of the possibilities here is both remote and bizarre, but

it wouldn't be out of character for this case: They could have a pact in which she takes the stand (immunized by virtue of us calling her to testify) and claims she did the murder, after saying differently through all of the interviews.

There appeared to be sound reason for the prosecution's concern. Sandy Glass failed to disclose a vital piece of information until ten months after signing the immunity deal. On February 7, 2002, her lawyer notified the authorities that his client had suddenly remembered the pair of wedding bands they had purchased at Dahlquists just weeks before the deadly fire.

WHEN SMALL DETAILS, HIDDEN FOR YEARS, WORKED THEIR way to the ears of those involved in Nick and Sandy's world, dramatic connections to the past were made. After Annette Anderson heard about the gold rings that Sandy said she and Nick had planned to exchange, the design of one caught her interest. The four stones—the diamond, ruby, sapphire, and emerald—jogged her memory of something she'd read in one of the books that Nick had once ranked above the Bible. Annette set aside what she was doing and combed through the pages of *The Final Quest*. Passages hailed those gems as "treasures of salvation." Each of the stones adorned a sword that was crucial to the book's plotline. Nick and Sandy saw themselves as players in the story: chosen by God, defended by angels, and loved by all those around them.

Nick and Sandy were getting married, Annette thought to herself. *They turned the rings into symbols of their romance, their supernatural love.*

MANY YEARS LATER, WITH SCOTT NICKELL, HER TRUE BEliever, sitting beside her in the wood-paneled breakfast room at the Poulsbo Inn, Sandy Glass tried to clarify her account. Everything had changed by then for everyone who'd been a part of the story. Irrevocably so. Her hands trembled. Her eyes flooded with tears.

"I can't do this," she said, weeping, as she ended her only media interview. "I'm sorry."

NICK HACHENEY WAS CONVICTED OF AGGRAVATED HOMI-cide on December 26, 2002—more than a year after his arrest and exactly five years to the day that Dawn died in the house fire on Jensen Avenue. Sandy Glass was the prosecution's chief witness. Nick did not testify.

EPILOGUE

THROUGHOUT HIS INCARCERATION, NICK HAS PRO-
fessed his innocence. In 2007, he won a legal victory
in the Washington Supreme Court when the panel of
justices agreed that the arson charge was not substantiated
by the facts, thereby striking down the "aggravated" aspect
of his conviction, which had carried a mandatory no-parole
sentence. He was resentenced on May 30, 2008, and now
will be eligible for parole as soon as 2025.

Annette and Craig Anderson and their four children live
in Oregon, their marriage having survived the ordeal of the
affair and the trial. Annette found her way back to God and
the church. She's never been happier. The Andersons remain
close to Gary and Julie Conner.

Pastor Bob and Adele Smith now make their home in
Poulsbo, not far from daughter Kim and her husband, Godwin. After a three-year hiatus, during which he worked as
an electrician, PB returned to the ministry and pastors New
Covenant Fellowship, now in Port Gamble. Adele still works
in the insurance business.

Lindsey Smith lives in South Africa with her husband
and two children. She's doing the missionary work that she
always knew God wanted her to do. She hasn't spoken to
Nick since the summer before his arrest and has no desire to
do so.

Robert Bily remains an apostle with Life Staff Ministries.
He and Pamela divorced and by 2009 had remarried other
people. The former Christ Community Church building has

been up for sale for several years. Robert Bily feels vindicated by the outcome of the trial but remains embittered by the fallout from the church split.

Sandy Glass married Scott Nickell and lives with her boys on the Glass compound on Bainbridge Island. She remains estranged from Holly Kloven and Annette Anderson.

Jimmy Glass undergoes dialysis three times a week and is on a waiting list for a kidney transplant. He told a friend in 2007 that he fears he might have been poisoned by someone. He's remarried and lives in Belfair, Washington.

Diana Tienhaara went back to her gut instincts about Nick and no longer feels that her former son-in-law killed her daughter. She's remarried and lives in the Bremerton area. In 2007, Nicole Matheson returned to Diana a box of cherished photographs—images of Dawn used at her memorial service that many were certain Nick had discarded.

Nicole owns and operates a successful granola and cookie business out of her home in Suquamish. She and Nick were married in a prison wedding in 2006. She sees him weekly at the state prison in Monroe, Washington.

A gravestone now marks Dawn Marie Hacheney's final resting place. The money for the marker was provided by a victims' rights organization.

ACKNOWLEDGMENTS

The author would like to thank David Chesanow, Daniel Bogaty, Shanna McQueen, Sara Sarver, Tina Marie Brewer, Jim Thomsen, Kenneth Jensen, Bunny Kuhlman, Gary Boynton, and Charles Turner for their support in seeing this project to its conclusion. To editors Charlie Spicer and Yaniv Soha, and literary agent Susan Raihofer, as always, I appreciate all that you do on my behalf. Also, a shout-out to Ellis Levine of Cowan, DeBaets, Abrahams & Sheppard, for his careful review of the manuscript.

Finally, I thank all of the people who gave me their time, shared their recollections, and—yes—bared their souls to get this story out. Many are named in the pages here, and many more are not. All, however, made an enormous difference.

Here are a few that I'd like to publically acknowledge for taking the time to meet with me for interviews, in random order: Dan, Sandra, and Theresa Hacheney; Diana, Donald, Daric, and Daron Tienhaara; Craig and Annette Anderson; Robert Bily; Holly and Einar Kloven; Nicole Matheson; John and Tanna Martin; Duane Martin; Ken Linden; Claudia McKinstry; Tami Walker; Carmen and Chet McKnight; Bob, Adele, Lindsey, and Kim Smith; Godwin Selembo; Adam Bily; Becky Burns; Jon McClung; Crystal Gurney; Jim and Ann Nardo; Eunice Zeitner; Scott Nickell; Kim and Ken Walls; Jimmy and Lisa Glass; James and Mary Glass; Debbie and Roger Gelbach; Amy Pitts; Kenny Goans; Sally and Rich LaGrandeur; Eric and Maureen Kruse; Sam and Julie Pennoyer; Michael and Julia DeLashmutt; Suzy and Danny

Claflin; Yvonne Basso; Lavern and John Melson; Dale and Peggy Brown; Gary and Julie Conner; David and Kathleen Curry; and Jim Hill.

Even though I didn't take the book in the direction of a police procedural or a lawyer's quest for justice, I appreciate the interviews and help given to me by Kitsap County prosecutors Neil Wachter and Claire Bradley; Bremerton Police Department investigators Dan Trudeau and Sue Schultz; and Bremerton fire marshal Scott Rappleye.

I interviewed Nick Hacheney on two occasions in prison.

I began, but was unable to complete, an interview with Sandy Glass.

—GREGG OLSEN
Olalla, Washington
July 2009

CPSIA information can be obtained
at www.ICGtesting.com
Printed in the USA
LVHW101146100123
736841LV00002B/280